Raised by the Courts

JUDGE IRENE SULLIVAN

ONE JUDGE'S INSIGHT
INTO JUVENILE JUSTICE

PUBLISHING

New York

© 2010 Irene Sullivan

Published by Kaplan Publishing, a division of Kaplan, Inc.
1 Liberty Plaza, 24th Floor
New York, NY 10006

Library of Congress Cataloging-in-Publication Data has been applied for.

Printed in the United States of America

10 9 8 7 6 5 4 3

ISBN-13: 978-1-60714-638-4

Kaplan Publishing books are available at special quantity discounts to use for sales pro-
motions, employee premiums, or educational purposes. For more information or to purchase books, please call the Simon & Schuster special sales department at 866-506-1949.

To

Mae and Harold Hyland,
with gratitude

Mary Kelly, Pat, and Andy Sullivan,
with love

Austin, Jordan, Shealyn, Andrew, and Maya Sullivan,
with joy

CONTENTS

FOREWORD

A YEAR OR SO AGO, Irene Sullivan shared with me her plans for writing about her experience as a judge in juvenile court. She mentioned it casually, almost in passing. I thought perhaps it would be in memoir format, offering advice for other judges. I was very wrong. What I read is a collection of insights, experiences, and observations about the juvenile justice and child welfare systems worthy of serious consideration by everyone who cares about kids. It is not for the timid; but if you want to know what really happens in our courthouses and to the youth who come there—what must change and why—this is the place to start.

I'd known Irene for well over 25 years, first meeting when we practiced law on either side of Tampa Bay. I suspect neither of us could have imagined how our paths would cross again to work on issues that were probably foreign to us as civil trial lawyers. In 1998, Irene was elected to the bench and became a judge in family and juvenile court. She began working tirelessly to understand what was bringing children and families into her court; why things never seemed to change and how to promote better outcomes. That same year, 1998, I left the active practice of law to join the Eckerd Family Foundation. We are a time-limited foundation concentrating on youth at risk in the juvenile justice system, youth aging out of foster care, and kids failing in school. We implement strategies that allow youth to succeed. Through that common interest, Irene and I met again.

Irene brings us into the courtroom and introduces us to the kids she sees each week. She tells us that Monday mornings are about violence. We meet Alyssa, Robert, and Tony, who sums it up by saying his "life sucks." We hear the stories of Déjà, Casey, Allison, and Lexie. These children tell us, in words difficult to hear, about the effects of mental illness, drug use, lousy parents, failure in school. And we learn about the extreme cases like Leo Boatman, the foster kid molded by the juvenile justice and child welfare systems into a cold-blooded killer. Judge Sullivan introduces us to the state attorney, the public defender and juvenile probation officers. We meet the mental health professionals, police, and social workers who deal with these kids and their families, and we see, hear, and feel what they do each day.

We venture outside to visit the places where youth live; we tour residential facilities, the detention center, and treatment programs. And what is so different here is that with each painful story comes a street-level explanation of why it happened and a perspective on a better way of doing things, within our reach right now. As we review the issues—mental health, parenting, substance abuse, foster care, incarceration—we meet change agents and see what can happen when sound policy is translated into practice; but we are also shocked and disappointed to find how major decisions are made and the consequences.

And so you ask, "What's different about this book?" It is more than merely an inventory of resources; it is a diagram for change. And unlike some discussions of tough issues, this work does not leave you with the sinking feeling of having been tasked with conquering world hunger. It is, in part, an answer to the frustration of Miami Judge Jerri Beth Cohen, whom we hear complaining in outrage that our systems willfully ignore "what works," despite the fact we know and have known what to do for a long, long time.

So who should read it? If you are a layperson, this gives you insight into some of the most frustrating issues that hit our papers every day. If you want your tax dollars spent to get better outcomes at a lower cost, read on. For the advocate, activist, educator, student, or healthcare professional, add this to your toolkit, and ask the question: *Why aren't we doing more of it?* For politicians and policymakers, please ask yourself, *Why are we not using strategies to produce better outcomes at lower cost?* For funders and foundations, *shouldn't we be investing in leadership?* The practices and policies Judge Sullivan writes about are not state secrets. They are in the public domain. The missing ingredients are leadership and the public will to make it happen.

As I worked on this introduction, it was with timely irony that I came across the piece "Hard Times Spur Ideas for Change," appearing in the May 25, 2010, edition of *The New York Times*. The correspondent wrote about the measures that leaders around the country have been talking about when reconsidering what government should be, having exhausted budget cutbacks during these challenging times. Scott D. Pattison, the executive director of the National Association of State Budget Officers, was quoted as follows: "We can incrementally hobble and muddle through, or we can stand back and be more strategic. That's the question: whether this will be the time when these ideas actually get carried out, or whether this is going to be a whole lot of reports that sit on a shelf...."

This book shows that we can take on the toughest problems with leadership and sound policy put into practice. It also offers hope; hope in the reality of the resilience of so many of these young people and often how little is required for them to succeed.

Let's use this work to strengthen the public will to change and not to occupy a slot on the shelf or, as Irene might say: Please, not another dream... a dream deferred.

—Joe Clark
CEO and President, the Eckerd Family Foundation

OPENING STATEMENT

I HAVE THE BEST JOB IN THE WORLD.

Watching kids stand before me—growing up in juvenile court—has been an honor, a privilege, an enriching but often frightening experience. No other division of the court provides a judge with such a chance to make a difference in a person's life, for better or worse. Juvenile judges hold delinquent or dependent children in the palms of their hands, looking for solutions: programs that work, caregivers who are nurturing and responsible, therapy that's appropriate, and punishment that's effective.

The contradictions break my heart.

Watching a ten-year-old jump for joy, pointing and screaming, "That's my judge!" brings a bittersweet smile. Why does he have so many criminal charges at age ten that he has his "own" judge? Where are his parents? Why is he living in a group home?

"You're my favorite judge." I've read that often in the letters kids write in hopes of an early release from a juvenile commitment. But how about the note that read, "…and I know from sitting in court all these years that I'm your favorite kid." Why is that kid in court so often, and not at the playground or the park or getting ready for the prom?

"You're the easy one on Forty-ninth Street," one kid wrote to me at my Forty-ninth Street chambers in Clearwater on the west coast of Florida. Then he stole another car and crashed it into a tree. I wonder, "Am I too tender and not tough enough?"

"Because you won't commit them," the blunt young prosecutor answers me when I ask why so many of our kids under age eighteen are being charged as adults in criminal court.

"All you want to do is lock 'em up, lock 'em up," a young mother says to me as I sentence her fourteen-year-old son to a residential commitment program, adding that it's "damned inconvenient" that I did this just as she was being released from prison.

"Send her away, Judge," a desperate grandmother pleads. "All she does is sex and drugs. She's going to wind up just like her mother, with a baby at fifteen."

Kids in court are like all kids. They are funny, sad, angry, hopeful, slovenly, and kind. Judges are like parents. They scold, encourage, admonish, flatter, punish, throw up their hands in dismay, and give second chances. "No one but a juvenile can so piss off a judge," says Scott Brownell of Bradenton, Florida, a kind-hearted, patient juvenile judge skilled at exposing the lies kids tell in court.

It's true that Judge Brownell and other good juvenile judges bring empathy to court. During Supreme Court Justice Sonia Sotomayor's confirmation hearing in August 2009, the word "empathy" was viewed by some on the political right as a negative. Senator Amy Klobuchar, a Minnesota Democrat, organized women senators to speak up for Judge Sotomayor.

"As a prosecutor," she said, "after you have interacted with victims of crime, after you have seen the damage that crime does to individuals and to our communities, after you have seen defendants who are going to prison and you know their families are losing them, sometimes forever, you know the law is not just an abstract subject. The law has a real impact on the real lives of real people."

The earlier you get kids in court, the more of an impact the law has upon them.

Nationally, only 5 percent of kids come in contact with the juvenile justice system, and only half of those commit a second crime. Thus, 95 percent of kids are obeying the law, hopefully doing well in school, engaged in sports or other activities, and preparing to be productive citizens. So why should we care about that 5 percent? Here's why:

- Approximately 93,000 young people are held in juvenile justice facilities on any given day, at an average cost of $240.99 per day per youth, according to the Justice Policy Institute, a Washington, D.C., think tank. Then some end up in prison as adults. Close to 3 million Americans were in jail or prison in 2008; that's 1 percent of our nation's population. If you count probation and parole, 1 in every 31 U.S. adults is under correctional control. The U.S. incarceration rate is four to seven times higher than that of other Western countries.

- We now lock up more young people than any other nation in the world, or about 1 million teenagers each year.

- Girls are the fastest-growing segment of the juvenile justice population.

- Minority youths are shockingly overrepresented in juvenile justice programs.

- High-school dropouts, teenage pregnancies, and the plight of foster kids aging out of care all contribute to our expensive, growing prison population.[1,2,3,4,5]

At one time, the world looked to the United States as the leader in juvenile justice. Indeed, the first juvenile courts created in Chicago well over one hundred years ago were models of humane, effective treatment of juvenile delinquents. In the last twenty years, however, we have become the "incarceration nation" for juveniles as well as adults. The Annie E. Casey Foundation, a private charitable organization dedicated to assisting disadvantaged children, was established in 1948. Bart Lubow, its director of programs for high-risk youths, says bluntly that "we are addicted to incarceration." In spite of this, pockets of excellent juvenile programs are scattered about the country, many of them financed by foundations and a mixed stream of public funds. These innovative programs are proving the adage that you can be both smart and tough if you understand *what works.*

So does looking to Europe. The Old World has a kinder, gentler attitude toward juvenile justice, says Petra Guder, international coordinator of the German Juvenile Court Judges Association. "In the vast majority of European States," she observes, "the minimum age of criminal responsibility is fourteen, waivers to adult court due to the severity of a crime do not exist, and there are no provisions that a juvenile can be sent to prison without parole or sentenced to death."[6]

I remember bringing my Norwegian cousin, Kjerstie Hylland, to my Florida court. She runs her own child welfare agency outside of Oslo. When she saw kids ages ten, eleven, and twelve in handcuffs, leg restraints, and jumpsuits, she scowled and asked, "Does Amnesty International know about this?" In Norway, children under fourteen who commit crimes are considered dependent, neglected children, and child welfare agencies take control.

Florida is a fascinating, challenging state for many reasons. Columnist George Will calls Florida "a geological afterthought...the last portion of what are now the lower forty-eight states to emerge from the ocean, and it emerged halfheartedly: Its highest point is just 345 feet above sea level." Its state rankings in terms of education and social services are near the bottom, incarcerations are often too frequent and cruel; yet, Florida can boast of some of the most progressive, effective juvenile programs in the country.

Even before the 2008 economic collapse, Florida ranked in the forties on state measurements for health and human services as well as education. In 2009, Florida ranked forty-fifth in personal income growth, forty-fifth in high-school graduation rate, and forty-ninth in combined state and local government spending on education, but *third* in spending for incarcerating children and adults. In 2008, for the first time in sixty years, Florida's population declined, by 50,000 people. One million people were unemployed. Food stamp requests almost doubled, to 2.1 million. Because Florida has been totally reliant on growth for its income, shrinking tax revenue meant further cuts to social services, juvenile justice, and education.[3]

Yet, from the Panhandle to Key West, the Tampa Bay area to Jacksonville, juvenile justice professionals—probation officers, therapists, social workers, guardians, state attorneys, public defenders, child psychologists, and, yes, judges—worked overtime and sometimes at great personal sacrifice for the kids in court. Over the years, programs that had been closed due to lack of funding were replaced by newer, cheaper community models that really worked. Foster kids' special needs in delinquency court, such as attorneys knowledgeable about their dependency case and need for independent living advice, were addressed. More first-time offenses were diverted from juvenile court through a network of youth/teen courts. Probation violations were handled less punitively, and gender-based services for girls improved. Ironically, it took an economic crisis to shift dollars from building expensive new prisons to creating "what works" programs that keep kids out of secure facilities. If we got there because of limited resources, that's okay—at least we got there.

In my circuit, the Sixth Circuit of the state of Florida, which hugs the Gulf of Mexico and Tampa Bay, a good deal of credit for progressive thinking and good programs goes to my key partners. Think of juvenile court as diamond shaped. The judge sits at the top point, with the child and the family at the bottom. The judge looks left and right, to the state attorney, public defender, and juvenile probation officer. All of them make recommendations regarding the youth, the delinquency charge, and the victims of the crime. I work with the offices of Bernie McCabe and Bob Dillinger, the elected state attorney and public defender, respectively, and Chief Probation Officer Tim Niermann. They represent what I believe to be the finest juvenile justice collaboration in the state of Florida. Their dedication and integrity make my job a lot easier, and together we create an effective process for decision making.

The good news is that trumpets of reform sound from the highest offices in the land. U.S. Supreme Court Justice Anthony Kennedy often speaks out against our growing prison population, urging us to look at the human being behind the prison bars. When we do, we usually find a high-school dropout—often illiterate, abused, and neglected as a child—growing out of the juvenile justice system. In the words of the Children's Defense Fund, the nonprofit child advocacy organization, we have created a cradle-to-prison pipeline. Justice Kennedy spoke on the topic of liberty at a lecture I attended at the Chautauqua Institution, in Chautauqua, New York, on August 27, 2009, the same day that a *New York Times* editorial castigated the California legislature for its "backward sentencing and parole policies that keep the state's prisons dangerously overcrowded with too many minor offenders sent to jail for too long. Democratic lawmakers," the *Times* editorial read, "who should know better are running scared of the prison guards' union and of being labeled 'soft on crime.'" Justice Kennedy criticized the lobbying efforts of prison guards for longer sentences. "That is just sick," he asserted, in an appropriate expression of outrage.[7]

"It's time for a 'new beginning' for adolescents in our criminal justice system," insisted Judge Judith S. Kaye, the recently retired chief judge of the state of New York, in a keynote speech given to the National Association of Juvenile and Family Court Judges in Chicago in July 2008.[8]

> The new beginning is not a search for new ideas. We do not need new ideas. We know what works, and we sure do know what does not work. The new beginning is with each of us: new resolve, new enthusiasm, new dedication to the return of America.
>
> It is what President Obama described as a "new era of responsibility, a recognition, on the part of every American, that we have duties to ourselves, our nation, and the world; duties that we do not grudgingly accept but, rather, seize gladly, firm in the knowledge that there is nothing so satisfying to the spirit, so defining of our character, than giving our all to a difficult task."[8]

Giving *our* all benefits all of us, according to retired U.S. Supreme Court justice Sandra Day O'Connor. "Society as a whole benefits immeasurably from a climate in which all persons, regardless of race or gender, may have the opportunity to earn respect, responsibility, advancement, and remuneration based on ability," she says.[9]

I hope that the readers of this book will agree that juvenile justice in our country needs that "new beginning" that Judge Kaye described. I hope many will be "giving our all to a difficult task" as President Barack Obama suggested, creating the opportunity benefitting *all* of us that Justice O'Connor mentioned. I'm proud that Justice Kennedy calls "sick" the lobbying efforts that keep minor offenders in jail.

For the youths and families served by those juvenile judges, I'll settle for no less than President Bill Clinton's hope for the people in the war-torn Middle East: "the quiet miracle of a normal life."

AUTHOR'S NOTE: I'VE DIVIDED this book into three parts that parallel my experience in juvenile court: "Awakening," "Despair," and "Enlightenment." I considered a fourth part, "Outrage," but decided that readers will find that for themselves, perhaps in different places. The stories and events are true; the children's names and identifying details have been changed to protect their privacy.

PART I

Awakening

CHAPTER 1

The Night Swimmers

I T LOOKED LIKE A twenty-first-century Norman Rockwell painting moving toward me in the narrow hallway.

The tall, black-robed judge walked toward his chambers, a wide, mischievous smile on his tanned and handsome Cuban face. His salt-and-pepper beard matched the hair that rimmed his balding head. His arms enveloped three black boys who were grinning and giggling, pulling on the judge's hands to make him move faster.

"Judge Sullivan," he said, rocking on his heels. The tone of his greeting echoed the twinkle in his eye and the puffed-up chest on his six-foot-two frame. "I want you to meet some very important friends of mine."

I had been a juvenile judge for just two weeks and had seen many kids in the courtroom, but not in a secure area reserved for judges and staff. But Judge Frank Quesada had a reputation for spontaneity in juvenile court.

"Okay, fellows, introduce yourselves to Judge Sullivan. She's our newest juvenile judge, and you just might be seeing her in court someday."

"I'm Javon!" the tallest boy shouted.

"I'm Deangelo," the next one giggled.

"He's Javaris," they both chimed in, pointing to the smallest boy, who was mostly hidden by the judge's robes.

I guessed them to be about nine or ten years old. They had huge brown eyes, gleaming white teeth, and close-cropped Afros. Each wore jeans with a belt and a neat plaid shirt with a collar. Well dressed for juvenile court.

"Javaris and Javon are brothers, and Deangelo is their cousin," Judge Quesada explained. "They live with their grandmother, who brought them to court, and right now they are giving her fits."

"What have they done?" I asked.

"Well, I call them the 'night swimmers.' It seems that when Grandma goes to bed, the three of them sneak out a window, hop on their bikes and ride down to the Pier in St. Petersburg—about a three-mile ride in the dark. They hide their bikes, take a leap into Tampa Bay, have themselves a nice swim, and ride home to Grandma's house about midnight."

Javon and Deangelo continued to smile. Javaris buried his face in Frank's robe.

"When they first came to court a few months ago, they didn't even reach the top of the podium. They had to step to the side so I could see them. Police gave them a few warnings, followed them home to make sure they were safe, and woke up Grandma. But they continued to slip out the window and head for the Pier. The older two were charged with misdemeanor trespass; they let the little guy off. I ordered them all away from the Pier, put in a strict curfew, and here they are again.

"This time," he went on, "I ordered them to report to our boot camp for a day—that should scare them into behaving—but I also made a deal with them. I told them I'd show them my private chambers, including the ship in the bottle and my refrigerator filled with soft drinks, in exchange for their sworn promise to keep curfew and never leave Grandma's house without permission. Or it's big-time boot camp, for sure. Right, guys?"

Frank bent down toward them, squeezing a few shoulders. "Right, Judge," they chirped, flashing those wide-spaced teeth.

Frank shooed them into his chambers toward the sailing ship and looked back at me. His eyes were misty.

"I'll be out of this division in a year, and I'll miss these little fellows, with their midnight swims and stupid misdemeanor charges," he said. "But if you stay here, you'll be seeing them through their teenage years. If they're slipping out of windows and disobeying Grandma now, God only knows what's in their future."

Judge Quesada, my mentor in juvenile court, seemed larger than life itself because of his shrewdness, intelligence, wit, and storytelling and culinary skills. He overflowed with compassion for the kids in court, but could be stern and tough when necessary.

His words that day were prescient: "You'll be seeing them through their teenage years."

Over the next seven years, I did see Javon, Deangelo, and Javaris often in court, with their weary grandmother and various other relatives; sometimes their mother but never a father. They grew taller and more muscular, clearly visible over the podium. They sported wide, bushy Afros and long, straggly dreadlocks. They wore hip-hop T-shirts and also tees printed with the faces of dead friends or relatives. As they grew older, Javon and Deangelo dressed in oversized pants—"saggers"—falling to midthigh, boxer shorts screaming for attention. Javaris was different, always neatly dressed in belted jeans and a plaid shirt.

Their fathers were in prison. One mother was dead, and the other chose a life of drugs over her sons but showed up occasionally. When Grandma became overwhelmed, the boys were shuffled among other relatives. They fell way behind in school and were chronically truant. Javon and Deangelo were diagnosed with conduct disorders but rarely took medication. Medicaid forms were lost, doctor's appointments missed. They were increasingly disruptive in school. Finally, the schools gave up on them. They were suspended frequently, which they liked.

Javon and Javaris became involved in a series of car thefts and house burglaries. Deangelo was convicted twice of selling crack cocaine. When placed on probation, they broke curfew, and all three tested positive for marijuana.

By ages twelve and thirteen, they were in separate residential commitment programs, hair shorn, wearing grey prison garb, handcuffs, and leg restraints when they came to court.

Javon and Javaris did well in the programs and were honorably discharged back home to Grandma. Deangelo resisted counseling and drug treatment, fought with the staff, and at age fifteen was transferred to a high-risk commitment program, where he remained for years.

Javon cooperated with his postcommitment probation for nearly a year but then fell victim to the temptations of the drug sales in his neighborhood. When he was caught on school property with a large amount of marijuana for sale, he was charged as an adult. He was ordered to drug treatment and put on probation. When he was arrested for stealing a purse from a woman, he was sentenced to three years in prison. He has an infant son by his first girlfriend, and his second girlfriend is pregnant.

Although none of the boys had reached the age of eighteen, Grandma and the other relatives had given up on them.

Javaris, the youngest, still skipped school and broke curfew, traveling back and forth among relatives. He'd stayed clear of the law for a while but was arrested again for stealing a car and trading it for cocaine. He then sold the cocaine to an undercover cop for $20.

As Javaris stood at the podium in front of me, dark brown eyes empty, shoulders sagging, looking completely disengaged, I thought of the first time I'd sentenced him, five years before. He was a spunky kid then, arrested for grabbing a couple of bait fish from a vendor on the fishing pier and throwing them to pelicans. This was his first arrest. Out-of-court diversion services were offered, but his grandmother didn't return the phone calls. So, like his older brother and cousin, he entered the juvenile justice system at age ten, charged with petty theft.

Javaris's defense to the petty theft charge was that he didn't know that tourists were paying for the bait fish; he thought they were free. He smiled broadly as he showed how many bait fish he could hold in one hand. His aim was accurate, and the pelicans loved him, he bragged. He showed me his toss. No doubt, he was good at it.

That may have been his last success. Now Javaris stood before me about to be committed again, for felony car theft and selling cocaine. He would be locked up for about two years in a facility just short of an adult prison. He might benefit from the education and counseling provided, or he might become a smarter, tougher criminal.

Standing before me, he looked younger than fifteen. Slim, with neat dreadlocks, sad brown eyes, his trademark jeans and plaid shirt, and silence. That set him apart, the silence, because most juveniles are anything but silent in court. Trying to avoid incarceration, they are agitated, pleading, imaginative, and dramatic. They flap their arms, raise their voices, beg, smile, and agree with everything you say. The clever ones write letters.

"I'm turning my life around, Judge, you gotta believe me."

"I'm sorry I disappointed my mom again. I'll make it up to her if you'll just let me stay at home."

"You can't send me away. I gots me a shorty [a child]"—or "a job," or "a test to take," or "a sick grandmother."

"I know you gave me a second chance before, but this time I really mean it. I won't go near those guys again. I'll keep my curfew. I really mean it."

When sentenced, some of those same youth scream, "Fuck you!" when taken into custody.

Javaris didn't say a word. He stood silent and alone. None of his relatives was with him in court. I wanted to hug him rather than sentence him.

"Javaris is a good kid, but we can never find him," said his probation officer, a large, kindly black man, his hand resting on the youth's shoulder.

"He's a smart kid, but…" his teacher added, summarizing his truancies, suspensions, and disruptions in school.

"He's a drug dealer and a thief," the victim in the front row interrupted, "and his family doesn't give a damn."

Family? What family? A bed or a couch at his grandmother's or aunt's house?

"He's basically been raising himself," the psychologist said at the podium, "roaming the streets at night, occasionally at school, finding his own food, violating curfew. Once in a while, a neglect report is investigated, but Javaris returns home, and the investigation is closed. Teens aren't given a high priority. Javaris hasn't had many successes."

Not since the bait fish episode, I thought.

"I'm sorry, Javaris," I said after sentencing. "I can't excuse your crimes, but somehow I think that we failed you, too. Your family failed you, the system failed you."

His sad eyes met mine, and he still didn't speak when handcuffed and led away.

DISPROPORTIONATE MINORITY CONTACT (DMC) is the elephant in my courtroom. Nobody mentions it, yet twice a week when I take the bench in delinquency court, I face a courtroom full of black faces. Most of the kids put on probation are black, as are the vast majority of kids committed or charged as adults.

It's true that more minorities live in the downtown and midtown areas of St. Petersburg that my court serves, but even so, the numbers are disproportionate. While blacks represent 30 percent of the population in my particular jurisdiction of south St. Petersburg, black kids make up 70 percent of my caseload.

Why? No one ever asks.

"A conversation about race and racism is so difficult," explained Dr. Rita Cameron-Wedding, professor of ethnic studies at California State University in Sacramento. "Color blindness means we're not supposed to talk about race, as if it's a level playing field." The professor spoke to a large group of juvenile judges and other professionals at a national juvenile justice conference in March 2008.

"Yet if you don't notice race and gender, you don't notice anything else. Unless your dining room table is totally multi-cultural, multi-age, multi-gender, race does matter."

Dr. Cameron-Wedding warns that it would be easy to "drop an anchor" and make biased conclusions based upon the numbers I see in my court, "as the DMC data weigh you down." Like, in court, just declaring that black kids commit more crimes than white kids.[1]

Race matters. Indeed it does in juvenile court.

Michael Eric Dyson is the author of many books, including the recent *April 4, 1968*, which examines how Dr. Martin Luther King, Jr.'s death changed America. He is a professor of sociology at Georgetown University in Washington, D.C. The current statistics he cites are frightening:

- Nearly 70 percent of black children are born to single mothers, compared to 27 percent of white children and 43 percent of Latinos.
- Blacks are incarcerated at 4.8 times the rate of whites.
- Black youths between the ages of ten and seventeen make up less than 20 percent of their age group in the United States but account for more than 50 percent of those committed or transferred to adult court.
- Black unemployment is twice that of whites, and the incomes of black men are lower today than they were in 1974.

Professor Dyson blames a "legal loophole" for incarcerating so many black adults: the disparity in sentencing between crack and powder cocaine abuses. Crack cocaine offenders, mostly black, faced minimum five-year sentences, while powder cocaine offenders were grouped with other controlled substance abusers and first offenders and received a maximum one-year sentence.

For black kids, however, we should focus the lens on an earlier time in their lives, before the lure of drugs, whether crack, powder, or prescription. Here's where Professor Dyson speaks to a kid like Javaris:

"Black families must shoulder some of the weight and responsibility for improving our lot: increasing parental attention to our children's education; examining and discouraging some destructive birth trends among vulnerable and desperate single young females; encouraging greater responsibility for black fathers."[2]

Look at the evolution Bill Cosby has made from actor-comedian to social commentator, while criticized by some in the African American community for heaping blame on irresponsible parents and gangsta rap music. Bill Cosby speaks to kids like Javaris in his book *Come On, People: On the Path from Victims to Victors,* which he cowrote with Dr. Alvin F. Poiussant: "We feel that an important element in this crisis is the breakdown in good parenting. We're not telling you something you don't know. In too many black neighborhoods, adults are giving up their main responsibility to look after their children. In all corners of America, too many children are getting the short end of the stick as extended family networks collapse and community support programs fail to replace them in any significant way."

So race matters. Or does it?

Academy Prep is a remarkable private school in St. Petersburg that provides a first-class, rigorous, well-rounded education to black boys by giving scholarships and other financial aid. The dress code is strict, attendance is mandatory, and the school day is long. Participation by parents or guardians is required. Most of the boys live in the areas that my court serves.

In my eight years as a juvenile judge, I have never had a delinquency case involving an Academy Prep student. Contrast that with Riviera Middle School, which also had a large minority population. A few years ago, it was chosen as the "default school" for parents who forgot to register their kid in a school of their choice. It is no surprise that Riviera was the school with the most disciplinary referrals, school arrests, and fights on campus.

Unfortunately, law enforcement, teachers, and judges often make biased conclusions about race and black youths. So race matters. But so does what Martin Luther King Jr. called the "violence of poverty" and the "black discouraged." And so does the failure of the community to recognize educational neglect and to intervene by establishing after-school programs, tutoring, and outreach to the parents in the schools, churches, and neighborhoods. And so does a prison mentality that makes the United States the world's largest jailor.

Recently a group of second- and third-graders came to observe my delinquency court. They hadn't been there ten minutes when I saw an alert black kid in the front row lean toward the teacher. I couldn't hear all his words, but I did catch "Why…so…blacks?" That cute little guy saw the elephant in the courtroom, and he wasn't afraid to ask why. Good for him.

He also looked so sweet, young, and innocent. So much like Javaris and the other two night swimmers on the day I first met them.

Race matters.

CHAPTER 2

Umatilla

THE WEBSITE LISTED IT as an alternative school: Umatilla Academy for Girls. Visitors entered the red-brick, one-story building by way of a wide circular driveway that enclosed a lush green lawn with an American flag flying high on its flagpole.

Located in rural central Florida, Umatilla is a small town of pretty little lakes and a tired-looking business district. Next door is Mount Dora, home to quaint bed-and-breakfasts, antique shops, fine dining, and bicycle pathways in Florida's "hill country."

Inside the school's double-locked doors, I learned later, security cameras regularly caught girls and staff at war with each other. Girls were dragged through hallways, pushed and struck repeatedly, and denied suicide watch or effective counseling. Girls retaliated by throwing plastic chairs and vacuum cleaners at staff and running wild through the common areas. Education was minimal. No one was safe. Girls who'd suffered years of family violence and abuse were abused again. And the operators of Umatilla Academy were trying to make a profit.[1]

Beginning in 1999, the state of Florida, under Governor Jeb Bush, began to privatize many state services, including those for delinquent youths, by contracting with companies that were to provide high-security residential treatment, education, recreation, and counseling. Diversified Behavioral Health Solutions (DBHS), a for-profit, Texas-based corporation, got the Umatilla contract for one hundred "high-risk" delinquent girls.

Our court had sentenced three girls to high-risk programs; all ended up at Umatilla. The sentencing process itself is complicated. The Florida Department of Juvenile Justice conducts a "staffing" of the youth with the parent, child, and probation officer present, then recommending a program level: low, moderate, or high risk. The judge either accepts or rejects the recommendation. The youth is placed on a waiting list for a particular program chosen by the department to meet her needs. While I hadn't chosen Umatilla, I was curious about the program. I wanted to visit unannounced to talk to our girls and report back to my colleagues.

In the summer of 2006, I pulled into the driveway. An old bronze plaque in the foyer described the facility as a hospital for crippled children. As such, it had been a major employer for the town. The hospital had closed, and the building was leased to DBHS in March 2005, well into Florida's privatization effort. I'd heard Governor Bush speak of his "dream" of a capital city with empty government buildings. I thought it somewhat grandiose, but I, like many others, respected his intelligence and energy. I was eager to see how well this privately run for-profit program worked. After all, my colleagues and I had sent three young women there.

Deja, sixteen, was a victim of physical abuse and a chaotic childhood. Her anger frequently got her in trouble. Angela, fifteen, was a constant runaway, violating probation. Her mother's boyfriend had raped her when she was thirteen. She turned from that early sexual experience to prostitution. Holly, sixteen, was openly, aggressively gay and hooked on the drug ecstasy.

When the security door swung open, I noticed the walls first. They were missing an identifiable color. They were neither white nor beige. It was the same for the few torn plastic chairs in the visitor's area. Colorless—unless "dirty dishwater" is a chip on a paint swatch. I didn't see any posters, murals, or artwork. No inspirational messages in the hallways. Nothing but... *nothing*.

My reluctant guide was the only assistant director working on a Friday afternoon. He began the tour in a grimy, smelly cafeteria and continued down a corridor of girls' single rooms. They were tiny and windowless, and contained only a cot, mattress, and blanket and a box for clothing. No photographs, cards, or other personal items. We passed a bathroom, which I assumed was under construction, as the toilet lacked a door, and the shower had no curtain. It turned out that there were never any doors or curtains in any of the bathrooms.

School was in session. As we walked toward the classrooms, I noticed a large pile of what looked like crumpled sheets stacked against a wall. I was surprised to see sheets, since I hadn't noticed them on any of the cots. Suddenly the sheets started moving! A mop of unruly black hair, a brown oval face, bright white teeth, and a dirty scrub suit rose from the colorless sheets.

"Judge Sullivan?" Deja asked, reaching up to greet me. I took her hands in mine. I'd handled her cases in dependency and delinquency court for the last three years. From what I'd already seen of Umatilla, I felt the sting of guilt. Although I'd legally followed the recommendation of the Department of Juvenile Justice and ordered Deja to a high-risk program of its choosing, I still felt guilt. A lot of guilt.

Deja had a string of misdemeanor battery charges and, finally, a felony for slapping a teacher. As a young girl, she'd been abused by a number of her mother's roommates and boyfriends. She lived with her great-grandmother, who died when Deja entered high school. She then bounced among foster homes, had multiple behavioral issues, and disrupted school when she did attend. A child psychologist diagnosed Deja with post-traumatic stress disorder, conduct disorder and depression.

"She's one of the tough ones that won't attend class," my guide said, swinging a chain of keys toward Deja. "Just as well, as she has a new charge for assaulting one of the girls."

I walked with Deja into the science class. Like most hospital patient rooms, it contained a tiny bathroom and space for two hospital beds. There were no beds, of course. Ten or twelve girls were sprawled against the walls; two or three perched on stools, heads resting on their hands on a round table. A very large man, the teacher, sat next to an old TV, watching a National Geographic video about the oceans. No conversation, no instruction, no interest from any of the girls.

"Deja, is this what it's like all the time?" I asked.

"Yes," she said.

My guide let us talk alone. Deja began to cry.

"The girls are running the place," she told me. "They sleep in class and then revolt all night. There's no order; no one cares. It's scary. I try to stay out of it, but I got a new charge when I jumped a girl who was starting trouble. The guards don't care. They're mostly men. New ones all the time. They laugh. They look at us when we're on the toilet or in the shower.

"And we don't get out to exercise. They say our 'meds' makes us unfit to go out in the heat. There's a basketball area outside. I haven't been outside in a month."

I couldn't deal with this. I wanted out. I wanted to talk to Dr. Judy Britt, the program's psychologist, or one of our child psychologists, or someone in the Department of Juvenile Justice, or another juvenile judge. I couldn't believe what I was seeing.

"I'll be back soon, Deja," I said, giving her a hug. I couldn't face Angela or Holly that day, so I asked my guide to take me out. Right before the security door, he paused and suggested that I take a look at the auditorium.

I found myself in a huge, banquet-size room, fully air-conditioned, with a large stage—and absolutely empty. I could imagine an indoor gym, fitness area, and art and theatrical classes. "Wow," I said to my guide, who smiled proudly. "We'd like to use this sometime," he explained, "but we haven't figured out how to get a secure lock on the outside door."

Upon returning home, three things happened very quickly. I called our administrative judge, Marion Fleming, and she immediately issued an order prohibiting the court from sentencing our girls to any high-risk program. I reached Anthony Schembri, then the secretary of juvenile justice, begging him to visit and audit the program immediately. And I found Dr. Britt.

"Most of the girls have mental health problems better treated in a psychiatric setting," she offered right away. "I'm very concerned that the girls are incurring new charges while here at Umatilla. Treatment and training dollars are scarce, and staff turnover is a huge problem."

Dr. Britt referred me to a mental health counselor, who put it another way: "There's not a lot of dangling carrots. No mile markers, rewards, reinforcers. Just what you see."

DJJ Secretary Schembri is a round man, funny, bold, and outspoken. He was recruited by Governor Bush to head juvenile justice after a stint running prisons in New York. His first stop on his visit to Umatilla was the cafeteria. "What kind of a grilled cheese sandwich is this?" he asked, holding up one thin piece of processed cheese. "Two slices are required, three taste better, and if my wife's not looking, I use four pieces of cheese." He expressed nothing but disgust for the facility and put it on a fast track for closure unless many things changed.

Ron Rambaldi, the program director, acknowledged problems but blamed the Florida legislature for not providing sufficient funding. Direct staff turnover exceeded 300 percent a year, and staff salaries started at a paltry $10 per hour. Guards worked double shifts to keep up with the high turnover. Rambaldi was suspected of running a program with half the necessary staff while billing the state for the full amount. He denied that this was profitable, claiming that overtime and worker's compensation ate up any profits.

I visited Umatilla two months later with two of the state's finest juvenile justice officials: Liz Gattarello, our circuit's commitment manager, and Michelle Jameson, then a senior probation officer. They knew Angela and Holly well from encounters in court. The three of us sat around a table while Angela, a tall, olive-skinned brunette, and Holly, a short, pudgy blonde, paced around us.

"So what's with the dirty clothes and the pants hanging off your butt?" Liz asked Angela.

"They don't give us enough clothes. Everything's dirty. We can't change shirts when we want to. It's disgusting."

"And the pants?"

"We do it to annoy the staff. It's boring here. The teachers suck, and the girls are out of control. It's so easy to get into fights."

"And whose bad choices are responsible for that?" Michelle put in.

"Well…mine, I guess," Angela admitted.

"Hey, Holly, do you have any new friends here?" Michelle asked with a little smile

"You betcha!" she replied, pumping her arm. "I've learned not to hit on them right away. Things are getting a little better here—at least the food is— but we shouldn't be here. The counseling's a joke. We want out."

To be fair, improvements had been made in the last few weeks. Dr. Britt had become the program manager. She was a caring, experienced psychologist, candid about the program's shortcomings. The improvements, while mostly cosmetic, were still important. Murals and posters decorated newly painted walls. The reception room was furnished colorfully. The girls were allowed personal photographs in their rooms. The auditorium had been used for a holiday party, and a number of brand-new soccer and basketballs sat in the exercise yard. The cafeteria was cleaner, and the food tastier.

But despite some progress, serious mistreatment and abuse continued. Gangs of girls roamed the halls. Some were punched by staff. A guard was arrested for dragging a girl by her ankles down the hallway, causing severe rug burns. A girl who'd swallowed nails wasn't taken to a hospital. Teens on suicide watch were left unsupervised. And the high turnover of untrained male guards continued. Toilets and showers remained open, so that the girls could be seen at all times.

Teenage female offenders are a difficult population, especially if they have been victims of physical or sexual abuse. They don't want to be touched. They seek solitude and privacy. Dr. Lawanda Ravoira, director of the National Council on Crime and Delinquency Center for Girls and Young Women, and an expert on effective and humane treatment of incarcerated girls, was brought in from her Jacksonville office on an emergency basis to try to stop the rampant mistreatment at Umatilla.

"The Umatilla program was a bad idea from inception," she told me. "Facilities designed to house large numbers of girls often create an environment for further victimization and abuse. That happened at Umatilla. Not only was it too big, but it was located in an isolated rural community, which made it hard to recruit qualified staff. The turnover rate of staff was incredibly high, and chronic staff shortages resulted in poor care of the girls.

"Basic community support services to address the mental and emotional health needs of girls were practically nonexistent," Lawanda continued. "There was a fundamental lack of understanding of how to treat traumatized girls. The result was a commitment facility that was chaotic, volatile, and unsafe for both staff and girls."

I've since visited a number of excellent residential programs for delinquent youths, in Florida and elsewhere. Some were state run, with excellent results and low turnover. Others were run by private corporations, with good results, stability, and efficiency. A few were substandard—none, however, as bad as Umatilla.

"Many mistakes are made by thinking that girls' programs are actually boys' programs painted pink," said Barry Krisberg, president of the National Council on Crime and Delinquency. Umatilla was this, and less: It would have been unfit for boys as well.

Girls in need of psychiatric care went untreated and were accused of assaulting other girls and Umatilla's untrained staff. Some of these charges were filed as felonies, with the girls often transferred to local detention facilities. Those who left Umatilla carried with them the scar of a record of violent crimes.

My colleagues and I removed Deja, Angela, and Holly from Umatilla before the state closed the program in 2007, cancelling its contract with Diversified Behavioral Health Solutions. Joshua Ford, the company president, complained that shutting it down within two years of operation was "unfair," claiming that his company was working out what he called the "bumps in the road." Really? *Bumps in the road?* The Umatilla Police Department received so many phone calls reporting abuse at the facility—124, to be exact—that it established its own booking station there. I guess that was one efficiency Umatilla could brag about.[2, 3, 4]

Three years after my visits, Holly had remained crime free, and Angela had racked up one criminal mischief charge, which was resolved. However, Deja, the girl with the most baggage, had spent considerable time in jail on fleeing and eluding charges. I was beginning to understand that for us judges, juvenile justice is a process of learning, *un*learning, and *re*learning.

CHAPTER 3

Crossover Killer

MAYBE AMBER AND JOHN would have married and had children together. Maybe they would have just stayed friends, hanging out, attending each other's weddings. They certainly had a lot in common. They loved the outdoors, camping, hiking, exploring the wilderness, and animals. They were both twenty-six years old, community college students in Gainesville, Florida, who worked part-time jobs and had close families and big dreams. Amber Peck wanted to be a veterinarian. She'd just been awarded a grant to study zoo conservation in Australia. John Parker served two tours of duty in Afghanistan as a marine and had returned home eager to be a real dad to his eight-year-old daughter, who adored him.

On January 3, 2006, Amber and John camped overnight in the Ocala National Forest, central Florida's wonderland of huge springs, winding streams, scenic lakes, and lush foliage. They parked Amber's red Jeep in public parking and hiked a few miles to the park's remote and pristine Juniper Forest section, where they made camp on a hillside overlooking Hidden Pond. Vehicles and machines were barred from the Juniper section of the forest. Even park employees used hand tools to maintain the soft, sandy hiking paths, pines, and palm trees. John knew the forest like it was his backyard, according to his mother, Vicky Parker, and he was eager to share its quiet beauty with Amber. They told their families they would return the next day, as they were both very busy with work and school. No one reported seeing them that night, but perhaps Amber and John saw raccoons, deer, armadillos, or even a bear.

ON THAT SAME DAY, Leo Boatman's future looked pretty promising, too. At nineteen, he'd recently been released from Omega Juvenile Prison, a maximum-risk facility. While there, he'd obtained his high-school diploma. He'd moved with his Uncle Vic into a mobile home in Largo, Florida. For the first time in years, he was living with family. He worked at a Hooters restaurant and had also lined up a part-time job at a bakery. In two days, he would begin community college. Boatman told his uncle that he wanted to stay out of trouble and be part of the family again. He told his friends that he was looking forward to college and wanted to become a veterinary technician.

Boatman had aged out of foster care while in Omega. The state had recently initiated a program to provide financial support to foster kids aging out of care, especially those attending college. So the state sent him $800 a month to help with rent and tuition. Boatman's simultaneous involvement with two state agencies, the Department of Juvenile Justice and the Department of Children and Families, meant that he was a "crossover kid."

Boatman boarded a bus in Clearwater to take him to Silver Springs, in the Ocala National Forest. He bought some camping equipment and stuffed it into a travel bag. He carried an AK-47 assault rifle he'd stolen from his Uncle Vic, who'd been keeping it for a friend. He began hiking to Hidden Pond.

Three days later, after an exhaustive search, Amber's father and brother-in-law found Amber and John shot to death, their bodies partially hidden in the bushes and banks of Hidden Pond.

After the shooting, Boatman had hitchhiked to a Holiday Inn, then taken a bus home to Largo the next day. He returned the rifle to its place, along with the remaining ammunition. He bought a pellet gun and put it in a blue nylon bag with his camping equipment. He attended his first day at St. Petersburg College before he was arrested for the slayings that evening at home while doing his homework. The tip came from Joey Tierney, a twenty-year-old visitor who'd remembered picking up a hitchhiker in the woods a day after the shooting. His passenger had told him that he'd been living in the forest for a few days but wanted a motel. Tierney knew the area well and wasn't surprised, even when Boatman told him that he had a hunting knife and rifle. Boatman didn't hide his identity from Tierney or the motel clerk. Tierney later collected the $5,000 reward and said he was through picking up hitchhikers.

Hotel records, store receipts, interviews, and ballistics tests tied Boatman to the scene. Police matched a slug fired from the rifle with a bullet recovered from one of the victims. They proved that the AK-47 was the murder weapon. Boatman's friend Briana Ryan told authorities that he had confessed to her, saying, "I went out in the woods and killed someone." When she asked whether he had killed a homeless person, he replied, "I wouldn't kill a bum, because they would have nothing to lose. I killed two preppies." In the videotaped confession Boatman made to detectives, he said, "I used to think stuff like that was appalling, you know...I'm not saying like I don't care emotional-wise or I don't have emotions or whatnot. I'm just saying I don't feel them like I should."[1]

Boatman's public defenders negotiated a life sentence without parole to avoid the death penalty. The families of Amber and John agreed, as it would spare them the heartache of having to hear the details of the crime. At the sentencing before Circuit Judge Willard Pope, on July 30, 2007, Boatman appeared emotionless, head down. "I can't offer an explanation, because there is none...I'm sorry," he said. John's mother, Vicky Parker, called the murders senseless and described her family's horrible, vivid memories of discovering the bodies. "Only one person in this courtroom knows the truth," she said, "and he, I hope, will spend the rest of his life wondering was it worth it."[2]

Amber's father, David Peck, read a poem his daughter had written about looking forward to her move to Australia for college. Then he spoke for the young woman, recalling the murders. "You are such a coward. You hid in the bushes and waited for me and Johnny to approach you, then came up to me as I was crying and screaming for you to let me live...Though I only had a flesh wound, you came up to me and put the rifle to my head and pulled the trigger to silence me forever...[but] you didn't silence my dreams...they will continue to be heard long and loud. I will not be silenced." Glenda Peck told the judge her daughter wouldn't have wanted Boatman put to death.[1,5,6]

I decided to correspond with Leo Boatman because I wanted something from him: I wanted to know what he was thinking when he stole the gun and boarded the bus. I wanted to know what he was thinking when he first spotted Amber and John, when he aimed the rifle, and when he fired the fatal shots. I wanted to know because every day in court I see crossover kids living in chaos, locked up in juvenile programs, bouncing among foster homes, lacking positive reinforcements, family, and true friends. I see their empty eyes, I hear their flat voices, and I sense their hopelessness, mistrust, and lack of empathy for others. We—citizens and taxpayers—are the surrogate parents of these children. How many of them will end up in prison? How often are we raising murderers?

I wrote to him at the Cross City Correctional Institution. His speedy reply surprised me. It was neat and well written.

Your letter came at a good time and was well received. Normally I would ignore such a letter, as I usually do, but recent events have caused me to do some deep thinking. Let me explain that before I respond to your letter.

Anybody with life in prison is always looking for some way out. I began to question if I had made the right decisions legally, and so I was thinking of filing a 3.850 [ineffective representation of counsel]. But my lawyers came out to see me and convinced me that my decision was best for me and gave closure to the victims' families. That's when I began to think of some other way to continue my life. As it was, my life felt like it was serving no purpose.... Anyways, to make a long story short, I came to a lot of conclusions. I now have the goal of trying to use my past, my knowledge of foster care and the juvenile justice system, to help others, maybe prevent kids from going through some of the things I went through. I even began dreaming of having certain foster homes shut down.

I say all this not because I feel sorry for myself or want a pity party thrown. Instead I want to draw attention to the flaws in our system.[3]

When Boatman mailed the letter, he must have called the only person in the world he believes cares for him, Steve Shick, telling him about my inquiries. Steve drove an hour in a heavy rainstorm to the courthouse to talk to me. When Boatman was ten, a juvenile judge had appointed Steve to be his advocate in court, officially called guardian ad litem. The relationship grew, and Steve, single and childless in his fifties, wanted to adopt Leo, but, he said, the state stopped the adoption process when Boatman kept breaking the law and running away from foster care.

"I still consider myself his father," Steve said to me, blaming the child welfare and juvenile justice systems for treating Boatman unfairly. Steve provided a list of eight "significant events" in Boatman's life that he claimed led to the tragedy at Hidden Pond:

1. He was abandoned by his mother, who had mental health problems and who later drowned. He entered state care at age four and was adopted by his maternal grandmother. He never knew his father.

2. He was abused mentally and emotionally by his grandmother and sister, Rosie, who was the grandmother's favorite child. He was called "stupid" at every opportunity.

3. When he was ten, his grandmother gave him back to the state of Florida as a failed adoption, but the state allowed visitation between them anyway because he wanted it.

4. He lived in a series of foster homes, some of them abusive, and he became a chronic runaway.

5. Between the ages of nine and nineteen, he was consistently locked up in juvenile justice facilities.

6. His child welfare caseworker seemed eager to classify everything he did as a felony and wanted him locked up. The caseworker seemed eager to have him committed as an adult.

7. He wanted to be adopted by Steve but still ran from his care at age thirteen and spent the rest of his youth in juvenile prisons.

8. When Boatman was released at age nineteen, Steve offered help, but Boatman told him to "get out of my life."[4]

Steve said that he still loves Boatman. He remembers a spunky, bright twelve-year-old with a horrendous background and a need to test boundaries. He remembers a foster child who complained again and again of severe abuse at the hands of foster parents, to no avail. He remembers a delinquent youth who was never given the opportunity of probation but locked away instead. Steve cried as he described to me the horror of reading the newspaper headlines of Boatman's arrest and confession. He has never asked him why he killed Amber and John. They've never spoken of it. That's what I still wanted to know.

Warden Claude Henderson and his assistant warden, Erich Hummel, welcomed me to the Charlotte Correctional Institution, the maximum-risk state prison in Punta Gorda that Boatman was moved to after he was accused of attacking another prisoner at Cross City. They provided a brief tour of the facility. They'd placed Boatman in the tightest level of "close management": a quad consisting of single cells, approximately ten by twelve feet, where prisoners lived at all times except for a weekly shower and biweekly exercise in a chain-link-fenced "dog run" adjacent to the cells. Meal trays were delivered through a slot in the door. These inmates had no access to TV or the prison library; however, they could order two books a week from the librarian.

Assistant Warden Hummel gave me an alarm device to wear on my belt and escorted me through security to a large visitor's room. After I sat down on a folding chair facing an opening in the wall, two guards brought Boatman into a small boxed cage. A grey mesh screen and heavy crisscrossed steel bars in the opening separated our faces. Physical contact, even by fingernail, would have been impossible. Slowly my eyes adjusted to the screening, and I could make out his face, a thinner version of the young man I'd seen in the newspaper clippings.

We talked for an hour about prison life, and his desire to get into "open population" and perhaps transfer to a prison where he could take some college courses. We liked the same mystery writers—Michael Connelly, Harlan Coben, Lee Child—and he told me he was angry with himself for staying up all night to finish one of the two books he got that week. "I'm so bored," he said, adding that it was difficult to face life without parole. He said that talk of prison rape was "highly exaggerated," as there are "so many gay guys in prison that, once you get into open pop, the sex is consensual," called "rocking you to sleep."

His voice grew hard, and he spat out hatred for an abusive foster father he had lived with during adolescence. The man would discipline the boys by making them "do ten thousand jumping jacks next to him," while he sat watching TV and drinking beer. "No," Boatman said. "You never finished the ten thousand—that was the point." He said most of the foster boys ran away, then went into detention and eventually prison. "They made you sit naked on a towel to keep you from running away." He claimed that the few gifts he received from family, like headphones, were taken from him. He spoke of sexual abuse by an older male relative of the foster dad. He claimed he saw his caseworker only when he was taken to court.

Sure enough, my research confirmed that the foster parents Boatman named were licensed as therapeutic foster parents; however, their home was closed in June 2004 when Boatman was in a juvenile prison. There were verified abuse reports of bizarre punishment, failure to protect, inadequate supervision, beatings, excessive corporal punishment, mental injury, and inappropriate and excessive isolation.

Bad as this was, Boatman saved his most bitter words for the five years he had spent at Omega, the juvenile prison in Bradenton, Florida, which has since been closed.

"I was the longest-serving boy in Omega, from age fourteen to nineteen," he said. "It was scared-straight shock. The guards made the difference. It went from strict discipline, like it was supposed to be, to guards who would pounce, yell, slam you into walls. I was taunted by guards who read my medical records and who would shout personal things, like 'No one wants you anymore.'

"We slept in separate cells on concrete bunks. The guards enjoyed the abuse. They beat the crap out of you for talking, wrote you up for minor infractions like not raising your hand in class or moving your eyes in detention.

"One guard made like he was pointing a gun at my head, and said, 'If I had a choice—pop!' But one guy, he was a good guard. He would talk to you."

Boatman said that his only visitor during those years was his grandmother. "We were starting to get to a better relationship. Then she died, and they didn't tell me for a while.

"When I was fifteen, I spent two months in solitary confinement. I snapped. You can't do that to a boy unless you want to make an animal." I had read Boatman's delinquency record, an escalating list of assaults and batteries that seemed to grow more violent. Most occurred in juvenile programs, with other boys or guards.

Boatman's sister, Rosie, didn't show up to get him when he was released from Omega, so the chaplain drove him to her Clearwater apartment. She didn't answer the door or the phone. The chaplain left him there with a $20 bill, and hours later Rosie opened the door. She told Boatman that she'd been arrested again—her third time for driving with a suspended license—and asked him for a loan to hire a lawyer. A few weeks later, he signed over his first checks from the state to Rosie.

Boatman then moved into a trailer with his Uncle Vic, who'd recently been released from jail. "It was a little tin can," he said of his new home, but he had a job at Hooters and an eye on a real apartment for the two of them. He'd received some vouchers for new clothing. He enrolled in college. He said he was "excited" about his life at this time. Then he found a motorcycle that he wanted, put a down payment on it, but crashed it before Uncle Vic gave him the lessons he'd promised. "He was gay, had a boyfriend in Fort Meyers, and was never home to teach me. He also took my rent money."

Suddenly Boatman felt saddled with debt and victimized by relatives. He relived his complicated Omega feelings. "I wanted a paramilitary life; I wanted to take care of myself alone in the wilderness. I also thought about hurting someone; what it would be like." Opportunity arose when Vic's friend, living nearby in his trailer, asked Vic to keep his AK-47 rifle while his parents were visiting, as he had a three-year-old daughter, and his parents would be angry if they saw the rifle in the trailer. "I wanted to buy it," Boatman said, "but I didn't have the money. I'd never seen a gun like that before. I'd never shot a gun."

Boatman startled me by becoming agitated when we began to talk about the murders. He paced the little box and then sat down, narrating a straightforward, factual, and chilling tale. "It took me two hours to hike in to Hidden Pond," he recalled. "I was climbing a hill when I saw a guy and girl taking down their tent. He was real nice, asking me where I was going. I told him I was hiking further in, and he gave me some good directions. I watched them carry some of their camp things downhill. I sat on the hillside, thinking I would take their campsite once they left it. Then I took the rifle out and watched them walk back up to get the rest of their stuff. I raised the rifle and aimed it at the guy, and then I thought, *What if they should see me pointing a gun at them?* I'd read James Patterson books, and I knew the difference a second could make. So I shot him. He fell to the ground. She screamed, and I shot her."

And then he walked down the hill, put the gun to her head and shot her again.

PART II

Despair

CHAPTER 4

No Peace at Home: Violence and Juvenile Court

JUVENILE COURT IS ABOUT VIOLENCE.

Kids are violent because they've experienced violence. A juvenile judge hearing dependency cases (involving abuse, abandonment, and neglect) and delinquency cases discovers this quickly. I learned it the first Monday on the job.

Mondays were my "duty day," which meant that I presided over the detention and shelter hearings beginning at a quarter to eight in the morning, as well as a docket chock-full of dependency motions. Monday afternoons alternated among delinquency arraignments, truancy cases, and a special girls court, which we called Girls Mission Possible.

Mondays were about violence.

Child protective investigators present evidence to me to justify "sheltering" the child, meaning removing the child or children from the parent(s) or caretaker(s). Their jobs are incredibly difficult. They respond to calls to the child abuse hotline at any hour, and gain entry to a house where drugs and guns may be present and where there are almost always signs of domestic violence. Then they have to remove crying children from their parents and find safe shelter placements for them immediately. Here's a sample of the actual evidence presented by investigators in my court to justify removal:

1. The boyfriend was smacking the mother in the backyard. The child, who is three, tried to stop the boyfriend. He hit the little girl in the face and said, "Get away, little bitch!" The mother was begging the boyfriend to stop. He grabbed her by the hair and told her to "take the little bitch to her room." When the mother is at work, the child is often heard saying, "Stop it, stop it, stop doing that to me." It's unknown what is being done to the child.

2. The sixteen-year-old mother became upset with her stepfather and threw her infant daughter on the bed in front of him, with a plastic bag tied over her head. The mom's seven-year-old sister had to remove the bag. The house was filthy, with dirty diapers lying around and little food present anywhere. The mom stays out late at night with friends and refuses to get up to feed her baby. All adults tested positive for marijuana.

3. For the last couple of years, Mom has used marijuana, ecstasy, mushrooms, and cocaine. Mom has put her "blunt" to her eight-year-old son's mouth and encouraged him to "take a hit." When he cries, "No," Mom and Stepdad punch him on the face, arms, and legs.

4. There is no furniture whatsoever in the home except for a TV. The children sleep on two thin mats on a filthy floor. They have bruises on their arms and legs and are not enrolled in school. Rotting chicken was in the refrigerator; the toilet was not working and full of feces.

5. The two-month-old infant has fractures to his right arm and left leg. It is unknown how he got these injuries. The mother blames the four-year-old sister, "who is very rough with him" and pulls his arms and legs through the crib. Upon examination at the hospital, he was found to have eight to ten rib fractures. The doctor stated there is no accidental explanation for any of the injuries.

6. The mother spends the twelve-year-old daughter's disability check on drugs and made her daughter have sex with the drug dealer so the mother could have more drugs. The mother threatens her with a knife, and she has to lock her mother out of her room. Witnesses have

seen the mother running in and out of the house nude while under the influence of crack.

7. During a verbal altercation, the mom's paramour threw items about the house, punched a hole in the wall, and pushed the mother to the floor. The children in the house ran to the window and shouted to children outside the house, who called the police. The paramour denied everything, although his hand was very swollen and appeared broken. He has an outstanding battery charge for pushing and slapping his ex-girlfriend while she was holding their six-month-old child.

8. The mother attempted to cut her wrists with a knife while the children were present. She wouldn't drop the knife until the deputy pulled his gun. The mother admitted to a history of having affairs during her marriage. One affair was with the father's stepfather in a motel room, with the children being told to stay in the bathroom until the sex act was completed. The mother's defense to the scenario was that she had not actually locked the kids in the bathroom. The mother was arrested as a teen after engaging in an agreement with her own biological father to kill her stepmother. The charges against the mother were not filed, as she testified against the father, who was acquitted.

9. When the mother was pregnant with her son, her boyfriend beat her. When her child turned three, the boyfriend came back into her life and threatened to kill the mother and child. In front of the child, he poured lighter fluid on the mother and began to strangle her. The mother admitted that he had threatened them both with a machete.

10. The child is in the care of her mother, who is engaged and planning to marry a registered sex offender who is serving time in prison for lewd and lascivious behavior. The mother has been exchanging letters and photos of her child with this offender. Handwritten letters from the offender were reviewed, and they were found to contain specific requests for nude photographs of the child, i.e., "I want pictures of her pussy and ass...she shaves there? How fucking naughty is that? I bet she has a cute pussy." The mother confirmed she read these comments but said that he wrote them in fun. The mother's computer

revealed pictures of the child in distress or crying and the mother shoving an item into the child's mouth so that her eyes would roll back in her head.

11. On a daily basis, the father hits the mother on her stomach and thighs, leaving bruises, because she is pregnant again. The father encourages the ten-year-old boy to take part in the beatings. He did so and then jumped over a fence and broke his arm. The parents refuse to get him medical attention. The five-year-old girl hides in her room because she is scared. The mother balls up to protect her unborn child, and has been hit with metal chairs, ash trays, and fists. The father was charged with aggravated battery, but the mother refuses to testify. The parents are from Egypt and have lived in the United States for three months. They speak only Arabic.[1]

PRECEDING THESE OFTEN HORRIFIC shelter hearings on duty days were the detention hearings, which took place each morning for children arrested and locked up the day before. Some were charged with property crimes such as burglary, shoplifting, and auto theft. More were charged with crimes of anger and violence, such as strong-arm robbery, fighting at school, assault, battery, and domestic violence. Our team—prosecutor, public defender, psychologist, probation officer, and judge—had a very short time for each case to determine whether the youth should remain locked up, be placed on house arrest, or be released, and if so to whom. Critical decisions had to be made in minutes.

All kinds of kids commit property crimes. Some do it once and never again. However, kids who have been victims of violence commit violent crimes, often again and again.

The violence that kids experience changes the development of their brains. They become angry and impulsive, unable to control their emotions. Magnetic Resonance Imaging (MRI) studies have confirmed a change in brain development in critical areas that control anger and emotions for this group of kids.

As reported by the American Psychiatric Association in its January 2002 newsletter, MRI studies and examinations performed by Michael

DeBellis, M.D., on a group of 41 abused and 61 healthy children confirmed that changes in brain development associated with chemical surges in the abused children cause cognitive, behavioral and emotional problems. These are the angry kids I see in court who frustrate teachers, behavior specialists, and law enforcement. Puppets of a violent childhood, like Casey.

Casey's feet didn't touch the ground when he sat on the courtroom bench at his detention hearing. Short for nine years of age, the blue-eyed, tow-headed kid leaned against his thin, frazzled mother, who sported a huge black eye. She'd leaned down to discipline him, she said, when he punched her in the eye with a closed fist, nearly fracturing her cheekbone. At the disposition of his case a few weeks later, I asked him why he had hit her. "I watched her boyfriend do it," he replied. "It's the way he gets what he wants."

Juvenile court is about violence.

Casey's case is far too familiar and easy to explain. He was imitating Mom's boyfriends to get what he wanted, and Mom became a victim of another kind of domestic violence. In our country over the last ten years, domestic violence homicides accounted for one in five of all homicides.

If I'm blessed or just lucky, it's because I work with three highly skilled, compassionate, and articulate child psychologists who evaluate the most troubled kids in our court. Their offices are across from the courtrooms, which they monitor by closed-circuit TV. They are just seconds away if a judge needs them. Drs. Cynthia Zarling, Christine Jaggi, and Adele Solazzo evaluate the child victims of violence who turn violent toward others: Mom, Dad, teacher, sibling, classmate, or stranger. We meet on occasion to discuss the evolving nature of domestic violence.

"It's easier for a child to be angry than frightened," Dr. Zarling said, explaining why a child reacts differently to being struck than to witnessing Dad beating Mom repeatedly. "With Casey, it was easy to see that he not only gained a role model in Mom's boyfriend—who got what he wanted by beating up on her—but he lost all respect for Mom, as he didn't think she could keep them safe. So it was easier to hit her." Casey was angry at his mother, not frightened for her.

"Kids rarely express it directly, but their undercurrents and actions, including running away, show that above all they want to be safe," said Dr. Jaggi. "It's often 'fight or flight,' and combined with raging hormones, it creates a situation where they are constantly checking their environment for potential abuse."

"Yes," Dr. Solazzo chimed in. "That's why girl victims can't stand to be touched, even by teachers or school resource officers. It's a primitive response to danger. They are wired to respond."

I've learned so much from these child psychologists about normal kids put in abnormal circumstances of stress. The violence affects their ability to trust, to attach, to feel secure with an adult. They push away.

"Kids exposed to violence are so attuned to their environment," Dr. Solazzo added. "They are never looking inside themselves. They are always looking for things to happen."

"Exactly," agreed Dr. Zarling. "They put themselves away on the inside. It's just their body taking the hits, hearing the violence. They are so adept at external toughness. They keep the good side inside. They join gangs as much for a perceived safety as for criminal gain. Someone to 'watch my back' seems reasonable to a child victim of violence, especially one with poor family support."

Dr. Solazzo reminded me of a teenager named Sarobia, whom we'd seen in our girls' court. She'd done poorly in a tightly structured day school for delinquents, constantly using profanity and picking fights. "She perceived everything as threatening, her acts as well as the acts of others," Dr. Solazzo said. The Department of Juvenile Justice wanted to commit Sarobia to a residential program out of town. Yet she'd been working part-time at a McDonald's for two years, with no problems, no profanity, no fighting. We decided to transfer her to another high school, and she did fine. "She didn't need her toughness anymore," Dr. Solazzo explained.

"Family violence needs a family solution," Dr. Jaggi said, and all agreed. "These kids are arrested for violence in the home, but nothing happens to the adults. Somehow, this doesn't seem fair, and how then do they view the justice system? Kids have a great sense of fairness."

Fairness may even increase if a working group of child psychiatrists and psychologists affiliated with the National Child Traumatic Stress Network has its way. The NCTSN, established by Congress in 2001, and comprising treatment centers around the country, seeks to improve access to care and therapy for youngsters subjected to various forms of trauma, including domestic violence. The team is proposing a new diagnosis called "developmental trauma disorder," or DTD, to capture the reality of life for the children that I see in court: exposed to multiple, chronic traumas, usually within their own families.[2,3]

With the help of our child psychologists, I make this diagnosis every day with kids like these:

Austin is an adopted youngster, depressed and pessimistic, who has experienced multiple, severe losses from violence in the family. His stepfather was killed in fight with his mother's boyfriend. His uncle, who mentored him, was imprisoned for domestic violence. He alternates between angry resentment and self-blame, with associated feelings of inadequacy and thoughts of suicide. He's rapidly accumulating a lot of fairly minor charges, like hitting schoolmates and shoplifting.

Kerona was placed in shelter care due to domestic violence in the home. She doesn't have much of a delinquency record, yet she's living between relatives, needs mental health counseling, and admits to having used marijuana since she was thirteen and drinking alcohol from the age of twelve. Now sixteen, Kerona smokes pot daily (probably with her mom) and has experimented with ecstasy, cocaine, and prescription medications such as Soma and Valium.

Tony, also age sixteen, reports, "my life sucks." His mother has severe anxiety and substance abuse issues. His stepfather has a history of aggression. Tony saw him beat his mother. Tony's situation worsened when his mother died from an overdose of prescription pills. His stepfather kicked him and his older sister out of the house the day after the funeral. Tony has been living with his maternal grandmother ever since, although his mother had claimed that his grandmother had kept him locked in a room for hours. Tony is doing poorly in school, as he feels overwhelmed by his situation and feelings of hopelessness. He is looking for a lifeline but doesn't want to be depicted as weak.

Allison's mother, in and out of prison for most of her life, received a fifteen-year sentence for drug trafficking with her violent boyfriend. At fourteen, Allison was formally removed from her mother's care and placed with the grandmother who'd essentially raised her. Grandma now says that Allison is too difficult to manage and should be placed in foster care. The girl admits to being "lazy" and having "an attitude," but she has no idea that her grandmother wants to place her in state care. Allison has been skipping school and was seriously truant for much of sixth and seventh grades. That has worsened, and she will have to repeat ninth grade. She acknowledges being sexually active and says she's stopped attending church with the family. Almost certainly, Allison will move in with a boyfriend who will abuse her. She would get food and shabby housing; he would get ready sex. The cycle will repeat itself when she has a child.

Tiwan, age ten, small and thin, was arrested along with his twelve-year-old sister and eleven-year-old cousin for purse snatching, which is filed as strong-arm robbery, and aggravated battery, both felonies. All three live with their grandmother, who is on kidney dialysis and unable to supervise the kids. Tiwan's mother recently got out of prison where she had gone for stabbing a boyfriend; the kids resent her, and she's no help to Grandma. The three kids often leave home in the middle of the night to meet a fourteen-year-old youth, James, who selects the victims of their crimes. James beat up on Tiwan so often that Tiwan felt grateful when he finally quit, happy to be "accepted" by James and his friends. Mom told the psychologist to "lock up the kids" and declined to be interviewed.

Lexie is a sixteen-year-old rule breaker whose mother describes her as angry and rebellious, "with an attitude." She's charged with aggravated domestic battery on her mother. Lexie spent time in foster care when her mother was hospitalized for severe injuries inflicted by Lexie's father, who later died of alcoholism. The girl's nineteen-year-old half brother recently moved back into the home, and Lexie resents him and his drug use, anger, and arguments, and blames him for the depression and stress she feels. Her mother is intimidated by him and offers her little reassurance or positive attention.

Robert's aggression spilled over into school. He fractured a kid's shoulder at the bus stop and dislocated his brother's finger. He has a long history of trauma, including exposure to severe domestic violence and bizarre physical abuse. During his parents' divorce, when he was four, his father exercised weekend visitation by tying him to a tree in a remote section of a woods. Although his mother had been beaten and controlled by the father, she didn't believe Robert until he was brought home by the police with ant bites all over his body. His father went to prison for aggravated child abuse. This twelve-year-old says he "has to let the anger out, and once I let it all out, I can't think straight."

Kevonte is a ten-year-old charged with threatening other kids with knives and throwing rocks at moving cars. He has a history of suicide threats at school, self-destructive behaviors, and aggressiveness toward others. His mother took him off medication, as she "got tired of giving it to him." Two years earlier, she'd been charged with child abuse when he and his brother were found wandering the streets at one in the morning. She denies that an abusive boyfriend lives with the family, yet Kevonte describes him, his clothes, where he sleeps, and how he yells at everyone. The boy has never known his father. When asked, if he had three wishes, what they would be, Kevonte couldn't think of one.

Roshelle, sixteen, is still angry at her mother for being sent away to her grandparents at age eight, as Mom chose not to leave her violent boyfriend. The paternal grandparents were both alcoholics and physically abused Roshelle and her younger brother, whom she tried to protect. Roshelle remembers her mother's boyfriend acting out sexually with her. She never received counseling for this and became sexually preoccupied with both males and females in her early teens. At a special school for troubled girls, she presented as dramatic and manipulative, and would lie on the floor and refuse to do anything when she didn't get her way. She resents her mother's attempts to discipline her and has run away over forty times.

Charlton's mother states that there is "not a peaceful moment at home." Fifteen-year-old Charlton is fascinated with weapons, especially knives, and is threatening and aggressive with his mother and siblings—that is, when he isn't clinging to his mother, wanting to sleep with her at night. His mother says that his extreme attachment to her began when he was a toddler: She was pregnant again, and his father, who didn't want another child, repeatedly beat her in front of Charlton, hoping to cause her to miscarry. Charlton is in court for having taken out his anger on his teacher, who called the police.

Tee Jay, a depressed, disruptive, and aggressive thirteen-year-old, is charged with domestic battery against his mother. He claims that *he* is the victim—that she "set him up" with the police. According to Tee Jay, the fact

that she refused to pick him up from detention backs up his story. He is failing in school, but his mother refuses to intervene. At home, he has given up;
still angry that he was allegedly set up," he seeks to avoid all confrontations.
Tee Jay claims that he woke up to find his mother choking him. He called
the police, but when they arrived, his mother and her boyfriend claimed that
Tee Jay had punched the mother. At the interview with the psychologist, he
was unkempt, with long, dirty fingernails and a mass of dreadlocks that he
twisted in an agitated fashion throughout the session.

Jonathan suffered through a chaotic and violent childhood, which con-
tributes to his explosive temper. His parents separated when he was two, and
his mother has had a succession of boyfriends, none of whom served as a
father figure to him. "I wouldn't let a man come into my life," he tells the
psychologist. Most of these men battered his mother, who was arrested for
attempted murder when she fought back. Jonathan and his mother are still
close. She refuses to consider that his aggressive behavior at school is related
to the domestic violence he's witnessed at home.

IF WE KNOW THAT KIDS caught in the crossfire of domestic violence are victims, what about kids exposed to yelling, screaming or even persistent family arguing? Beginning in 1977, researchers at the Simmons College School
of Social Work, in Boston, followed roughly four hundred kindergartners
from Quincy, Massachusetts, into adulthood, to assess the key experiences
that are likely to contribute to mental health problems down the road. Family conflicts ranked high. A 2009 study from the Simmons series, published
in the *Journal of the American Academy of Child and Adolescent Psychiatry*,
examined the effects of parents fighting with each other and with their children. Not too surprisingly, eighteen-year-olds who reported physical violence at home had higher rates of mental and physical illnesses. But even
just family arguments during adolescence had negative long-term effects
at age thirty. Children exposed to household fights were two to three times
more likely then kids who grew up in healthier households to be unemployed, wrestle with major depression, or abuse alcohol or other drugs by
age thirty.

"We've known for a long time that family violence is terribly bad to be
around," said Dr. William Beardslee, a psychiatrist at Children's Hospital

Boston, and coauthor of the 2009 report. "Now we also know a climate of argumentativeness, of frequent verbal arguments, is not good for children."

"You almost have to give a prescription to parents who are fighting not to fight in front of their kids," said Joseph Powers, a family therapist at McLean Hospital, a psychiatric facility outside of Boston.

"It's not just yelling and screaming that does the damage," added his colleague Dr. Martin Teicher, a developmental psychiatry researcher at McLean. "It's 'I wish you were never born' or 'You're not as good as your brother.'" Teicher tracked this to major depression and anxiety and also related it to physical changes in the brain if it experiences stress.

"Take the drama out of the trauma," said Dr. Steven Gold, clinical psychologist and professor at Nova Southeastern University in Fort Lauderdale, looking at childhood violence from a different perspective. "Imagine instead what's *not* happening in these violent homes. What's *not* happening is teaching responsibility, praising achievement, modeling good behavior, prioritizing education—all the things that go into the making of a healthy, productive adult. These kids are still children at age thirty, making bad choices, unable to hold a job, a relationship, and suffering addictions, all because of early childhood violence and the lessons they never learned."

Do you know why zebras don't get ulcers? That's the fascinating title of a book by Robert M. Sapolsky about stress. The Stanford University professor writes about the psychological and sociological disruptions that stress induces, especially chronic, long-standing stress, and often in children. Zebras experience acute physical stress, he says, trying to outrun the attacking lion so as not to be eaten. But it's over quickly, and either way—for the escaping zebra or the well-fed lion—the stress is over rather quickly. Children who have lost or have been removed from a parent, or who have been exposed to violence suffer chronic stress that affects brain development, as well as makes them angry and then more vulnerable to addiction and adult diseases. Professor Sapolsky says, "Not getting enough sleep is a stressor; being stressed makes it harder to sleep. Yup, we've got a dreadful vicious cycle on our hands."[4]

"Although there are no good statistics on kids killed by boyfriends," *St. Petersburg Times* senior correspondent Susan Taylor Martin reports in "Love At What Price?" in July 2010, "one study found that children living with unrelated adults are nearly 50 times as likely to die of physical abuse as kids living with both parents. And the injuries often come at the hands of young adult males." She quotes Josephy Vandello, a social psychologist at the University of South Florida: "'Both for biological and social reasons young adulthood—18 to 24—is a time of a lot of conflict and violence.'"

So what does it mean when a mom tells me in court, "I told my boyfriend I wouldn't tell anyone about the bruises if he'd just pay the bills."?

Juvenile court is about violence.

CHAPTER 5

Amateur Psychologists: Juvenile Judges and Mental Health Issues

RACHEL BEGGED TO BE released from custody. She glared at me with her wide-set oval eyes, tears trickling down her cheeks. She clenched her fists until her knuckles turned white. She bit her lips, shook her head, twisted her hair, and crossed and uncrossed her legs. Short and thin, she looked younger than seventeen. She'd appeared before me in court since she was ten years old.

She looked up at me from the witness box and spat out these words one by one: "I'm. Sick. And. Tired. Of. Being. Locked. Up." She turned to the psychologist, the probation officer, the social worker, and her father, all standing at the podium. "I promise, I really, really mean it, that I won't run away this time. I'll keep my curfew. I'll go to school. I'll listen to my father. I'll go to counseling. I want to get better. I really mean it this time."

Could I believe her?

I first met Rachel when she began to be arrested and charged with battery on her father, some teachers, and eventually law enforcement and detention staff. Her father had sole custody of her, and he would often bring her into court for violating probation, trouble at school, and defiance. They would sit in the back of the courtroom, he with arms folded over a barrel chest, and she quietly by his side. When her turn would come, she would readily admit to anger and violence toward others. Standard psychological evaluations, anger management counseling, and brief periods in detention didn't resolve her problems. Neither did a few short psychiatric commitments. Eventually Rachel was placed in a residential commitment program for delinquent youths, where she did fairly well for nine months in a structured setting.

I'd committed many kids to juvenile justice programs over the years, often suspecting that mental health issues were driving their crimes. I felt frustrated by a lack of options, waiting lists for services, and the need to keep kids safe. I felt inadequate and relied upon the recommendations of others, including parents, treatment providers, and probation officers.

I remembered visiting Rachel recently in detention after she'd been arrested for running away again. "I'm so proud of myself, Judge," she said to me with a big smile, despite her grey detention shirt and baggy pants. "I'm proud that I wasn't arrested for battery, for hitting someone. Do you know how good that makes me feel?"

With that remark, Rachel stole my heart and burrowed into my conscience. Had we let her down, terribly so?

We put a team in place: psychologist, probation officer, social worker. They recommended an inpatient psychiatric placement for Rachel, hard to come by in Florida until you've exhausted outpatient services—and especially difficult to manage when you're a runaway. Rachel wasn't cooperative. Her father didn't have her Medicaid in place. We were overcoming obstacles, hoping that a psychiatric bed would soon open up for Rachel.

In the meantime, she sat to my right in the courtroom, requesting that she be released. Unless I committed her to a high-risk delinquency program for girls, her detention time was up, and she was due to be let go. Rachel pleaded her case, begging not to be recommitted and agreeing to cooperate with rules and counseling. "I just don't want to be locked up," she repeated deliberately.

I didn't want to make this decision. Just as I started to speak, Rachel's father interrupted. "If you release her and something happens to her, if she's killed or dies of an overdose, I will hold you responsible," he said, tight lipped and jabbing his finger at me.

"He hates me!" Rachel cried out. "He doesn't want me home. He doesn't care what happens to me!"

"Rachel," I said, "you don't belong in detention. You need intensive mental health treatment. Dr. Solazzo has arranged for in-home counseling to start right away. You may need residential mental health treatment, but you shouldn't be locked up here. Will you cooperate with what we've put in place? Will you live at home, keep your curfew, go to school, and get this counseling?"

"I promise I will, I promise," she begged. She watched as I hesitated, then signed her release order. As I passed it to the clerk, Rachel turned back to her father and the others at the podium. She seemed completely comfortable in the courtroom. "Finally, after all these years, you guys got it right," she said. "I need help. I don't need to be locked up." She handed me the letter I'd asked her to write, describing her life's goals. Here it is, verbatim:

Dear Jude Selvion,

I feel if I Rachel oke to be put on adut porbshion intell Im 18. Today I ake this to be on adut probshion and imatupayshion I undsanding that the firtst time I say I not going to do want my p.o. say I will go to the Big house no more jdc if I go. Ole porson I should be mad at is my selfe no one to baml bu me my goels are I plain 2 jobs baging at Winn Dixie Monday thow Firday after school I also want my drive liein. I would do this at home with my Dad but he said no he wold not believe me my Dad all was said that active speech loder thin word. I tryer of seeing dispoind faces I feel if I do this I will make everone poud of me I have a good frend home ann she live in painelles park in aprants she has 2 kids and a diversliein I plan to have 2 jobs Wannn Diexe bagging Monday thow Firday after school on the weekends I well bust table go to school ever day and summer school.

I've translated Rachel's letter as follows:

Dear Judge Sullivan. I feel if I Rachael am okay to be put on adult probation until I'm 18. Today I ask this, to be on adult probation and inpatient. I understand that the first time I say I'm not going to do what my probation officer says I will go to the Big House. No more juvenile detention center. If I go, the only person I should be mad at is myself. No one to blame but me. My goals are I plan two jobs:

bagging at Winn Dixie Monday through Friday after school. I also want my driver's license. I would do this at home with my Dad but he said no he would not. Believe me my Dad said that actions speak louder than words. I'm tired of seeing disappointed faces. I feel if I do this I will make everyone proud of me. I have a good friend at home, Ann. She lives in Pinellas Park in apartments. She has two kids and a driver's license. I plan to have two jobs: Winn Dixie bagging Monday through Friday after school. On the weekend I will bus tables. I will go to school every day and summer school.

Rachel ran away the day after I released her. The police picked her up a week later, passed out drunk on a bench in downtown St. Petersburg. They took her to a detox facility, where she told staff that she'd slept with homeless men in exchange for alcohol and drugs. The police returned her to our juvenile detention facility. Our team continued to work on her application for in-patient psychiatric treatment.

Dr. Solazzo provided the background for the application:

Our office saw Rachel in 2002, 2003 and 2006. In reviewing the file, I am struck by the number of psychiatric admissions. There appear to be over 25 crisis admissions in her history. In 2006, while in an inpatient psychiatric facility, a neuropsychiatric exam was conducted because of processing concerns and aggressive behavior. There appears to be a history of mild language delays and two head injuries. The same examiner conducted a neuropsychological in 2001 and found low-average IQ, impairments in language, attention, impulse control, writing, and memory. An underlying organic etiology suspected to be related to in utero drug exposure was suspected. Her history of witnessing domestic violence between her biological parents and being a victim of physical abuse and sexual molestation were additional complicating factors. She was sexually abused by her mother's boyfriend and by at least two juveniles.

The 2006 neuropsychological suggests that she continues to have weakness in language processes and subtle communication difficulties that contribute to miscommunication and emotional and behavioral reactions by Rachel. She has difficulty multitasking and strategizing, becoming easily overwhelmed. She's defensive, with limited insight, intolerant of frustration and disappointment. When she is confronted with sanctions, she becomes excessively angry.

Very early records suggest that both biological parents had a history of crack cocaine usage and both had physically abused her. The father admitted that he would frequently spank her for no reason, and the mother bit her on a least two occasions and drew blood. Authorities intervened, the father stopped using, the mother continued to use, and she went with her father.

Hospital records indicate there is a family history of schizophrenia and alcoholism and other abuse problems with multiple relatives.

So many of the behavioral manifestations present today have been there since she was 2 or 3. She should be getting disability checks. She would be best served by a psychiatric stay, not a juvenile justice commitment. There is no cure here, only amelioration.[1]

Eventually the team was triumphant, and Rachel willingly entered residential treatment for her mental illness instead of a juvenile prison. Many people from juvenile justice and child welfare agencies advocated for Rachel, cutting through bureaucracy, waiting lists, and agency requirements.

In court again before she left, Rachel shyly thanked everyone and promised to cooperate. Detention staff drove her to the psychiatric facility to prevent any attempt at escape. The doors locked behind her once again, but for the first time in her life, Rachel was in a psychiatric facility that specialized in advanced behavioral programming for girls who were victims of severe abuse and trauma.

A few months after her admission, our team visited Rachel.

When she walked through the door of the conference room, she looked like a ballerina: Pencil thin, tiny face with those large oval eyes and a pointy chin. The unkempt hair that used to hide her features had been swept off her face into a braided knot at the top of her head. She looked beautiful in a beige shell and khaki pants, and she flashed a wide smile at familiar visitors.

Dr. Solazzo had interacted with her often in court. Michelle Jameson had showered her with personal attention when discussing "alternative sanctions" to commitment, which was Michelle's new job in juvenile court. And Jill Gould, special projects coordinator for the Department of Juvenile Justice, had participated in the staffing that led to Rachel's present mental health commitment. Before Rachel had joined us, we had met privately with the treatment team, which included her psychiatrist, psychologist, nurse, and teacher. They gave us a gloomy report of Rachel's first month: lots of anger, cursing, fighting with staff and peers, low frustration tolerance, and two instances where she tried to harm herself.

"She looks at the worse-case scenario for everything that happens," the psychologist said. "She feels hopeless."

"Her psychosis has been exposed," the psychiatrist added. "She's showing the symptoms, along with her bipolar disorder." (To us, this explained her manic-depressive states and her broken promises.)

"A rather typical beginning for a girl with her history of trauma," the director assured us. "This is where she belongs."

Rachel looked so good that I hoped the team was exaggerating. She sat down, I asked her how she was doing—and she exploded.

"I'm locked up again, it's all the same! This place is too strict for me. I don't need a psych ward; I have anger issues." Her eyes bore into mine across the table.

"I'm way different now, smarter, wiser than the people here. Why can't I be home? I'm learning to work on my anger. Before, I was hitting people just to hit people first. I don't get how not going home puts you in a psych ward," she cried, teeth clenched and eyes filling with tears.

"Rachel," the psychiatrist interjected, "are you hearing voices?"

"Trust me," she snapped, "if I hear voices, you'll be the first to know, as I'd be freaked out." We laughed with her.

When the treatment team left, she began to smile again, telling us of the few friends she'd made, mostly staff. She worried that she might be given more medication. "I'm here for the counseling," she said, "not for more medication." She admitted that "going home isn't on the table because I wasn't staying home." She took us on a tour of her room and proudly showed off a bed made as tight as the army might require, and a clean bathroom and shower that she shared with a roommate.

"You are my favorite judge," she said, smiling again. "I saw some of the others, but you are my favorite. And guess what? I know—I figured out sitting in court—that I am your favorite kid. Right?"

How many Rachels are there?

Driving home, we shared our impressions of the facility: very clean, clinical, sterile, warm, Pottery Barn wood floors with a Rooms to Go lobby, motivational posters on the cheerfully painted walls. Then we discussed Rachel.

"I fell under her spell," Jill said. "She's a great debater and argues like a lawyer, but all the time, her lost-kid eyes were fixed on me."

"Yes, she's a good advocate for herself," Dr. Solazzo said, "in spite of her special needs. She's basically been institutionalized her entire teenage years. She's seventeen now, she knows how to act in treatment, although I'm not sure of the psychosis diagnosis. She's reacting to long-standing trauma. Whenever a traumatic situation arises, her mind goes back to the initial traumas, and she reacts aggressively. She's not sophisticated. She's rigid. What she said makes sense in her mind."

"She's such an actor," Michelle put in. "She challenges you— 'Why? Why? Why?'—and it starts to sound reasonable, but then you remember that her thinking is impaired, and she's so negative. Then you remember her history and why she's so negative. And she's resisting medication, as she thinks it will turn her into a robot."

"I was surprised that she called herself 'wiser,'" I said. "It's a word I wouldn't have expected her to use."

"Dialectical behavior therapy." Dr. Solazzo jabbed her finger in the air. "She's getting that type of counseling that teaches her to develop a 'wise mind'; to learn how to separate your emotions from the trauma. It's a type of therapy designed to help patients deal with strong, often debilitating emotions, with both group and individual counseling. It's exactly what she needs."[2,3]

I so hope Rachel develops a wise mind.

A few months later, midway through her treatment, she sent us a touching note:

Dear Judges Sellven. I think I finded the nice Rachel. The one that do not hit people. The one never cuse. The good one that I miss so much.

We heard that Rachel had a meltdown after our visit, refusing therapy, trying to cut herself, unable to control her anger. Perhaps she had thought that I was going to order her release. When that didn't happen, she exploded. We were hesitant to visit again, but the program said that Rachel was back on course, making good progress. We took Jill's West Highland White Terrier, Benji, who had been trained as a therapy dog, working with sick children and nursing home patients.

Rachel hugged Benji tightly as he slobbered on her, showing off his tricks, earning treats, and making Rachel laugh and talk about her goal of becoming a veterinary technician. She looked great, was at ease with herself, and was pleased with her progress in therapy. Well on her way to becoming "the good one that I miss so much."

CHAPTER 6

The Teen Brain: They're Still Just Kids

THESE TWO WERE a real brother and sister act. They committed some crimes together and schemed to commit others. Their dad, a single parent, worried about them, but he had to leave for work every day to support them. They snuck onto a neighbor's porch, intending to frighten a handicapped man. The boy stole things. The girl fought at school and in the street. In my court today, they would have been charged with felony burglary, as well as assault, theft, battery, and school disruption.

But this was Maycomb, Alabama, during the Great Depression. The kids, Scout and her brother, Jem, lived with their dad, Atticus Finch, the crusading lawyer who defended a black man wrongly accused of rape in Harper Lee's 1960 Pulitzer Prize–winning novel, *To Kill a Mockingbird*. Scout and Jem were never arrested and prosecuted for their cheeky behavior, although I can't imagine any reader wanting that outcome. The brother and sister were inquisitive, risk-taking kids exploring their boundaries and discovering the larger world around them. After Atticus Finch (portrayed by Gregory Peck in the 1962 film adaptation), they were the book's heroes.

Every week in my court, kids are charged as delinquents under criminal statutes written for adults. Only the penalties are different. Here are a few who have come before me:

Ricky threw an egg at a moving vehicle, and he's charged with a felony for throwing a "deadly missile." Kierra tossed an orange and gets the same charge. Theo threw a baseball bat at a squirrel in a tree, bruising the animal's face and spraining its paw. He's arrested for felony cruelty to animals. Alexia grabbed her friend's cell phone out of her hand at the bus stop and threw it in the grass. She, too, is charged with a felony: robbery by sudden snatching. Javonte smacked a girl's butt at school because he thought she was cute; now he faces a charge of lewd and lascivious behavior. Jessica knocked on the bedroom window of her best friend, who'd been grounded. Police were called, and she faces a trespassing charge. Kevin flicked an eraser, striking a teacher, and was charged with a felony: battery on a school board employee.

Don't misunderstand. These behaviors are wrong and should be addressed with appropriate punishment by parents and schools. But do they warrant arrest and prosecution, creating public records that could potentially affect future employment, military service, and loan and scholarship applications? In most of these cases, the state can prove the technical elements of the crime, and the kids either admit guilt or are found guilty.

It's a source of frustration for juvenile judges like Raymond Gross, who became my "partner" judge when Frank Quesada rotated to a civil division. Tall and handsome, with thick, grey hair and bushy eyebrows, Judge Gross cares deeply about every youth in his courtroom. He can be stern and foreboding with the kid who needs it but is just as stern with the state for prosecuting in court what he deems frivolous, like the theft of a candy bar. He's also one of the smartest men I know and a deep thinker. I enjoy and sincerely value our discussions.

"When did misbehavior turn into misdemeanor?" I asked him, confessing that I stole the question from Anthony Schembri, former secretary of the Florida Department of Juvenile Justice.

"Look at it in terms of the first juvenile courts created in Chicago, and their purpose," Judge Gross instructed me. "Just because you *can* prosecute doesn't mean you *should*."

Judge Gross is the type of juvenile judge contemplated by the famed Julian Mack (1866–1943), the second judge on the juvenile court in Chicago. Judge Mack addressed the 1909 annual meeting of the American Bar Association and published his speech the next year in the *Harvard Law Review*. "The judge must be willing to search out the causes of the delinquency and to formulate a plan for curing it," he stated. "The problem for determination by the judge is not has this boy or girl committed a specific wrong but what is he, how has he become what he is, and what had best be done in his interest and in the interest of the state to save him from a downward career?"

No one thinks that Judge Gross isn't tough enough on the kids who deserve it. In fact, some parents in my courtroom complain that their kids would behave better if they had Judge Gross. But he truly understands adolescent development, as clinical psychologist Dr. Michael Lindsey, an expert in disproportionate minority contact describes it: "Adolescents are not children but also not adults. Some adolescents enter this transitional period with poor regulation and affect tolerance skills. They do not have what is required to negotiate the challenges, particularly those in high-risk, low-supportive environments."

Linda Burgess Chamberlain, Ph.D., of Homer, Alaska, is a health scientist and sought-after speaker on teenage brain development, as well as family violence. "Recent scientific discoveries are helping us to better understand and respond to the sometimes unpredictable, frequently frustrating, and totally amazing teen years," she says. "Around puberty, the teen brain begins to undergo major changes, many of which will not be completed until the early to mid-twenties. The massive surges of hormones teens experience are associated with gender-specific changes in the brain that may help explain some of the differences between male and female brains.

"The teen brain is a work in progress that is far from complete," she continues. "Adolescence is also a time of enhanced vulnerability. Rapid changes make the teen brain more sensitive to stress and neurotoxins such as alcohol, tobacco, and drugs.

"Teens lack all of the hardware in their brains to think like an adult. The outer covering of the brain, the cortex, goes through extensive remodeling during adolescence. Often referred to as the 'intellectual brain,' this upper region is responsible for reason, logic, and rational thinking. Teens may not be able to respond rationally when asked 'What were you thinking?' because they reacted impulsively without the benefit of a mature prefrontal cortex to think things through first." Dr. Chamberlain, quoting Dr. Lawrence Steinberg, an expert in teen development, compares the teenage brain to "a car with a good accelerator but a weak brake."

She goes on to explain: "While part of adolescence is about seeking new experiences and independence, teens still need lots of quality time with healthy adults to help shape their brains and learn the skills to transition into adulthood. They need the guidance of adults' mature prefrontal cortexes, even more so when they have histories of trauma." Dr. Chamberlain is also the founding director of the Alaska Family Violence Prevention Project.[1,2]

Tough cases often put the judge in the position of analyzing the adolescent brain. A tragic case with Tampa connections was handled exceptionally well by Cobb County juvenile judge A. Gregory Poole in Marietta, Georgia, in 2009.

A twelve-year-old boy from Tampa was charged with murder and child cruelty in the July 2009 death of his five-week-old cousin. Judge Poole tried the case in juvenile court without a jury. The facts not in dispute were these: The boy was visiting relatives near Atlanta when he got into a car with his mother's twenty-two-year-old first cousin and her infant daughter. The mom and cousin stopped at a Target store to shop, and left both children in the car with the engine running. They returned fifteen to twenty minutes later to find the boy playing on his cell phone, and the baby limp and not breathing. Her lips were blue, her mouth swollen, and her eyes hard to the touch. She died the next day.

Crime tests found no physical evidence in the car. The boy's statements, many made without an attorney and while he was crying himself, were confusing but seemed to indicate that he might have jammed the pacifier into the baby's mouth to stop her crying. The judge found the boy not guilty of murder or child cruelty but guilty of two counts of battery. In his ruling, as reported in the press, Judge Poole said:

> I find beyond a reasonable doubt that the baby suffered major trauma during the eighteen minutes the juvenile was alone with the baby.... I find that the juvenile caused the injuries and that the baby later died as a result of the trauma.
>
> Now, what do I think happened? This child was left alone with the baby. I don't know that should have happened, but it did....
>
> The baby, a child he really didn't know, started crying, and it got louder....

He didn't know what to do. I think he was scared. He tried using the pacifier to make this baby stop crying. It didn't work. What did he do next?

He got out the bottle of water.... He gives it to the baby. The baby won't be quiet. Turns up the radio so he won't have to hear this baby crying. That didn't work. He might have even turned it up again. Well, the pink pacifier didn't work. Let's use the purple pacifier....

This juvenile was trying to get the baby to quit crying.... He was scared, and he didn't know what to do.... I wouldn't expect him to know what to do.

I find that in order to get the baby to be quiet, using his own means as a twelve-year-old, that he committed batteries, plural, against this baby....

Did this child mean that his actions would kill the baby? No....

Technically, I think I can find possibly, if I wanted to go further, some type of an involuntary manslaughter. In my mind, I've still got to place this child with some expectation, some appreciation for the horrific damage that it has done, and I find nothing along those lines.

Did he do wrong? Oh, yeah, he did. I wish it hadn't happened, but it did.

The boy and his parents cried. The baby's mother left the courtroom without comment. Judge Poole later placed the boy, a first-time offender doing well in school, on lengthy probation and ordered counseling.[3]

A tough decision and a good one by Judge Poole.

Dan A. Myers, M.D., a well-known child psychiatrist from Dallas, wrote to me: "This case is a tragic result of a common parenting error: If a teenager looks, walks, and talks like an adult, *never* assume that he *is* an adult. Clearly, the twenty-two-year-old cousin misjudged the maturity, competence, and discernment of the twelve-year-old boy to handle what for an adult would have been a only a moderate degree of stress. If there was a lobe in the brain for 'discernment under stress,' and we could inspect it, we would have found that this twelve-year-old's lobe was much smaller than that of a mature adult."

According to Dr. Myers, whose clients include kids from wealthy families as well as those adopted out of orphanages, "Today's culture, with its glorification of youth and its acceptance of youth's entitlement, can cause parents to overestimate the capability of their children—particularly their teenagers. Parents have the mistaken notion that if they can teach their teenager the consequences of his actions, the teenager will have the discernment to modify his behavior. The result is that parents may feel prematurely 'free' of their obligation to provide protection, direction, structure, and control of their 'looks like an adult' teenager. The consequences are that their teenager regularly finds himself making unwise and unsafe choices. Fortunately, maybe because of guardian angels, few have the dire consequences of the Georgia case." Dr. Myers writes further on this subject in his book *Biblical Parenting: A Child Psychiatrist's View*.[4]

If I could wave a magic wand over the parents I see in court, I would make them better teachers of their children, and teaching would include setting boundaries. So often, the parent "speedometer" revs from zero to one hundred as parents utterly fail to address a problem and then hurtle into screaming, blaming, and abuse.

Ruth A. Peters, Ph.D., a clinical psychologist and author of *Don't Be Afraid to Discipline*, observes wisely, "So often parents ignore a behavior issue, or they overreact to it by scolding, screaming, or even striking the child, when it's really a matter of *teaching* the child the proper behavior. A huge part of discipline is *teaching* the right way, not punishing the wrong way. A child who is *taught* rather than ignored has a better relationship with the parent—one that's more open, communicative, and problem solving."[5]

Teaching is mentioned so rarely in my courtroom that I'm often startled when I see it in another setting. On a hot summer night, I was tired and frazzled after checking into a Baltimore hotel for a speaking engagement the next day. Two very cute, brown-skinned boys in bathing suits, who looked to be about six or seven, cut in front of me entering the elevator. "Boys, boys, come back here!" I heard as I held the elevator door open. It was their mother. "Don't you run in front of her!"

"Why not?" one boy asked as the other piped up, "Do you know her?"

"No," the mom said, "but she's a lady, and she's older than you. She goes first." No punishment—that wasn't necessary—but a great teaching moment.

TO KILL A MOCKINGBIRD is filled with quality adult time and teachable moments. Scout's and Jem's insatiable curiosity, impulsivity, and risk-taking behaviors ran smack into their father's patient, wise advice. Atticus Finch taught by word and example, and by setting boundaries. "Don't you *ever* fight in school," he admonished Scout, while allowing her and Jem the freedom to explore their world.

A *Mockingbird* parenting class would be first rate, I believe. Drs. Chamberlain, Myers, and Peters could write the curriculum. The mother in the elevator could teach the class. And, of course, we'd show the movie with Gregory Peck as Atticus Finch.

And to put it all in proper perspective, we who labor in the juvenile justice system should recall that Harper Lee's memorable book begins with the Charles Lamb quotation "Lawyers, I suppose, were children once."

CHAPTER 7

Connect the Dots: Gangs and Guns in the Juvenile Court

EIGHT-YEAR-OLD PARIS loved parades. So she would have beamed and blushed to have seen her picture on the posters that roughly two hundred people carried as they marched through her neighborhood in south St. Petersburg in April 2009. It showed her smiling shyly, dressed in school clothes, her hair braided with barrettes. The message on the banner also would have appealed to the pretty little girl known as "Princess," who loved puzzles: "Help Paris Connect the Dots."

She lived with her aunt because her mother, Robin Whitehead, died from an accidental fall when Paris was six. Her father, Robert Hamilton, was a soldier in Iraq. She and her aunt lived in a house full of people who loved her, some of whom were in trouble with the law.

But on the day of the parade, Paris lay in a casket the color of cotton candy, dressed in white with pink barrettes, along with a Minnie Mouse doll, a soft cotton bunny, and her tiara. Paris was the innocent victim of a gangland-style assault on her house, dying in a flurry of nighttime gunfire, as gang members shot more than fifty bullets into her house. Three of the bullets struck her in the back when she got up from her bed to see about the noise. She was the only victim of the random attack, carried out in retaliation against a rival gang.

Police quickly arrested two nineteen-year-olds who they say supplied the weapons, which included semiautomatic AR15 rifles. The family of Paris

Whitehead-Hamilton joined with community leaders to urge residents to "snitch" on the shooters and "Help Paris Connect the Dots," in hopes of identifying the rest of the gang members and locating their stash of weapons.

At her funeral, Elder Tony urged people to turn in the wrongdoers. "When Paris fell, a neighborhood stood up and said, 'That's enough!'" he shouted from the pulpit of the packed Mt. Olive Primitive Baptist Church.

"We know what they are, where they are, and often who they are!" cried State Representative Darryl Rouson, a long-time neighbor. "This isn't snitching!" he challenged. "Do the right thing."

"I grew up here," said city councilman Ernest Davis. "People whose hands look like mine are killing people whose hands look like mine." Pinellas County commissioner Ken Welch was blunt: "It's time to get rid of the thugs."

Third-grade teachers from the Promise Academy charter school cried as they spoke of Paris's good nature, generosity, and spunk. "She wanted to be president of the United States," a classmate said. "She was always smiling." Everyone agreed, remembering that she'd lost her mother and hadn't really lived with her father.

I felt awkward at the funeral, as one of a handful of white people in the church. But I had a reason for being there. I was horrified that Paris was senselessly murdered in her home in a neighborhood that was part of my court jurisdiction. Furthermore, one of the nineteen-year-olds arrested, Stephen Harper, had appeared in my court two years before. He now had a five-month-old son and a first-degree murder charge.[1,2,3]

My courtroom had been shaken two years before when fifteen-year-old Deandre Brown, nicknamed "Squirrel," was killed in a drive-by shooting outside his home as part of a similar gangland feud. The police arrested eighteen-year-old Tyree Gland as the gunman. A jury convicted him of second-degree murder. Both boys had appeared in my courtroom.

Tyree was so steeped in gang culture that he wrote threatening letters to the judge, the prosecutor, and their families from jail. He walked into court with a tattoo on his right arm offering a bounty for the detective responsible for his arrest. "Wanted," it read. "Detective Gibson, $100,000."[4]

I'd had enough of guns, gangs, and shootings, and I mourned for Paris and her family. Although emotions peaked at her funeral, and commitments were made to "connect the dots," the passion fizzled, and police alone were left trying to identify the shooters. A year later, Preston Avenue South was renamed Paris Avenue South.

Two months later, fourteen-year-old Jamonte stood before me in court, stone faced, waiting to hear his sentence to a high-risk program for boys, for charges that included auto theft and selling cocaine. "He's one of the most depressed young men I've seen," Dr. Jaggi said in her report. "He sees nothing positive in his future, no way out of his crime-ridden neighborhood, and no one to look up to. He's given up and given in to all the wrong temptations."

Jamonte also had a deep sense of guilt. He was a member of the gang that had supplied the guns in the murder of Paris Whitehead. A few months before that, Jamonte had stumbled upon the body of fifteen-year-old Mikasha Gamble, a runaway shot to death in an alley following a nighttime argument with a man presumed to be her boyfriend, drug dealer, pimp, or all three. Jamonte's father was serving a prison sentence for drug dealing; his uncles and older brothers still sold drugs on the street, one step ahead of the undercover cops.

Jamonte was repeating the eighth grade, as he skipped school a lot. He left home often, spending nights with friends and relatives, to escape the violence between his mother and her boyfriends. He excelled during his five months in a moderate-risk commitment program, finishing schoolwork on time, not angry or disruptive. He thrived on structure. Then he returned home to the same family and the same neighborhood.

Jamonte could be the poster boy for gang recruitment.

"Young people join gangs because they want to," says Dr. Phelan Wyrick, a youth gang expert in the U.S. Department of Justice. "They think it's a good idea. They look to gangs as a solution. The world we set up for them doesn't work for them. 'I've got a better idea,' they think."

Dr. Wyrick cites "pushes and pulls" that make gang life attractive. "Pushes are the negative conditions in the environment that make a gang-free, crime-free life seem unattractive or inaccessible. Pulls are the attractive features of gangs." Among the push factors are disadvantaged neighborhoods, access to drugs, high crime rates, frequent truancy and suspensions, low parental expectations, broken homes, and neglect. "Most of the gang members have either been victims of violence or have witnessed it," Wyrick says.

Pull factors include status, identity, fun, excitement, a family feeling, security, protection, and money. "Some of this is pure adolescent development," Wyrick says, "but for young people exposed to violence as a young child, one way of dealing with that fear, of taking control in adolescence, is by joining a gang. Young people get a feeling of confidence. They've punched someone; they've been punched themselves. They've shot someone, and they've been shot at.

"For girls who've been sexually abused," he adds, "sex involvement is a means of control."[5]

Our circuit state attorney's office obtained a federal grant to prosecute gang members while providing education and training to keep kids out of gangs. Gang members were identified by their style of dress, tattoos, hand signals, and, very often, their own admissions. Many kids bragged openly of gang membership. Not a smart thing to do, as sentencing was enhanced if a crime was connected to gang activity.

"One of my biggest regrets is joining a gang," Ted Braden wrote on his blog, *Teen in Jail*, which he created with the help of his mother; she takes the letters he sends from our jail and posts them on www.teeninjail.blogspot. com. Ted's juvenile record included felony burglaries and drug charges, including marijuana, cocaine, Xanax, and ecstasy. When he turned nineteen, he was arrested five times in one year on drug charges, the last for selling fifty ecstasy pills in a Wal-Mart parking lot. The drug trafficking charge was reduced to a sale and possession and bought him a three-year prison sentence with credit for time served in jail.

Of gangs, Ted writes on his blog: "All my teenage years as a gang member, I learned to hate rival gangs. One gang that I hated most was called 'Folks,' or 'Folk Nation.' I have never talked to one or have never liked one, but over the last 4 or 5 months, I've become really good friends with a Folk gang member (in jail). It turns out that we were sentenced to prison on the same day, so we will both leave on the same day to go to prison.

"If you really think about it, gangs don't do nothing for you. The only thing it will do for you is what it did for me—and that is twice as much time for anything you get in trouble for. It only enhances the penalty."

Ted's account of his first day in prison is chilling:

You get totally naked in front of whoever is there. You face the guard that is strip-searching you, and you hold your hands and arms up so they can see that you don't have anything in your hands or taped to your armpits. You open your mouth and move your tongue around so they can see that you don't have anything in your mouth. Then you run your hands through your hair (if you have any) and pull your ears forward so they can look in and behind them. Next you turn around. You pick up your feet one at a time to show that you don't have anything taped to the bottom of your feet. Lastly, you bend over and cough. The guard inspects your butthole to see if he thinks you have any drugs or weapons stuffed in there. If they think you have something in there, they do a cavity search on your [sic] immediately so you don't have a chance to get rid of it. And, no, I didn't receive one that day (thank God).[6]

In court, I frequently see members of the 8 Hype, Bethel Heights, Latin Kings, and Asian Pride gangs. The difficulty is that many of these boys grew up in the same neighborhood. Some are related, sharing the same absent father, stepfather, or mother's boyfriend. Most are looking for a male bonding experience but frequently turn to crime. It is hard to separate the natural and innocent inclination to be part of a neighborhood "gang" from the frightening gang activity that leads to stealing weapons, trafficking in drugs, and committing murders.

Six months after gang members gunned down eight-year-old Paris in her aunt's home, further investigation revealed that two people living there had connections to warfare between the Bethel Heights and 8 Hype gangs. Paris's cousin Richard "Junior" Lamar and his "blood brother," Markeath "Monster" Fielder, were living in the house. Fielder allegedly told Lamar to move Paris away from the front of the house that night. More than fifty bullets tore through the house; one killed Paris, who was still sleeping in the front bedroom, its windows facing the street. In addition to Stephen Harper, two nineteen-year-olds, Dondre Davis and Mario Lewis Walls, were indicted for murder.

The very existence of rival gangs creates the warfare, claims Detective Bryan Sims, head of the St. Petersburg Police Department's gang unit. "They love to fight as a way of expressing their manhood," he said. "This is called fight 'for free.' There's no criminal return other than the fight. Gangs exist so they can shoot each other."

"But where do they get the guns?" I asked him.

"By burglarizing homes and businesses and stealing weapons; by trading drugs for guns with adults who've bought them legally, at gun shows or wherever."

I thought of the frightening increase we'd had in home burglaries, where weapons are taken, and young kids arrested and charged with armed burglary. I thought of the street violence in Florida, often occurring after high-school football games, when a kid high on alcohol or drugs shoots a gun into a crowd, a car, a home. We don't have an epidemic of strangulations, poisonings, or stabbings; we do when it comes to violence with guns.

The Florida Department of Juvenile Justice reported a 55 percent jump in the number of young adults charged with murder or manslaughter between 2003 and 2009. Guns. You can bet on it.

Detective Sims is a huge African American man who looks like he'd frighten the pants off any kid involved in a gang. Actually, his mild manner and the warmth he projects allow him to infiltrate youth gangs, prevent some of the violence, and offer protection to youth leaving gangs. At a workshop on gangs for law enforcement and juvenile justice personnel, he described symbols of gang culture, some seemingly innocent.

"Red and black laces in the shoes, the number 5—like when you see five guys wearing jerseys with the number 5 on them—that's not a coincidence. Bandanas, you can't wear them to school, but you can try to poke one out of your pocket. Graffiti in your school notebook. And tattoos—oh boy, those tattoos. Some wear 'Life' tattoos on one eyelid; 'Death' on the other eyelid. A teardrop tattoo below the eye means a loss in the gang. If it's open, it hasn't been revenged; colored in, it's been revenged.

"Young boys are so vulnerable," Sims continues. "You can talk a fourteen-year-old boy into just about anything."[7]

Especially one who doesn't have a father, I thought.

CHAPTER 8

Who Is My Father Today? Fatherless Children in Juvenile Court

THE THERAPIST LEANED OVER Tony's neatly clipped Afro as he finished drawing pictures of what he liked to do on the weekends. She'd asked him to draw because he'd clammed up when talking about his family, even though he was very vocal about his problems at school. Tony drew pretty well for a ten-year-old. He labeled two stick figures "Tony" and "Dad." Then he colored shirts and shorts onto them as they played basketball and soccer and rode bikes. Tony gave the drawing to the young therapist, who was just about Tony's size.

"Your Dad does a lot with you?" she asked Tony. She was surprised, as his mother hadn't mentioned a father.

"He sure does. I see him on weekends. We have a lot of fun. He's really good at basketball."

"That's great," the therapist said, eager to speak to Mom in the waiting room.

"You didn't tell me about Tony's relationship with his Dad," she said, showing her the drawing.

The mom looked up, puzzled and annoyed.

"Tony ain't seen his father in seven years," she hissed. "The deadbeat lives in the neighborhood with his girlfriend and a few kids. He stopped paying child support three years ago. He don't give a damn about Tony, and he sure don't give a damn about the fights and suspensions at school. He's a piece of shit."

The therapist copied the drawing and asked Tony whether he wanted the original. "Sure," he said, with a big smile, clutching it to his chest as he and his mom left with a referral for counseling.

Tony was one of my court kids, charged with battery on a schoolteacher—a felony—and many school disruptions. His encounter with the therapist bothered me. I worried about Tony and all the charges he was incurring at school. I opened the file in my mind labeled "Absent Fathers" and slid Tony's experience into it, next to Sir Edward's.

Sir Edward Jones II had a distinctive name, as did the man he was named after, Sir Edward Jones. Sir Edward II was big for fourteen, compact and muscular. He was charged with striking his mother, a thin, petite woman who'd brought Sir Edward's ten-year-old half brother to the trial. Family violence cases make for difficult trials. The winners and losers have to go home and try to live together.

"Sir Edward has a difficult early history," Dr. Jaggi said in her evaluation. "He explained to me that he's had bad luck with parents, as his parents haven't been very parentlike. His mother was sixteen when pregnant with him. He believed that his father was Sir Edward Jones, for whom he was named. He liked this man, who did a lot with him, although they never lived together. When he was six years old, he said, there was a court case, and both of them had to take a blood test. He then learned that his real father is a man named Roscoe Smith. Mr. Smith has no interest in him at all, never sees him or remembers his birthday or Christmas. His younger brother, Tyrone, has a different father, who takes Tyrone places and buys him things. One of Sir Edward's happiest memories is when Tyrone's father took the two of them to a theme park for Sir Edward's birthday. That happened just once.

And the man he thought was his father, Sir Edward Jones? He stopped visiting once he learned of the blood test results. Yet in just a few years, Tony or Sir Edward may be one of the young men in court who pleads for an early release, saying, "I gots me a shorty" or who violates probation by moving in with "my baby momma."

Mothers and fathers play different roles in juvenile court. Both can be helpful or harmful to their children. Both can nurture or neglect them, teach them or taunt them, work with them or walk out on them. Because of pregnancy and childbirth, we always know who the mother is, but we often spend thousands of dollars trying to identify and locate the biological father and get him to step up to his responsibility.

Think of a twelve-inch ruler. On the left end, write "sperm donor" and on the opposite end write "biological father married to and living with mom in a monogamous relationship." Going from left to right, at every inch mark, you can pencil in a sexual relationship that leads to fatherhood: "prostitution," "tryst in backseat," "one-night stand," "casual sex partner," "dating seriously," "fiancé/paramour," "living together, not monogamous," "living together, monogamous," "married, but sleeping with someone else," and then at the right end of the ruler, "traditional marriage and fatherhood."

Sexually active, uncommitted males can father dozens of children within a few years. Those are the children I see in court, psychologically damaged by anger, disappointment, and feelings of rejection and abandonment. They cling to father substitutes whom they often call stepfathers but who come and go as if through a revolving door, sometimes staying just long enough to abuse them emotionally, physically, or both.

Alex had a high IQ and should have been shopping for colleges with his mother, a nurse, instead of appearing before me as a chronic truant. Alex's mother valued hard work and education and took pains to remind Alex that his father, a sperm donor, was a medical student. That's all Alex knew about him. It drove him crazy to think that he could never find his biological father. It was worse than being adopted. So he took it out on his mother, skipping school, smoking pot, laughing as his grades plunged.

Keyona and Joe had four sons and had lived together for twenty years. The Florida Department of Revenue brought a child support case against Joe, as Keyona, a single woman, had been collecting food stamps and rent subsidies. To avoid a support order, Joe and Keyona married, but she threw him out a year later for a new boyfriend. The revenue department re-entered

Joe's life, and to make matters worse, one of his teenage sons was charged with sexually assaulting the youngest son. Joe blew up and told his sons not to call him until they were adults.

Juvenile judges see legal fathers, stepfathers, boyfriends, paramours, fiancés, and friends. Many men want DNA tests to prove or disprove fatherhood. A few love the child and want the blood relationship; others appear shocked and in disbelief when child support is ordered for a child born of a one-night stand. Some mothers claim they don't remember the names of their casual sexual partners. "It was a wild weekend in Tampa, Judge," the attractive redhead said at the podium. "We didn't have time to exchange names."

From this lifestyle of neglect, children are conceived and born with two strikes against them.

Strike one: Their single, poor, stressed-out mothers often send them to live with relatives. Modern-day nomads, the kids live everywhere and nowhere. School attendance suffers when no one is in charge. While it may take a village to raise a child, it really takes one responsible parent—ideally, two—to get the job done. Financially strapped mothers often invite the nearest man to move in and support them. Domestic violence occurs. No one gives or receives respect. "I won't tell anyone about the bruises if you pay the bills."

Strike two: These kids often know nothing of their father's side of the family. They grow up angry, wondering about their missing half and fantasizing about what dad's family might be like.

I sat in the front row of the New Orleans Convention Center when Bill Cosby spoke at the Essence Music Festival in July 2008. He was angry, frustrated, and less restrained than in his book *Come On, People*.

"For God's sake, use a condom!" he cried. "This isn't the most romantic sex. It happens in the backseat of a car if you are lucky. You're sixteen years old, so use a condom. Don't have a child. Don't break a child's heart."

Cosby went on to say, "It's feast or famine. A feast of men, a famine of responsible fathers."[1,2]

Cosby has been criticized by other African American commentators on social issues, most notably Michael Patrick Dyson of Georgetown University. Professor Dyson claims that Cosby is simplistic and punitive, and that he is ignoring social conditions responsible for black men abandoning their children.

The predominately African-American festival crowd loved Cosby, applauding even his harshest remarks. Afterward, I stood in line for an hour for Cosby to autograph my copy of his book, and then caught a cab to the airport. The black taxi driver, Henry, saw the book and declared that Cosby was his hero. Henry told me how much he loved and cared for his four children, working two jobs to support them, including the oldest, born when he was just sixteen. Two of his kids had good jobs and families, and two were in local colleges, he said proudly. He stopped the cab to show me their pictures. At the airport, Henry parked illegally and carried my bag to the US Airways counter. His oldest daughter was a ticket agent there, and he wanted to show her the autographed book.

Her friend behind the counter said that she wasn't working that day. "She's probably taking her girls shopping," he said, taking out his wallet again. "Did I show you the pictures of my grandkids?" I gave him the fare, a tip, a hug, and the Cosby book. I smiled every time I thought of Henry, all the way home.

I'm a miserable failure at hiding my disgust when it comes to women identifying three or four possible fathers for a newborn, or biological fathers appearing shocked that they have to pay child support. On the other hand, give me a dad like Henry or a dad who hopes that DNA testing will prove that he *is* the father, and I melt with admiration.

THOSE EARLY ABANDONMENT issues devolve into trouble in delinquency court.

Single fathers trying hard to raise a daughter through her teenage years have a tough time. They are often baffled. "Look, Judge," Kelly's father said to me. "When my car breaks down, I take it to a mechanic, and he fixes it. I've been bringing my daughter to court all year, and you haven't yet fixed her. She's still running away, hanging out with older guys, violating probation. I'm tired of bringing her here."

Single mothers of teenage boys have a tough time. They are bullied into playing cook, housekeeper, and chauffeur for a youngster who won't do a chore or keep a curfew. "I have no control. He runs the house. I drive him everywhere. He still curses me out." I hear that almost every day.

Sixteen-year-old Antwan so intimidated his mother that he wouldn't let her talk to his probation officer outside of his presence. He refused to leave the room. His mother saved her story for court. No longer afraid, because Antwan had been committed to a high-risk program, locked up in detention until a bed could be found, she lamented that he was a drug dealer and often high on marijuana and cocaine.

As her son was led away, he tried one more plea for leniency by announcing that his girlfriend was four months pregnant.

As Bill Cosby would say, "Wear a condom."

CHAPTER 9

Crossover Kids:
Lost in Both Systems

RYAN LONGED FOR a pet of his own. He didn't complain when his dad got evicted again and sent him to live with his mom and her boyfriend, who beat him. He didn't complain when he bounced among foster homes or when he failed to pass fifth grade in the third school he'd attended in a year. He just kept telling his caseworker that he wanted a pet. Then he was sent to live in a group home that adjoined the large backyard of a man who raised exotic monkeys.

Ryan sat on the fence and watched the monkeys play, eat, and scratch themselves. He loved the screeching and the chatter, their tiny mouths and large, black-circled eyes. He watched the man feed them and clean their cages. To the red-headed, hazel-eyed, freckled boy, they seemed friendly.

So, one day, Ryan climbed the fence, opened a cage, and took out one of the two monkeys. He played with the animal all afternoon in a corner of his yard, feeding it potato chips and pieces of cheese. At dusk, he climbed back over the fence, and just as he opened the door of the cage to return the monkey, the owner grabbed him by his shirt and ordered him to wait for the police.

Ryan was charged with grand theft, for stealing the first monkey. The owner sought $1,500 in restitution for the second monkey, which had dropped dead that afternoon. Apparently, the monkey's veterinarian testified, the monkey suffered a heart attack when Ryan took away his companion. That's when I first met Ryan, now a crossover kid with both dependency and delinquency cases.

Jasmine's history of abuse was far worse than Ryan's. Her mother's boyfriends raped her before she was ten years old. Her mother ignored a court order to get her to counseling and instead tortured Jasmine to punish her for her outbursts of anger and rage. Her beautiful black skin became a pincushion of bite marks, scars, rug burns, and scrapes. Law enforcement responded, charges were brought, her mother's rights were terminated, and she and her sisters were placed in foster care. The sisters, who had not been raped, did well in care, but for Jasmine, each new placement broke down because of her behavior.

The counseling and therapy that I ordered for Jasmine never seemed to take. Placed in a residential mental health facility, she struck other clients and staff. She rotated in and out of detention facilities. Soon she had a delinquency record two pages long, full of domestic and felony batteries. Like Ryan, Jasmine was a crossover kid. The paths that she and Ryan would take, while different, are predictable.

At about age fourteen, many crossover kids "chuck" the system and forge out on their own. The boys very often choose a criminal path, selling cocaine, stealing cars, burglarizing homes. Police close in, arrests are made, and the charges quickly result in long-term commitments in juvenile correctional facilities. Although the state is the surrogate parent of these foster kids, the child welfare case workers often throw in the towel. Rather than fighting for stable housing, better services or more effective counseling for the youth, they agree to a commitment. It's one fewer runaway to worry about. And, the costs shift: The Florida Department of Juvenile Justice, rather than the Florida Department of Children and Families, bears the cost of their incarceration.

Crossover girls often choose a different route. They rarely sell drugs, steal cars, or burglarize homes. They don't need to. As runaways, their bodies become their currency. They hook up with older men, pimps, drug dealers, and gang members, exposing themselves to sexually transmitted diseases and drug use. They hang out in their old neighborhoods. They drop in on relatives who won't raise them but will feed them dinner or let them sleep on the couch, never calling the police to bring them to safety.

When crossover girls under my care go missing, it's scary to listen to the evening news or read the newspaper. Three of mine have been beaten or shot to death. Mikasha spent the night before her death visiting her "auntie," who fixed her favorite dinner of pork chops and mashed potatoes and admired her $50 French manicure. The aunt never thought to ask where the fifteen-year-old runaway got the money for the manicure or to call the police to bring her home. Gunshots followed a loud argument in an alley where Mikasha's body was found the next morning. Auntie cried at her funeral.

Monkey-loving Ryan burglarized another house, stole an automobile, wrenched an iPod out of a classmate's hand, and was direct filed to adult court at age sixteen. He was sentenced to a maximum-risk program for boys, where he remained until he aged out of foster care. The sentencing recommendation mentioned that Ryan had been in and out of foster care since the age of two, that he called his father "a total screw-up," and that he had been using marijuana regularly since he was thirteen.

Jasmine finally found a placement she liked: a group home in the country that had horses she could care for. She got a job at a fast-food restaurant nearby. She was happier than she'd been in years, but then the group home lost its funding and closed. Jasmine was placed in another group home in the city. She ran away again and came back with new clothes, unwilling to say where she'd been. Her older sisters, both working part-time and in local colleges, want her to live with them when she turns eighteen. These young women have had a positive impact on Jasmine, and for the first time in years, she is happy, stable in a group home, visiting her sisters, and doing well in high school.

Judge James Seals of Fort Myers, Florida, and Judge Lynn Tepper of Dade City, Florida, speak and write passionately about the state's failure to meet the needs of foster kids incarcerated in juvenile justice facilities. "No one visits," says Judge Tepper. "Not their case manager, not their probation officer, and they no longer have parents. If their good behavior earns a weekend pass home, there is no home to go to, as their foster bed has been given to another child." Judge Seals urges very close case management by a single judge overseeing both the delinquency and dependency cases, so that these children are not simply lost in the system and then released when they turn eighteen. Without connections in the community, these youths often become homeless, turn to prostitution and crime, and land in jail or prison.

Like twelve-year-old Maria, whose mom, Janet, fled from Ohio with her to escape a violent, abusive boyfriend. The two moved in with a friend in Jacksonville, Florida. Maria was enrolled in seventh grade.

Janet couldn't find a job, and the friend tired of supporting them, kicking them out after two months. Maria missed the next two months of school while her mother drove them from town to town, looking for work and living in their car. They arrived in our county and got lucky. Janet got a job as a bartender, and Rita, who owned the bar, took pity on them and invited them into her home.

Maria was re-enrolled in seventh grade.

Janet returned to Ohio to "give it another try" with her abusive boyfriend. Rita agreed to keep Maria. Rita's husband, Joe, was accused of sexually abusing Maria. Rita took Joe's side, and law enforcement placed the girl in a foster care group home.

Now thirteen, Maria was re-enrolled in school.

Living with strangers in an unfamiliar state, now failing the seventh grade, Maria ran from her group home and kicked and flailed at the police officer when she was arrested as a runaway. She was charged with felony battery on a law enforcement officer.

That's when I met Maria, in court. She was more alone than anyone I'd met. All she wanted was to talk to her mom, who no longer wanted her.

Shay Bilchik, the director of the Center for Juvenile Justice Reform at Georgetown University Public Policy Institute, speaks and writes eloquently about the needs of crossover children and the relationship between child welfare and juvenile justice. He begs for better communication between agencies and a coordinated response when a dependent youth is charged with a crime—a crime that often takes place in anger at a foster home. Shay, previously the administrator of the U.S. Office of Juvenile Justice and Delinquency Prevention under President Bill Clinton, sometimes begins his presentation with a story I'll paraphrase somewhat:

Before the days of Facebook, MySpace, Twitter, BlackBerrys, and iPhones, there were Indian tribes that roamed the continent, moving to find better hunting or fishing, or more protected land. When they would meet other tribes also on the move, they would share information. How was the weather ahead? How many buffalo had they killed? How many battles had they fought? How many white men had they chased? Likely, there was a bit of bragging.

But the smartest, most civilized, most secure, and happiest Indian tribe among them always asked this question first: "How are the children?" This tribe knew that if the children are well, all else falls into place.

CHAPTER 10

Recreational, Reactive, and Really Bad Crimes: Uncovering the Role of Sex and Drugs in Juvenile Court

I BEGAN TO SORT JUVENILE crimes into three broad categories, which I called "recreational," "reactive," and "really" bad crimes.

Recreational crimes include teenage pranks such as knocking down mailboxes, pulling fire alarms, and covering the school bathroom with graffiti—all wrong deeds and all misdemeanors.

Reactive crimes require more analysis. Did Ashley stab her mother's boyfriend because he'd been coming on to her for weeks? Did Donnel steal his friend's iPod after being taunted that his mom and dad were in prison and could never buy one for him? Did Christopher set fire to his grandmother's house because he overheard her telling child welfare workers that she was returning him tomorrow? Aggravated battery, robbery by sudden snatching, arson. Those are all felonies.

Really bad crimes frighten everyone, particularly the innocent victims. Burglaries, home invasions, gun thefts, drug dealing, carjacking, rape, and murder. They need to be resolved swiftly, sternly, and punitively.

Sex and drug crimes fit into all three categories. Sex between a seventeen-year-old and a fourteen-year old might be recreational and consensual, even

Romeo and Juliet–type young love. Yet, in juvenile justice, it is considered sexual battery. A pat on the fanny can result in a charge of lewd and lascivious behavior, even though the "patter" is imitating mom's boyfriend. Forcible rape is always a horrendous crime; in many cases putting the perpetrator behind bars for life. Likewise, popping an occasional beer or puffing a joint puts you in the category of recreational drug criminal if you are a minor. Treating serious depression or bipolar disorder by self-medicating with marijuana, cocaine, or stolen prescription drugs is clearly reactive behavior. Drug trafficking is a really bad crime that can send a kid straight to prison.

I hold very strong opinions about sex, drugs, and hip-hop music and culture:

1. We should almost never require juveniles to register as sex offenders.

2. We should never legalize marijuana, as it is the most dangerous gateway drug for kids to use.

3. We should enjoy the intellectual ingenuity of *certain* hip-hop artists.

There, I've said it, and many will disagree.

Sex Offenses: Labeling a youth a sex offender has far-reaching, often unintended, diabolical consequences. Under the federal Adam Walsh Child Protection and Safety Act of 2006, and some state laws, the juvenile's picture, name, age, and address become public record, accessible on the Internet by pedophiles and adult sex offenders. Registration requirements can last many years or even a lifetime. Yet research shows that juvenile sex offenders are highly responsive to effective treatment and rarely reoffend, in contrast to adult sex offenders, who have a high recidivism rate. Many youths are reacting to having been sexually abused themselves, or imitating the adults who live in their home. Others may find pornography that's carelessly left for them to view. These are problematic cases for the juvenile judge. Of course, there is empathy for the victim. Regardless, many judges think the juvenile defendant doesn't deserve the punishment of lifetime sexual offender registration, in spite of the fact that he is found guilty of lewd and lascivious conduct, or even a sex battery, a touching not amounting to forcible rape.

Like Brad. An honor student with no prior record, and a member of the wrestling team, the teenager lost his temper when his former girlfriend taunted him in front of her friends in the high-school weight room and training room they both used. As she stood at an exercise machine in nylon shorts, her left leg fully extended behind her, he passed by and stuck his hand into her shorts, digitally penetrating her vagina with the tip of his finger. She screamed in alarm, and he was arrested. Because this was nonconsensual, and involved some force and penetration, the charge was a capital sexual battery. Clearly, Brad deserved punishment, anger management and sexual counseling, and perhaps probation. The victim needed vindication. But should Brad be required to register as a sex offender for at least twenty-five years?

After a trial, I found Brad guilty as charged but ordered the counseling and probation rather than the commitment the state was seeking. I declined to find the "force" necessary to invoke the sex offender registration requirements, fully aware that the state could appeal—which it didn't.

Drug-Related Offenses: Research shows that severe, chronic drug addiction is more predictable in youths who (1) have been abused, (2) start using drugs or alcohol at a very young age, or (3) inherit an addictive trait, as some people are born genetically predisposed to the effects of alcohol and other drugs. Abused kids as young as eleven or twelve often use marijuana to relieve the stress created by an alcoholic or drug-addicted abuser. It's three strikes against the kid out of the box, and if we make marijuana more available by legalizing it for adults, we'll lose the whole ball game, as marijuana is the most common illicit drug used by youths in the United States. Kids model their parents who use marijuana illegally. They model their neighbors gathered on street corners, buying, selling, and using marijuana. They model their peers.

In poor neighborhoods, marijuana is cheaper and easier to get than alcohol, cocaine, ecstasy, or the powerful prescription painkiller OxyContin. The very kids who need all the help they can get must confront another obstacle when surrounded by adults who smoke marijuana. And the kids, stressed and depressed, are really reaching out for help.

The scene repeats itself again and again in my truancy and delinquency courts. Mom and fourteen-year-old Ashley stand at the podium. Mom begins her litany of complaints about her daughter: skipping school, failing grades, surly attitude, disrespect, a different child from last year. "If we drug tested you today," I ask Ashley, "would you test positive for marijuana?" In many cases, the answer is yes, and in well over half of those, Mom isn't really surprised *because the drug is available at home.*

Kids don't lie about this in court. They know their lives are unhappy, and they are reaching out for help. Individual or family counseling, drug treatment, a psychiatric or psychological exam, a change in schools or caregivers—give them all these things but don't give them greater access to a drug that robs them of ambition to do well in school and encourages them to drop out of a productive life.

How does marijuana do this? Physiologically, it creates a sense of euphoria, calmness, and sedation in kids, masking stress and real problems. It's the "avoidance" drug for teens. Teens have to learn to deal with success and failure, praise and rejection, happiness and disappointment, choices and consequences. Adolescence is a time of intense change, in which a child transitions to an independent, functioning adult.

As pediatrician Edward A. Jacobs wrote in the *Journal of Global Policy and Practice,* "If one turns to the use of marijuana to avoid or blunt the negative experiences or to try to enhance the positive experiences of adolescence, he/she never learns these lessons and the coping mechanisms necessary to successfully manage them." Basically, these kids never grow up.

I see them as little slacker soldiers, marching into court as early drug users at age twelve or thirteen, then marching out to jail or prison at seventeen or eighteen—not for marijuana use, mind you, but for the felonies they've committed during an adolescence of poor choices, little education, and unmet needs. But I blame the marijuana and the culture it creates.

"It was with great sadness that I sat through your truancy court hearings, watching one young person after another stand before the judge," Calvina Fay wrote to me. Ms. Fay is the executive director of the Drug Free America Foundation. "Although all of these young people were very different, with varying backgrounds, almost all of them had one link in common: drug use, primarily marijuana.

"As I asked myself why each one of them might have turned to drugs, the answer varied. For some it was probably a case of 'self-medicating' to feel better about their circumstances and to cope. For others it was possibly an act of defiance or even a tactic to get attention. For still others it may have been to counter boredom. And there is no doubt in my mind that for quite a few it was peer pressure—the desire to fit in.

"One thing that I have learned about youthful drug use is that many youngsters do not really have a strong desire to try drugs the first time. They simply do so to fit in when it is offered to them by a friend. That is why I see drug use as a 'contagious' behavior. It spreads among friends just as fashion trends spread," she concluded.[1,2,3]

I'm not advocating for more prosecution of juvenile drug charges or misdemeanor sex crimes, nor am I ignoring the use and sale of cocaine and prescription drugs and other substances. I'm advocating to get help for kids and for an understanding of the teenage brain and the danger of an entry drug. The kid who "cops a feel" or "takes a toke" while listening to hip-hop is not a sex offender or a drug dealer. He's a teen engaging in age-old risky behaviors. We shouldn't make it any easier for him to do so by making marijuana more accessible, as his behavior will likely get a whole lot worse.

Hip-Hop: Here I agree with Professor Michael Eric Dyson, of Georgetown University, in his book *Know What I Mean? Reflections on Hip-Hop:*

"And what do great artists do? They see and they say. They don't have to live it, but they can make you believe they've lived it. It's the same with the politics of authenticity. Within hip-hop, the elevation of the ghetto is often a metaphysical complaint against society's failure to recognize the humanity of those who come from the ghetto. And by the same token, hip-hop artists are rarely given credit for the kind of intellectual ingenuity it takes to create narratives that spark debates about whether what they say is true or not. That's a great deal of the ingenuity of the art form itself. Also, I think very few people are willing to acknowledge the genius of our black children."[4]

How can we not admire the rhetorical genius of the rapper Nas, an eighth-grade dropout from the projects in Queens, New York, in one of his earliest verses:

> It's only right that I was born to use mics,
> And the stuff that I write, it's even tougher than dice
> I'm takin' rapping to a new plateau through rap slow
> My rhyming is a vitamin held without a capsule.

In four rhymed lines, Nas has shown kids creativity, personal expression, toughness, and an alternative to drug use, while not using profanity, promoting violence, or degrading women.

Genius!

CHAPTER 11

The Deuces:
Disproportionate Minority
Contact and Juvenile Court

O N THE BENCH, especially when facing a sea of black faces, my mind drifts back to the 1940s and 1950s, when midtown St. Petersburg, part of the area my court serves, was a far different place. It was vibrant, bustling, and homogeneous, populated with the homes and offices of professionals, doctors, dentists, lawyers, and successful business people. It was centered around family, church, club, and community. It was black. It was segregated. It centered on Twenty-second Street South, known locally as "the Deuces."

Twenty-second Street in St. Petersburg resembled other African American promenades such as Atlanta's "Sweet Auburn," Beale Street in Memphis, or Ashley Street in Jacksonville. When blacks built it, back in the 1920s, they could have called it a first "black suburb," as the dirt road that grew into a thriving black community resulted from blacks being pressured to leave the city of St. Petersburg when whites objected to Negroes congregating in a new downtown movie house. One night in November 1921, two explosions rocked the venue. They weren't powerful enough to destroy it, but they succeeded in permanently shutting down the theater.

The Manhattan Casino stood on this street. Nicknamed "the Home of Happy Feet," in the forties and fifties it was a place for nightlife, good times, and, most of all, great music. Louis Armstrong, Count Basie, Ella Fitzgerald, and, later, James Brown all packed the Manhattan Casino. Men and women dressed up in fine suits and gowns. Alcohol was prohibited. Dapper George Grogan, a chemistry teacher at all-black Gibbs High School, served as booking agent. The Manhattan Casino hosted graduations, club meetings, fashion shows, and proms. On Friday nights, everyone danced. Club 16, a local men's club, held white-tie events at the Casino.

Of course, this cozy and cohesive community coexisted with the disgrace and injustice of racial segregation. The African American men and women who attended those dances couldn't live elsewhere in St. Petersburg. They couldn't sit at the drugstore lunch counter. They couldn't drink from water fountains, swim in pools, play in parks, or watch movies at "whites only" theaters. Their kids attended segregated schools. And while they could spend their money in St. Petersburg's shops and clothing stores, getting ready for the dance, they weren't allowed to try on clothes in the fitting rooms.[1]

In 2009, on a whirlwind tour up and down Twenty-second Street and throughout midtown, State Representative Darryl Rouson told me of growing up in the area in the 1960s. Although the Manhattan Casino had long since closed, midtown bustled with black-owned businesses, and black lawyers, doctors, and dentists served as role models and mentors to the neighborhood kids. People like Dr. Fred Alsup and Dr. Ralph Wimbish, both physicians and civil rights leaders; Dr. Robert Swain, a dentist and community activist; businessman William Strong, known as the first black in St. Petersburg to buy a Cadillac; Doretha Cooper Bacon, who opened a catering business and Doe-Al restaurants, specializing in southern cooking; Ernest Fillyau, a city councilman; and James B. Sanderlin, a young lawyer whose office was on Twenty-second Street South, and who became the county's first black judge in 1972.

Frank Peterman Jr., state legislator, preacher, and later the secretary of the Department of Juvenile Justice, grew up knowing these role models, along with his father, a prominent lawyer, and his mother, Peggy Peterman, a longtime staff writer for the *St. Petersburg Times*.

As segregation ended, and neighborhoods that were previously off-limits opened up to black families, many took advantage of these new opportunities and moved out to the neighborhoods of Lakewood, Bartlett Park, and Childs Park, and north of the city. That mass migration, and the influx of drugs in the late 1960s, doomed the Twenty-Second Street South community. Dope dens engulfed the abandoned Manhattan Casino. Interstate 275 and the new baseball stadium (now called Tropicana Field, home to the Tampa Bay Rays) added to the decline of the Deuces in the 1990s.

Revitalization efforts have taken place in the last fifteen years in an attempt to bring banks, grocery stores, and small businesses into the area. There are successes, but guns, drug dealing, and other crime always seem to be winning in the battle for a secure neighborhood.

"The cats aren't out yet," Representative Rouson said as we began our tour at five in the evening, "but just wait a bit." Darryl is a lawyer, a former cocaine addict, and a longtime resident of midtown who developed the first black gated community just south of midtown a few years ago. In 2010 he successfully sponsored legislation limiting the sale of drug paraphernalia in Florida's tobacco shops. Simultaneously speed-dialing contacts on his cell phone and pulling up to their businesses and churches, Darryl introduced me to businessmen, community activists, and preachers, as well as two drug dealers and a whole bunch of kids who fled when they saw me—all within an hour. All the while, he kept up a running commentary on the neighborhood's family centers, health centers, relations with the police, and upcoming mayor's race.[4]

Here's my problem in court: Although I see single white moms raising difficult kids, it doesn't compare to the number of single black moms raising sons I can fairly accurately predict will end up in prison. That's very scary. To see kids, African American males ages twelve to seventeen, enter that pipeline to prison without knowing how to stop it is more than devastating; it frightens me and makes me see *Failure* written across the courtroom walls.

My courtroom serves the part of town with the highest crime rate and the largest minority population. Those really bad crimes I mentioned—home invasions, auto thefts, robberies, gun thefts, gang involvement, felony drug sales—occur most frequently in the area I serve. As for child abuse investigations, we have the most in Pinellas County. Far too often, and disproportionate to their population in the community, those crimes are committed by young black males between the ages of fourteen and seventeen.[2]

Mayor Rick Baker brought some banks and businesses and a supermarket to midtown before his term ended in 2009.[3] His successor, Bill Foster, promised during neighborhood debates that he would find money to create tutorial, recreation, and job programs for youths, as well as improve public safety. That's smart, and let's hope it happens, as the first warning signs of a troubled youth are often neighborhood crimes and disrespect, suspensions, and failures in school. Like what happened to Darion.

Darion's rap sheet swelled in a year and a half. He was caught shoplifting fireworks a few blocks from home, giving a false name and date of birth to law enforcement, using a screwdriver to bust the ignition of a car outside his home, throwing a brick through a neighbor's window, possessing marijuana, disrupting class, and spitting at a teacher.

In school, he scooped rocks out of a waterfall exhibit and threw them at a guidance counselor, then ran outside, where he picked up handfuls of mulch and lobbed them at nearby children before scaling a fence. He doodled in class, drawing pictures of people shooting others, the word *kil* [*sic*] on top of each person's head.

When discussing his behavior with a counselor who happened to be pregnant, Darion threatened, "I don't give a fuck if you pregnant, bitch, I'll hit your ass. You bitch, you got me fucked up, hoe." He began rapping, saying "ozzie pussy," "fuck ya girl," "that nigga got a hit coming out of the house," and "this junk is fucking dumb."[5]

Darion's mother was "concerned" for her son, as he was the oldest of her four boys and in and out of detention. A single mom, she worked two jobs and said she couldn't supervise him in the neighborhood. Darion's grandmother lived in the country and agreed to take him for the summer. Darion brightened up in court at this opportunity and told me he wanted to go there because "I would get to fish and to ride a dirt bike."

This plan fell through when the grandmother took sick. Dr. Jaggi, our child psychologist, worked with the mom on another safety plan for Darion. They found an uncle who agreed to supervise him after school and on the weekend while the mom worked. The uncle had a lawn service, and he put Darion to work for him, picking up clippings.

Well supervised, mentored, hot, and tired from working outside with his uncle, Darion remained crime free.

Darion, you see, was only ten years old.

PART III

Enlightenment

CHAPTER 12

What Works in Juvenile Justice? A Dynamic Duo and Napoleon Show the Way

I T'S "AHA!"

It's when the lightbulb clicks on, the last piece of the puzzle slides into place, or "it" suddenly dawns on you.

In French, it's *coup d'oeil*, a flash of insight from intelligent memory.

Strategic intuition is that creative spark in human achievement that makes the impossible possible and carries you over that last stumbling block, when one good idea leads to a better one.

"What works" is a twenty-first-century, evidence-based method of analyzing success that evolved in part out of the business successes of Bill Gates at Microsoft and Jack Welch at General Electric.

That flash of insight that gives you a strategy is personified by Bill Duggan. The experimental method to test what works is likewise embodied by Lynn Ellsworth. Married, they live with their daughter in a cozy loft in TriBeCa, with a beautiful view of Lower Manhattan. They present an amazing synergy of wit, intelligence, and deep commitment to reform. They are both tall, auburn-haired with a touch of grey, with wide smiles and sparkling eyes.

I'd not yet met Bill, an associate professor of management at Columbia Business School and the author of *Strategic Intuition: The Creative Spark in*

Human Achievement and *What Works: How Success Really Happens,* but I knew Lynn from a presentation she'd given for the Eckerd Family Foundation in Florida, analyzing the state's juvenile justice system. Lynn invited me for dinner in October 2009. I read Bill's book beforehand, and the result was a lively discussion that set the framework for "Enlightenment," the third part of this book.[1]

Although I'd never studied military history, Bill's analysis of Napoléon Bonaparte I's battlefield victories helped me understand the concept of strategic intuition. With Bill's permission, I'll paraphrase a bit and quote some, and try to do the complete version justice.

Napoléon was known for flashes of insight throughout his life. As the nineteenth-century Prussian military historian General Carl von Clausewitz explains those flashes of insight, Professor Duggan asks that we "look at a modern re-creation of Napoléon's *coup d'oeil* in action" in the landmark 1927 silent movie *Napoléon* by the French director Abel Gance. In a few short minutes of the film, Gance portrays with remarkable economy the role of *coup d'oeil* in Napoléon's first victory.

Bill says:

The scene takes place during the siege of Toulon in September 1793. Toulon was the French navy's most important port on the southern coast. The British invade and take it. The army of the French Revolution surrounds the city and prepares a counterattack. Napoléon, twenty-four years old at the time, had the rank of major of artillery. He arrives in Toulon and reports for duty.

The scene begins when Napoléon comes through a doorway and steps inside a spacious country café. He wears a simple black uniform and his famous hat with the crown like an upturned boat—it was standard issue for officers of the day. Under one arm, he carries a thick book. He pauses to look around. The café is filled with soldiers in uniform lounging and drinking. There are politicians in fancy dress, dandy hats, and all sorts of hangers-on from the countryside. A French general sits at the center of a long table. There is no sign of military discipline. Napoléon strides over to the general. He salutes, hands the general his orders, and stands stiffly at attention.

Napoléon's orders post him as second-in-command of the siege artillery. The general looks at the paper and scoffs. They don't need artillery: "We shall take Toulon with the sword and bayonet!" Napoléon gives the hint of a smile, salutes, and turns to go. The general catches his arm and asks, "If you were in my place, little man, what would you do?" Another soldier brings a map and spreads it out on the table before the general.

Napoléon looks down at the map of Toulon for a moment and then looks off into the distance. The filmmaker shows what Napoléon sees in his mind as a swirl of activity on the map. Then Napoléon blinks, as if coming out of a trance. He places a finger on the map and says, "Once the fort of L'Aiguillette is taken, the English will abandon the town."

The general explodes with laughter, along with everyone else. But Napoléon just stands still with his face calm. The laughter dies down, and it becomes clear that with a single *coup d'oeil*, Napoléon has won everyone's allegiance away from the general.

As it turned out, the general went ahead with his plan. It failed miserably. Paris fired him. The next general listened to Napoléon, who took the little fort instead. Napoléon's idea worked. His career took off from there.

Military historians know the elements that Napoléon put together to come up with his winning idea: contour maps, plus the light cannon, plus the American Revolutionary War, plus Joan of Arc's legendary resolve.

At Toulon, these four elements came together in Napoléon's mind. The contour maps showed him L'Aiguillette, a small fort around the main fortress, as at Orléans. Light cannon hauled up there could command the harbor and cut off the British army from its navy, as at Boston and Yorktown. We can see from this Toulon example that a flash of insight for strategic intuition has the same basic structure as expert intuition, except that the elements that combine in the mind come from farther afield, usually from outside the strategist's direct experience. That makes the flash of insight so much bigger when the pieces come together.

The four components of *coup d'oeil* are intelligent memory, presence of mind, a flash of insight, and resolution. Napoléon had them all that day in Toulon.

Now, what does Napoléon have to do with kids, other than being short, and what does strategic intuition have to do with juvenile justice?

Nearly thirty juvenile judges found themselves experiencing a flash of insight that could be called strategic intuition during a "'What Works' Presentation" by Lynn Ellsworth in Naples, Florida, in the summer of 2005, the day before the annual circuit judges conference. Joe Clark, CEO of the Eckerd Family Foundation, created by Jack and Ruth Eckerd of Eckerd drug stores to fund rehabilitative programs for troubled kids, had invited her to speak to the judges. Joe is a strategist who directs the generous foundation to seek very specific interventions where foundation dollars can make a difference. Joe put me in charge of filling the room with judges—no easy task when the competition consists of the beach, pool, tennis court and families on a Sunday afternoon.

Joe and I were pleased with the size of the crowd, and Lynn began her PowerPoint presentation of what works in Florida's juvenile justice system. Ten minutes into it, she was interrupted by a loud *"Bullshit!"*

"Bull. Shit!" Miami circuit judge Jeri Beth Cohen said a second time, leaning across the table and jabbing her finger at the screen.

> We know what works. We know that treatment is better than incarceration, and that prevention is better than treatment. We know diversion is better than detention. Every judge in this room knows that. We've known what works and what doesn't work for years. We just can't get the legislature, the governor, the county commissioners, the folks with the money, to *pay* for what works. That's our problem. We know the answers, but we have no power, no clout. No one listens to us.

A lively discussion began; the liveliest I'd seen with judges. We talked of ways to engage the public. Protests, marches on the State Capitol of

Tallahassee, press conferences, and rallies. Lynn and Joe helped to plot a strategy, which was the missing piece of Judge Cohen's flash of insight—"bullshit," if you will. Orlando Judge Maura Smith provided the structure. We've had ups and downs since, but the four dozen-or-so of us have formally organized into the Florida Council of Juvenile and Family Court Judges, a branch of the national organization, and our voice is heard and respected in Tallahassee as we speak on matters important to the kids in our courts.

The judges let Lynn finish her presentation, and we all agreed that she'd analyzed Florida's juvenile justice system well. She knew what worked and what didn't. Her methods were evidence-based and accurate.[2]

We are still working to achieve what Lynn Ellsworth laid out that day as a series of evidence-based best practices. Many are found in subsequent chapters of this book, centered on keeping kids out of court, civil citations rather than arrests, alternative sanctions to commitment, more effective counseling and intensive family therapy.

Lynn also had the evidence to prove what *doesn't* work: indiscriminately locking up kids, removing them from their communities, ignoring mental health needs, charging kids as adults, and failing to provide adequate treatment. In the area of postcommitment aftercare alone, Lynn finds that probation, curfews, military drills, electronic monitoring, and probation rules enforcement are ineffective at preventing a youth from committing another offense.

Lynn's and Bill's plan to put what works *first* in juvenile justice strategy challenges conventional planning, which sets out a goal, a strategy to achieve the goal, and then a way to measure success. If we flip that around and start with *what works,* as Napoléon did, and then, like Napoléon, have presence of mind, flashes of insight, and resolve, we're well on our way to successful juvenile justice reforms.

If Napoléon's approach is a little too abstract, you might want to turn to management advisor Mark Friedman, who takes a different route but reaches a similar conclusion in his book *Trying Hard Is Not Good Enough: How to Produce Measurable Improvements for Customers and Communities.* Friedman's "Results Accountability" framework has been used in over forty states and in countries around the world as a how-to route to successful outcomes. Mr. Friedman worked for the state of Maryland, then for the

Center for the Study of Social Policy, in Washington, D.C. He then founded the Fiscal Policy Studies Institute, in Santa Fe, New Mexico, for a total of thirty-three years in "accountability." I attended a presentation he made to our Tampa Bay area Children's Services Councils, local taxing authorities that fund services for kids and families.[3]

Mark's fast-talking, practical approach focuses first on finding common language, common sense, and common ground. In describing the language of accountability, he uses a funny slide he calls "the Jargon Construction Kit" to illustrate what happens when we string together words like *benchmark, result, goal, objective, target, measure, indicator,* and *outcome* with modifiers such as *measurable, urgent, priority, targeted, incremental, core, qualitative, programmatic, performance, strategic,* and *systemic.*

"I guarantee, if you combine words in this way, you will get away with it because people will be too embarrassed to ask you what you mean," he maintains. "I have a rule about language: If anyone uses three or more of these words in the same sentence, they don't know what they're talking about."

"Common sense" to Mark Friedman is what "strategic intuition" and "what works" are to Bill Duggan and Lynn Ellsworth. "Common sense is about the way the rest of the world works," he explains. "Any successful human enterprise starts with 'ends' and works backward to 'means.'"

Common ground is the outcome, or end result, where people can come together and agree on a desired result. It is *not* the means used to achieve the result. "The result (or outcome or goal) is a condition of well-being for children, adults, families, and communities, stated in plain language. Results are conditions that voters and taxpayers can understand," Mark instructs.

"Recreation services are among the most important things we do for young people," Mark continues. And recreation is so cheap compared to other services. But recreation services in many of our cities and states have been cut back dramatically. The short paper "A Recreation Entitlement," on the Fiscal Policy Studies Institute's website (www.resultsaccountability.com), proposes creating a recreation entitlement for all youths ages seven through seventeen. Benefits would be widespread throughout the education, juvenile justice, and other systems. Costs would be less than 2 percent of a typical city budget.

Hip-hoppers, are you listening? For those who sing, rap, play an instrument, dance, or follow the beat, hip-hop is a fine form of recreation that also provides cultural connections. Recreation isn't just ball games or art classes. In "Hip-Hop Cultural Outcomes," a presentation made to the National Council of Juvenile and Family Court Judges in July 2009, Anthony Harris defended hip-hop as part of a positive cultural experience. As president of Raise Up Community Development Corporation, in Las Vegas, Harris speaks nationally about the history and culture of hip-hop. He defines culture as "the way that a group of people functions as it relates to values, norms, and beliefs. Your neighborhood has a culture; the legal system has a culture. It describes the rules, the norm of what's going on.

"Hip hop began in the 1970s in the African American community in New York City as a form of expression using break dancing, deejaying, graffiti art, and rapping. It was a cultural response to and against the establishment to express what was going on in their communities.

"It's not: rap music only, sagging pants, gold teeth, bling bling, or Ebonics. These are all expressions of hip-hop. It is not black people but a subculture of black people who use this message to express. *Hip* means current or informed; *hop* comes from the word *dance,* as in *sock hop.* We are expressing ourselves in hip-hop," he says.

"In 1979, the Sugarhill Gang's 'Rappers Delight' crossed over and became a popular hit nationwide, which put hip-hop on the map, [got it] recognized in the country. The song crossed racial lines into the national spotlight.

"In 1982, Grandmaster Flash and the Furious Five recorded 'The Message,' which gave voice to the social ills and issues of the black community. There became an avenue to express what's going on in the community: 'I'm frustrated.' Now there is a motive I'm expressing: 'Don't push me, I'm close to the edge. I'm trying not to lose my head.'"

Harris says that white suburbanites purchase over 70 percent of hip-hop music and that it's the number-one form of musical expression in other countries, including Germany, Australia, the Philippines, and Japan. Although he acknowledges some of the negative messages of hip-hop, misogyny and the exaltation of money, sex, and violence, Harris claims that the positives—a legal form of income, talent, having fun, art existing anywhere, and love of community—outweigh the negatives.

"When hip-hop crossed to white culture, people took notice. A lot of our young people now are now engaged and productive because of the commercialization of hip-hop. Music is central to the establishment of youth subcultures. It is used as the major way that youths express themselves. It reflects their attitudes and moods more clearly than they can otherwise. We can keep kids' attention with music. If it takes a rap song to do that, let's do that! Pulling them out of their culture and into ours doesn't work. Going into their culture to shift their thinking works a lot better," Harris concludes.

The funders of juvenile programs certainly understand these concepts. To shortcut the steps taken in *Strategic Intuition* and *Trying Hard Is Not Good Enough*, look no further than the generous foundations that underwrite programs for juveniles, such as the MacArthur, Annie E. Casey, Robert Wood Johnson, Eckerd Family, and Jessie Ball duPont foundations. To receive their support, you have to propose what works and have the evidence to back your results up. You have to be specific and prove that you can make a difference. Joe Clark, of the Eckerd Family Foundation, calls it "exquisite points of intervention." His foundation, like many others, is dedicated to funding projects that change a child's life in a specific way at a point that makes a real difference. For example, building community connections for kids who age out of foster care and improving the quality of legal representation that public defenders give to their juvenile clients.

In the following chapters, we'll meet other innovators who have had those flashes of insight that have raised the bar and who have become heroes within juvenile justice. They speak in plain English, seeking common ground and outcomes we all rely upon. Finally, they have the evidence to measure results and success. Like Lynn and Bill and Mark—and Napoléon.

CHAPTER 13

Healthy Families: How Preventing Child Abuse Prevents Delinquency

THE LINK BETWEEN child abuse and juvenile delinquency is well established; indeed, irrefutable. According to the National Child Traumatic Stress Network, "Child trauma is endemic in the juvenile justice system. At least 75 percent of youths involved in the juvenile delinquency system have experienced traumatic victimization, and 11 percent to 50 percent have developed post-traumatic stress disorder (PTSD). Children involved in dependency cases generally have experienced at least one major traumatic event in their lifetime, and many have long and complete trauma histories."[1,2]

What Miami's juvenile judge, Cindy Lederman, did was to try to prevent the abuse at the earliest stage of child development. Judge Lederman told me:

In 1993, I felt confident that all the programs and services I sent families to every day actually helped them. I was quickly and firmly disabused of this notion by the researchers and academics I met during my ten-year involvement with the National Research Council (NRC). The NRC is the largest operating arm of the National Academy of Sciences, an organization created by Congress during Abraham Lincoln's presidency to advise the government on scientific matters.

My involvement with the NRC was the most critical professional experience of my career. My professional life has never been the same. I began to wonder how to make responsible, evidence-based reform in practice and policy in our juvenile courts.

When I first was assigned to dependency court in 1994, Florida was not routinely evaluating any children when they came into care. Children were rarely in court, and young children were invisible. Eventually, around 2002, with great fanfare, the Secretary of Florida's Department of Children and Families implemented psychosocial assessments for all children in care ages five and older.

We began to look at the impact and extent of family and community violence on our children over five in the child welfare system. The results were so startling, so disturbing, that we began to wonder if younger children were equally affected.

I was skeptical about working with infants and toddlers. I was not sure how productive it would be in terms of learning about the impact and extent of violence on such young children. Then, once we learned, what could we do? I was ignorant of the science of early childhood development. Dr. Joy D. Osofsky, our project's expert on childhood and trauma, assured me that we needed to embark on this work. She taught me about her clinical work with infants and toddlers. And so we began.[3]

That was Judge Lederman's *coup d'oeil* in juvenile court.

Judge Lederman is now the dean of dependency court judges in Florida and a nationally recognized expert on court interventions in early childhood development. A graduate of the University of Florida and University of Miami Law School, she was the presiding judge of the Juvenile Division in Miami from 1999 to 2009. She's the chair of the Florida Department of Children and Families Child Families Services Reviews Task Force. In May 2007, she was invited to address House Speaker Nancy Pelosi's National Summit on America's Children.

How early do we act to prevent child abuse? Ideally, before conception, by educating those who can't afford a child or responsibly raise a child to wait a bit. Or at least during pregnancy, by encouraging quality prenatal care, parenting classes, and drug and alcohol abstinence. Realistically, from birth through the toddler years, as Judge Lederman learned.

"Science confirms that babies are not blank slates," Judge Lederman asserts. "From birth, babies feel, remember, learn, and communicate. The adults who care for them are the mediators of all their experiences, for good or ill. The early years are critically important. What happens to children in their first three years shapes their future success in school, in their relationships, in all aspects of their lives. Young brains are resilient. They can heal from early maltreatment with the right treatment and services. Judges hold the integrity of a developing child's brain in their hands when deciding the disposition of maltreatment cases. They can play a central role in securing the services very young children need to support their physical and mental well-being."

A DVD from the national educational nonprofit organization Zero to Three, titled *Helping Babies from the Bench: Using the Science of Early Childhood Development in Court* (2007), is used to educate child welfare judges on the significance of attachment needs and disorders affecting babies and toddlers. It graphically demonstrates the earliest childhood connection between abuse and neglect, and the potential for delinquent behavior.

The DVD's most compelling moment captures a young mother playing with her five-month-old son as he sits facing her in an infant seat. She smiles wide; he smiles and gurgles back. She tickles his stomach; he laughs and kicks his feet. She leans in close and coos to him; he laughs. She points her finger at him; he points his back, waving it toward her.

A therapist then asks her to continue to look at him without any expression, words, or activity, which she does. The baby's eyes widen, and he fixes on her, immediately knowing the difference. He makes loud noises to get her attention, but she remains impassive. His face turns red, and he begins struggling in his seat, as if to get away; she remains still. Finally, he bursts into tears and a loud wail, less than a minute after she became silent. At the therapist's signal, she starts kissing his face and holding his hands, and he relaxes, smiling again.

This scene in the video, called "Still Face," was created and narrated by the eminent child psychologist Dr. Ed Tronick of Children's Hospital Boston. It impressed me so much that I wish it could be shown more than once to every new mother. I remembered Dr. Steven Gold's admonition, quoted earlier, that it's not just the abuse that's done to children, it's what's *not* happening during the period of abuse: the attachment, bonding, trust, comfort with routine, human connections, and pleasure in relationships, leading to love. If a mother is withdrawn, distracted, depressed, or emotionally absent—perhaps because she's a victim of domestic violence, financially distraught, and/or addicted to drugs—her child, like the little boy in the infant seat, suffers emotionally.

Harvard professor Jack P. Shonkoff, M.D., an expert on early childhood development and a Zero to Three presenter, speaks frequently to child welfare specialists: "Abuse and neglect literally change the brain development of babies," he says. "Not just behaviors, but brain development. Formation of attachment is critical. Moving children from home to home is absolutely the worst thing you can do to them; worse than a mother who's far from perfect."

Dr. Shonkoff participated in an Internet discussion following the publication of his report "From Neurons to Neighborhoods: The Science of Early Childhood Development." In the interview, Dr. Shonkoff distinguished between "critical" and "sensitive" periods in a child's development. He explained:

> We do know that there are some functions that emerge, in terms of brain development, in critical periods. And the well-described ones are in the sensory area—vision and hearing—to some extent. But there has never been demonstrated in humans a critical period of anything related to cognition or emotional development or social development.
>
> We have instead what might be called 'sensitive periods.' In critical periods, again, there is a certain period of time in the sequence of brain development where particular kinds of experiences are very important, and if you have those experiences in the right way, you develop the normal architecture; and if you don't have those experiences, your brain can't develop normally.
>
> In a sensitive period, there isn't a time when the window closes and it's too late. But what it means is that when you pass the sensitive period, it's harder for these things to develop in an adaptive way, or they may develop in a way that is not as efficient as it might be, and that you have to try to overcome later. Unlike a critical period where

it's too late, missing a sensitive period means that it just gets harder as you get older. It's harder to get it right.

So the messages that come out of that basic principle of brain development are that getting things right the first time is better than trying to fix them later.[5]

In my work as both a delinquency and dependency judge, my colleagues and I are constantly exploring the transition of abused, neglected infants and toddlers into angry, delinquent kids.

Zero to Three presenter Lynne Katz of the University of Miami works closely with Judge Lederman at the Linda Ray Intervention Center, a play-time facility for young children and their moms and dads. There skilled therapists teach appropriate bonding, play, and discipline, and the parents and children are videotaped. "The best thing is to improve the relationship with the parent," Dr. Katz says. "The goal is to turn an abusive, neglectful relationship into a nurturing, healthy, positive one. Babies must think their existence matters." She concludes by saying forcefully, "We need to break the cycle of abuse at the beginning, not at the end." Judge Lederman praises the center, calling it "the best intervention in the country. If parents can't get their children back after that experience—so be it, we tried."[4]

Dr. Mimi Graham, director of the Florida State University Center for Prevention and Early Intervention Policy, suggests that the courtroom is an appropriate place for the judge to ask the following questions:

- Is the child on target developmentally for his age? If not, why not? Key developmental milestones easy to discuss in court are: walking, talking, eating, and being easily soothed. How is the parent involved? If the child is delayed, is he or she receiving intervention?

- Is the baby forming healthy attachments?

- How does the baby interact with others? Does the baby easily go to the parent or turn his back? Does the parent seem like a stranger to the baby?

- Is the baby happy or fussy? Does the parent know how to soothe the baby? Has the baby received a mental health screening or evaluation?

Healthy Families Florida is a program that provides voluntary in-home services to families of small children, with a goal of keeping the family intact and nurturing and keeping the children safe. It is administered by a private-public partnership, the Ounce of Prevention Fund of Florida, which we call "the Ounce." The mission of the Ounce is to identify, fund, support, and evaluate innovative prevention programs for Florida's at-risk children and families. A twenty-year success story in the health and human services arena, it is efficiently and enthusiastically run by CEO and president Douglas Sessions Jr. and a staff dedicated to reducing child abuse and creating healthy families. I'm proud to sit on the board, along with tennis champion Chris Evert and others committed to improving the lives of Florida's children. Chris sponsors an annual celebrity tennis tournament in Boca Raton, Florida, and has raised millions in funds over the years.

Ounce of Prevention Fund President Doug Sessions is an affable and effective advocate who has a bottom-line, evidence-based, research-oriented, type A personality and a long history of excellent relations with the Florida Governor's Office, the legislature, and the agencies that serve children.

Doug confirms the relationship between child abuse and delinquency, including the economic impact. According to his organization's review of national studies, 27 percent of children who are abused or neglected become delinquents. In Florida in 2006, over 42,000 children age three or younger were victims of child maltreatment. The number of youths served by the Department of Juvenile Justice for the same period was 129,210, at an average cost to the state of over $5,200 per delinquent child. Doing the math, and just using the numbers of children in the birth-to-three-years age range, the Ounce estimates that nearly $62.3 million in 2008 dollars would have been spent on delinquent kids who themselves were abused or neglected as babies or toddlers. That's in just one state.[6]

Healthy Families' services begin during pregnancy or within three months of a baby's birth and can last for up to five years, depending on the unique needs of each family. The program equips parents and other caregivers with the knowledge and skills they need to help ensure that their children can grow up healthy, safe, nurtured, free from abuse and neglect, and ready to succeed in school and in life. Here are some of the ways that trained home visitors provide parents and other caregivers information, guidance, and emotional and practical support:

- By modeling positive parent-child interaction to enhance the child's development.

- By providing education on child health and development and the importance of immunizations and well-baby checkups.

- By teaching about safe and unsafe sleeping environments for infants, coping with crying, and other prevention topics.

- By screening children for developmental delays.

- By screening mothers for maternal depression.

- By identifying and connecting families with natural support systems such as family, friends, neighbors, and faith-based organizations.

- By connecting families to medical providers and making referrals to other community services.

- By teaching how to recognize and address child safety hazards in and around the home, in the car, in and around water, and in other environments.

- By helping to develop appropriate problem-solving skills and identify positive ways to manage stress.

- By promoting personal responsibility for their future and the future of their families by helping them to set and achieve goals, such as furthering their educations and finding stable employment.

Doug, citing study results, notes, "A rigorous, independent five-year comparison evaluation concluded that Healthy Families Florida prevents child abuse and neglect so successfully that those participants had 58 percent less child abuse and neglect at twenty-four months compared to an equivalent group of parents and children who had little or no services."[7]

News anchor Katie Couric interviewed Jim Hmurovich, president and CEO of Prevent Child Abuse America, on the *CBS Evening News* on February 4, 2010, about a study finding a 26 percent decrease in incidents of serious child abuse, especially sexual abuse, between 1993 and 2005, when "massive investments were made in evidence-based strategies" such as Healthy

Families. Hmurovich and others in the field worry that a weak economy and budget cuts will unravel these gains.[8]

Those fears came true in May 2010, when the Florida's legislature slashed the state's investment in Healthy Families from $28 million to $18 million, meaning that 3,500 fewer families would receive services. "We all fear for the children of these families," Doug Sessions wrote in a message to the Ounce board.[9]

Sometimes the connection between child abuse and delinquency is driven home by news coverage of horrible cases. Late in 2009, I presided over a detention hearing for a fifteen-year-old who was accused, along with his eleven-year-old girlfriend, of pouring gasoline around the girl's mother's mattress and lighting it, attempting to murder her. As she was taken to a hospital burn unit, the two stole her car and drove away.

The chubby, crew-cut boy standing before me didn't look a day older than twelve. The families of both kids had long histories of dependency court action for drug and alcohol abuse, domestic violence, and beating their children. Both kids had been removed from their mothers and then returned. The fathers were in prison. Complaints that the girl was "oversexualized" began when she was *seven* years old. She had a provocative MySpace page at age eleven and a history of running to neighbors to avoid her mother's drunken rages and her mother's boyfriend's violent retaliation. Intensive psychotherapy and psychiatric evaluations were ordered, but I didn't see evidence that they were carried out.

Earlier in 2009, the boy had been charged with assaulting his sister with a knife and kicking his mother while she was hitting him. As for the girl, the state listed her as a witness in a child abuse case against her sixteen-year-old brother. He was accused of providing her with marijuana.

Our child psychologists intervened to work with the state and the public defenders for the children. It was as good a result as we could imagine: in return for guilty pleas, the boy was sentenced to a juvenile commitment program, and the young girl moved to live with an aunt in Orlando, on intensive probation.

"Among the Worst Offenders": The Supreme Court Bans Life Without Parole for Many Young Offenders

JUVENILES WHO COMMIT crimes other than murder cannot be locked up for life without the opportunity for parole, the U.S. Supreme Court ruled in a 5–4 decision in May 2010. To do so constitutes cruel and unusual punishment under the Eighth Amendment. In the case of Terrence Graham, a Florida teen sentenced to life without parole for a home invasion he committed while on probation for armed robbery, Justice Anthony M. Kennedy wrote for the majority: "The state has denied him any chance to later demonstrate that he is fit to rejoin society based solely on a nonhomicide crime committed while he was a child in the eyes of the law."

Kennedy added, "Life in prison without the possibility of parole gives no chance for fulfillment outside prison walls, no chance for reconciliation with society, no hope."[1]

The ruling affects 129 inmates in this country, 77 of them imprisoned in Florida. The *St. Petersburg Times* editorialized, "Florida now has to reform itself and quit denying counseling, education, and rehabilitation programs to certain young prisoners with life sentences. Ian Manuel, for example, was 13 when he shot a woman during a robbery in Tampa in 1990 and received a no-parole life sentence. As reported by *Times* staff writer Meg Laughlin, Manuel has spent nearly all of his time in prison in solitary confinement for disciplinary infractions that include storing food and cursing. He has been denied an education and the development of any work skills. While in solitary, he could not have books or television."[2]

Manuel has an unusual advocate: his victim in the botched robbery, Debbie Baigrie, who was twenty-eight at the time. She recovered from the shooting and "tried to help Manuel get a high school equivalency diploma in prison," wrote Laughlin. "But because he was a lifer in solitary confinement, the Florida Department of Corrections wouldn't allow him to participate in rehabilitation programs." Following the Supreme Court ruling, Baigrie told the *Times,* "After all of these years, to be able to put the words *rehabilitation* and *Ian* together in the same sentence makes me want to cry with relief. For some people, getting vengeance is closure. For me, knowing Ian can finally have hope is closure."

Many Florida teens received harsh sentences in the mid-1990s as a result of two high-profile cases in which local youths killed British and German tourists. Laws were passed making it easier to direct-file youths to adult court and eliminate parole. Although "second chance" legislation providing parole hearings was introduced in Florida in 2010, it didn't pass.

The Supreme Court's ruling in *Graham v. Florida* does something more: It ends the status of the United States as the only country that punished juveniles so severely. Israel discontinued the practice in 2008. Admittedly, many cruel regimes kill youths who commit crimes, but I'm referring to legal sentences passed by lawmakers.

The ruling also ended six months of anxiety experienced by the lawyers and child advocates across the country following oral argument of the case in November 2009. A week after the decision was announced, an ebullient Brian Gowdy, Terrance Graham's attorney, told me:

> It's very, very special. It's a once-in-a-lifetime experience. I felt good after the oral argument. It was obviously an issue that bothered the justices.
>
> My belief was that we were going to win, but how broadly, categorically, or case by case, like Justice [John] Roberts wanted, was in doubt.

It's a very strong opinion. It couldn't have been any better. The justices sometimes seemed to be talking to each other, like when Justice Kennedy asked Justice Roberts if juveniles had a constitutional right to hope.

[A companion case, *Sullivan v. Florida*, argued by Bryan Stevenson, was dismissed on procedural grounds.]

Brian got the case the old-fashioned way: He was retained by Terrance Graham's family to handle the first Florida court appeal after the youth was incarcerated in 2004. Brian lost that appeal, and the family ran out of money. But the attorney stayed on the case for the next six years without payment, all the way to the U.S. Supreme Court's ruling. He will continue to represent Graham in the resentencing.

"Terrence has been a pretty good citizen in prison and should do well on the outside when released," he contended. "He made some serious mistakes as a juvenile, but he has family support. He got his GED in prison, and his graduation ceremony was the night of the oral argument. I'm going to do all I can for him," Brian pledged, adding that the fate of all seventy-seven Florida inmates affected is unclear, especially those who'd exhausted their appeals.

As part of my work with the MacArthur Foundation Juvenile Indigent Defense Action Network (JIDAN), I'd been invited to a post–oral argument panel discussion at the Georgetown University Law Center in November 2009. It was an opportunity to hear the experts in this area slice and dice, mince and parse the questions and comments of the justices.

"We were all there to serenade Justice Kennedy," panelist Marsha Levick said, referring to the group of advocates who wrote amicus briefs in support of the defendants and their attorneys, Stevenson and Gowdy. It's easy to see why. In 2005, Justice Kennedy wrote the 5–4 majority opinion in the case of *Roper v. Simmons*, declaring it unconstitutional to execute anyone younger than eighteen at the time of the crime. In that opinion, Kennedy relied upon scientific evidence, including the work of noted psychologist Laurence Steinberg, concluding that juveniles "cannot with reliability be classified among the worst offenders" for whom capital punishment is reserved. Of course, *Roper* dealt with the death penalty for juveniles. The court has always recognized that "death is different."

For her advocacy, scholarship, and passion, Marsha has received a number of child advocacy awards. In addition to her public interest work, she has been an adjunct professor at the University of Pennsylvania Law School and Temple University Beasley School of Law, her alma mater.

"'Kids are different,' the rationale used by Justice Kennedy in the *Roper* decision, ran smack into the 'death is different' argument of Chief Justice John Roberts and others in today's hearing," Marsha summarized, admitting that the lines are more blurred when you speak of a period of years or even life sentences. *Roper* was more black and white, definitive, as it involved a death sentence. "What about sentencing a kid to sixty-five years in prison rather than life without parole? We'll be back to argue that as cruel and unusual as well," she promised.[3]

That was no surprise to anyone in the audience. Marsha has a thirty-year legal career advocating for the rights of juveniles and women. She is a nationally recognized leader in juvenile law, challenging conditions of confinement in detention centers and other youth facilities, and the quality of education for incarcerated kids. She describes the Juvenile Law Center in Philadelphia, which she cofounded—and which the MacArthur Foundation supports financially—as a public interest law firm created to advocate on behalf of children in juvenile justice and child welfare systems. A slim, striking brunette, incredibly articulate and deep-thinking, she tackles issues large and small, from writing amicus briefs on juvenile matters for the courts to assisting a single lawyer representing just one child. The MacArthur Foundation presented its award for creativity and efficiency to the Juvenile Law Center in 2008.

I first met Marsha at a MacArthur Foundation meeting in Miami in February 2009, when she took the microphone to announce that two juvenile judges in western Pennsylvania had been indicted in federal court in a "kids for cash" scheme. The Luzerne County judges, Mark Ciavarella and Michael Conahan, were charged with railroading kids into a privately run detention center in return for $2.6 million in kickbacks. The youngsters were not represented by lawyers, the hearings were brief, and the scheme went undetected for years. The fraud allegedly began when the judges helped the center land a county contract worth $58 million, guaranteeing the operators a steady income. The judges sent juveniles to that facility, often for petty charges.

I could hardly believe the allegations. If true, I thought at the time, this was the worst judicial crime imaginable.

The Pennsylvania Supreme Court dismissed thousands of juvenile convictions issued by the two juvenile judges charged in the corruption scandal. Only the most violent youthful offenders could be retried. Marsha was quoted in the national media, saying, "This is exactly the relief these kids needed. It's the most serious corruption scandal in our history, and the court took an extraordinary step in addressing it."[4,5,6]

The *Jewish Daily News* reported:

When Marsha Levick, 58, and her colleagues from the Juvenile Law Center in Philadelphia first began probing the harsh sentences imposed on young people after lightning-fast hearings in the courtrooms of Pennsylvania's Luzerne County, they had no idea what they would uncover. They knew only that the children were being sent away, sometimes in shackles, for first-time crimes as minor as pushing a classmate into a school locker. Levick and other JLC lawyers eventually built a comprehensive case, alleging that for years, Judges Mark A. Ciavarella Jr. and Michael T. Conahan were sending the youngsters, who often had no legal representation, to private jails whose owner had paid the pair a total of $2.6 million in bribes. The JLC—founded in 1975 by Levick, executive director Robert Schwartz, and two other Temple Law School classmates—pursued justice for the juveniles involved, fighting against the vast political bureaucracy of Pennsylvania's legal system, and finally won.

A few months earlier, U.S. District Judge Edward Kosik had rejected a plea agreement for a seven-year prison sentence for the two judges, who resigned from office and pled guilty. Judge Kosik held that the judges hadn't accepted responsibility for the kickback scheme. They would admit to fraud and tax fraud but not to locking up kids for money. Conahan pled guilty again in return for a sentence of one to twenty years. As he awaited sentencing, Ciavarella was preparing for trial on racketeering charges.

In the meantime, they face civil rights lawsuits brought by the children and their families. One group of plaintiffs includes a fifteen-year-old with no prior record who committed a third-degree misdemeanor when she created a MySpace page that mocked her high-school assistant principal. Taken from the courtroom in shackles, she was locked up for a month. She'd waived her right to a lawyer, as did many of the kids who were encouraged to sign waivers of counsel at every opportunity.

Patti Puritz, executive director of the National Juvenile Defender Center, cheered the Supreme Court's decision in *Graham* and the work of lawyers and child advocates at a MacArthur Foundation–sponsored meeting in Chicago a week after the decision. "*Roper* and *Graham*, two victories in five years! What is next?" she asked.[7]

Marsha Levick, smiling broadly and freed of anxiety waiting for the Supreme Court's decision, praised Kennedy: "The wonderful words of Justice Kennedy, the expansiveness of his decision, his questioning of what's wrong with making irrevocable decisions about the future of kids—we couldn't have asked for more." But the work lies ahead, she said. "In *Roper,* death sentences were simply converted to life without parole. This situation is much more complicated, as we have one hundred twenty-nine individual cases with different crimes, changes to legislation, and possibilities of resentencing or parole hearings. We're trying to develop model policies and work with psychological associations to get out ahead. We were catching up after *Roper.* We're getting out front after *Graham.*"

Our Florida team plunged into the task of how to resolve the seventy-seven Florida cases. "There is no easy answer," said Professor Gerard F. Glynn of Barry University School of Law in Orlando. "Life *with* parole doesn't exist in Florida. There are no parole standards, as there is no parole."

It will be fascinating to study the cases of those seventy-seven inmates as their cases evolve. For teenagers who spent years in prison without an opportunity for education and rehabilitation, the future is uncertain.

Now, I thought, Justice Kennedy's "worst offender" analysis in *Roper* and his pitch for rehabilitation in *Graham* could be used to overturn the Adam Walsh Act's punitive requirement for certain juveniles to register as sex offenders. I was persuaded by an exceptionally bright Stetson University College of Law graduate, Jessica E. Brown, who interned in our court. Jessica's law review article began with a chilling example of the consequences of sex offender registration for juveniles, taken from a July 2007 *New York*

Times Magazine article by Maggie Jones, "How Can You Distinguish a Budding Pedophile from a Kid with Real Boundary Problems?"[8,9]

> Johnnie is a registered sex offender. When he was eleven, he touched his four-year-old half-sister's vagina (over her underwear). A few months later, she performed oral sex on him at his request. Johnnie's mother found out. She called the police, and Johnnie spent sixteen months in a residential juvenile sex offender program, where he successfully completed treatment. When he was released, Johnnie's mother wanted nothing to do with him, so he ended up living with his grandmother. Two months after he started at a new middle school, someone found Johnnie on the state's Internet sex offender registry. Two days later, Johnnie walked into oncoming traffic and told a police officer he wanted to die. He transferred to an alternative school for juvenile delinquents. Even there, the harassment continued. Some of the other boys confronted Johnnie on the school bus, calling him a sex offender and yelling "You tried to rape your sister!" As a result of anger and depression, Johnnie has twice been admitted to psychiatric hospitals. Not only is Johnnie suicidal, but when he transferred to yet another school and the harassment continued, he told a counselor that he wanted to kill another student for taunting him. Johnnie knows what he did to his sister was wrong and continues to feel guilty about it. Johnnie has never committed another sex offense. Nevertheless, his name, photo, address, and school information continue to appear on the Internet registry, where they will likely remain for the rest of his life.

In her law review article, Jessica argued that registration requirements under the Adam Walsh Act contradict traditional rehabilitation and confidentiality goals. The result is more punitive and public proceedings, increasing the risk that adolescent offenders will become adult criminals.

Are adolescent sex offenders such as Johnnie "among the worst offenders," as defined by the U.S. Supreme Court in the *Roper* decision, Jessica asked, and thus required to remain on publicly accessible sex offender web sites for the rest of their lives? Could the *Roper* decision be used to overturn all or part of the registration requirements as they apply to certain juvenile sex offenders? After all, she reasoned, the Supreme Court concluded in *Roper* that juveniles are less culpable because of their immaturity and therefore are exempt from the death penalty.

"To reach this conclusion, the *Roper* majority identified three distinct characteristics that make juveniles less culpable than adult offenders," Jessica wrote. Summarizing, juveniles are prone to impetuous acts, have less control over their environment, and have more transitory personality traits.

Jessica concluded that both the public safety and the interest of juveniles would be better protected if the most serious juvenile sex offenders were tried as adults after an appropriate hearing before a juvenile judge. Sex offender registration would apply to that category of youths, without casting a wide net over kids like Johnnie, many of whom are themselves victims of sex abuse. It's that abuse that needs addressing.

Dr. Kenneth Wooden, investigative reporter and author of *Weeping in the Playtime of Others: America's Incarcerated Children,* an exposé of the industry of incarcerated kids, has developed a prevention program to educate potential child victims of sex abuse to the lures that sexual predators use, such as the grooming, the "lost puppy," and the "family emergency," in which the predator tells the child that he's a friend of the family, some kind of crisis has occurred, and he's been sent to take the child home. Speaking to child welfare specialists in April 2010, Ken said, "Sex abuse is so massive in this country. The adult predator is an expert con artist in pushing back responsibility to the victim."

Thanks to the hard work, foresight, and cooperation of our state attorney, public defender, and behavioral psychologists, our county has one of the most effective juvenile sex offender programs in the country, administered by Dr. Christine Jaggi. The beauty lies in its simplicity, but it broadly takes into account the behavior of the adults in the juvenile's life. Have they exposed the juvenile to pornography? Are they bringing sex partners into the house and forgetting to close the bedroom door? Do they ignore or deny early warning signs of incest? Are there other children at risk in the home? Is the juvenile sex offender actually a victim of adult sex abuse?

In our county, juveniles whose first charge is a sex offense—lewd and lascivious conduct, indecent exposure, sex battery—are evaluated by our psychologists prior to entering a plea. If it appears that the youth would benefit from sex offender education and counseling, and the youth and parent(s) are cooperative, the juvenile and the state enter into a plan that provides for an admission to the charge, probationary supervision, and the opportunity to have the charge dismissed if the juvenile successfully completes the plan and doesn't offend again in any manner. The victim and the victim's parent(s) must agree, too. This not only eliminates the Adam Walsh Act registration requirements, but because the charge is dismissed, the juvenile doesn't have a sex crime on his or her record, and the victim doesn't have to go through the agony of a trial. For those juveniles with a prior misdemeanor record before they are charged with a sex crime, there is still the possibility of a negotiated reduction in the charge—to a simple battery, for example—if they agree to enter sex offender counseling.[11]

Our first-time sex offender program has been hugely successful, with only a few failures of the plan. In 2009, in Florida, more than fifty juveniles were required to register as sex offenders. In our county of over one million people, only two juveniles are registered. Our enlightened assistant state attorney, Joe Walker, supports the plan and the treatment it provides.

Our plan is not for everyone, however. There are some serious juvenile sex offenders who need treatment in a residential commitment program. The value of our plan is that each case is analyzed individually: the facts, the motivation behind the sex offense, the youth's cooperation, the victim's wishes, and the likelihood of success. It certainly sorts out juveniles who are not "among the worst offenders" and relieves the juvenile judge of a difficult decision.

CHAPTER 15

Curses and Compassion: Victims' Responses to Juvenile Crime

S IX-YEAR-OLD TIFFANY jumped out of her mother's car, clasping the house key in her small hand. For the last few months, her mother had allowed her to open the front door while Mom struggled with her baby brother, Sam, and the groceries. Tiffany liked being a helper. She felt grown up.

Today, however, she didn't need the key. The front door was cracked. Tiffany pushed it open, stepped inside, and screamed so loudly that her mother dropped the groceries, grabbed Sam, and ran to her. Mom screamed louder than Tiffany.

The Christmas tree lay on top of the presents scattered on the floor. The ornaments were smashed; many of the boxes were ripped open and emptied. The flat-screen TV had been yanked from the wall and was missing. Someone had slashed the sofa and chairs; stuffing from the cushions covered the floor. The refrigerator door was open, and there was food all over the dining room table.

"As horrible a sight as that was," the mom said months later at the sentencing of the two fifteen-year-old boys who had ransacked the house, "the worst thing they did was take the video camera. Sam's first birthday party was the day before. We took movies of him with his cake, his cousins, Tiffany, and his presents. I never got that back. I don't care about the camera, but I'll never forgive them for stealing Sam's first birthday and for giving Tiffany such horrible memories that she won't go in the front door alone." Tiffany and her family were victims of juvenile crime.

HERE ARE THE STORIES of other victims in my court:

Jackson's father finished totaling the $7,000 in medical and dental bills incurred when the boy's jaw was broken and teeth knocked out in a fight with a former high-school buddy. "We treated Scott like one of our own sons," Jackson's dad said on the stand. "He spent weekends with us. We took him camping and to baseball games. We felt sorry for the kid. And what did he do? He nearly killed our son."

Walter was a poster guy for Florida retirement. He moved from Chicago to St. Petersburg after serving thirty years with the city water department. A widower, he lived on a small pension and his social security in a mobile home community next to a public golf course. He played golf three or four times a week and improved enough to play competitively on a local senior circuit. He considered it a luxury that he owned two sets of golf clubs: the old set he'd brought from Chicago, and the nearly new Big Berthas he'd bought "dirt cheap" at a garage sale. He kept both sets in the trunk of his ten-year-old Chevrolet.

The sound of tires screeching in his driveway woke Walter at two in the morning, and he looked out the window just in time to see the taillights of his car disappear down the street. Three weeks later, the police found Walter's Chevrolet in an alley behind an abandoned house. The ignition had been punched, the radio and four tires had been taken, and the trunk had been pried open. Both golf bags lay on the ground, but all the clubs were missing.

"I'd just qualified for the senior tournament at a public course in the next county. I didn't have a way to get there. I didn't have any rental insurance. A friend offered to lend me his golf clubs, but my heart wasn't in it. What do those losers want with golf clubs?"

Walter glared in court at the boys who stole his car. "Damn it, those punks ruined the only thing that brought me pleasure. I was really looking forward to that tournament."

Kaylee's aunt jabbed her finger at the defense table, where Kaylee sat with her public defender. "I did so much for that girl. Took her in when her mother went to prison, bought her clothes, and helped her with her schoolwork. And what did she do? Stole my credit cards and the sapphire ring I got from my mother—her grandmother—and ran off with her pothead boyfriend, racking up charges, pawning the ring. I never want to see her again in my life."

Here are the stories of other victims in my court: Victims of juvenile crimes bring a boiling cauldron of emotions to court—and, often, tears to my eyes. The random, senseless destruction committed by kids, compounded by the victims' feelings of betrayal, disbelief, and anger, create palpable tension in the courtroom. Victims often suffer economic and emotional losses that conflict with their instinctive desires to like kids and to want to help them.

Tension finds expression in many ways. A small number of victims call the defendants "scumbags," "potheads," or "pieces of shit" before I stop them. More often, though, I'm amazed at the generosity that victims show to the juveniles who've harmed them.

Mario, 16, stared straight ahead at the podium, but his mother turned toward the victim in disbelief. Did he really mean what he said? Mario had just pled guilty to breaking into an RV dealership and ransacking one of the vehicles; he removed the electronics and, for good measure, defecated on the sofa bed. Now Mr. Walker, who owned the dealership, was offering Mario a job at the dealership at $12 an hour if he would attend school each day, stay crime free, obey curfew, and use half of his earnings to begin to pay for the damage he caused.

Three or four other parents raised their hands in the courtroom. "We'll take that offer!" I heard. Mario's mother elbowed a weak response from him. The probation officer agreed to give it a try. Sadly, two weeks later, after just three days of working at the dealership, Mario was caught selling cocaine to an undercover cop at two in the morning. He was arrested for violating probation *and* the new drug charge, and then sentenced to a high-risk commitment program.

Victims suffer in so many ways. They are out of pocket financially, their sense of security is lost, they are inconvenienced by losing time from work to come to court, and they're angry—often at the judge and "the system" as well. Although the RV dealer was unusual, countless other victims in court have faced the juveniles who had brought them harm, and wished them well:

"I don't want to see you in prison."

"I wish you a good future."

"I hope you get an education and a family you love so that you can see how much this hurts."

"I hope you turn your life around and make your mother proud."

"I don't want to read about you shot to death in a gang war."

I look at the faces of the kids as they look into the eyes of the victim they've harmed, some of them shaking, in tears and apologetic, and I think they get it. Victims in court make a greater impact on the guilty young person than a parent or juvenile judge.

"SHE'S KNOWN ON THE STREET as 'Judge Hug-a-Thug,' the Fox News reporter told the television audience after filming a sentencing in my court. The victim of the burglary, apparently anticipating that I might not commit the kid, had called Fox. Indeed, when I heard that six weeks after the burglary the youth was doing well in school, playing on the basketball team, and working twenty hours a week at Wendy's, I suspended the commitment and kept him on probation as long as the good grades, basketball, and job continued. I also ordered him to use the money he earned to pay back the victim for the damage from the break-in. But this victim, like some others, wanted retribution as much as restitution. I don't blame them.

Kristin Henning, a Georgetown University Law Center professor, takes an unusual, but perceptive, position on what is wrong with victims' rights in juvenile court. She favors removing victim testimony from the courtroom, arguing that it interferes with the rehabilitative goals of juvenile justice and that the juvenile may not be ready or appropriately prepared to hear victim testimony at a courtroom sentencing. Professor Henning makes a case for neighborhood accountability boards, mediation, and other avenues for victims and juvenile defendants to meet and work out issues of remorse, apologies, and restitution.[1]

I disagree. While I think those measures are helpful and constructive following sentencing, I think it is part of the necessary rehabilitative process for the juvenile defendant to see the victim in court testifying to his or her emotional and financial losses. The youth may not fully comprehend the extent of the harm he has caused, but he gets the picture. And if he's shaken, ashamed, embarrassed, and upset, that's a good result and a first step toward rehabilitation.

Professor Henning, however, makes excellent points. She writes that "victim impact statements, delivered in the highly charged environment of the courtroom, without trained mediators to facilitate discourse between the victim and the offender, are also unlikely to foster the emotional healing and restoration that victims seek." She suggests that because "many youths are not intellectually and emotionally equipped to experience and articulate sincere remorse in the days after an offense, victims are often disappointed in the child's response to the victim impact statement, and judges are likely to penalize the child for an apparent lack of empathy."

It is true that juveniles often stammer or divert their eyes or even laugh nervously in court in front of the victim. But it's my responsibility as judge to explain the reaction and certainly not to aggravate a sentence because of a tepid response. The victim deserves to be heard in court, the youth needs to face reality, and although I think the postsentencing forums are helpful, I think the child's true emotions are indeed expressed, or can be explained, at the sentencing.

Professor Henning advocates for an Impact of Crime curriculum that the Florida Department of Juvenile Justice required be taught in all residential commitment programs. Program facilitators use a series of student exercises and quizzes designed to help young people understand the impact of crime and accept responsibility for the harm they have caused. The program facilitates a dialog about ways in which offenders may begin to restore victims and communities. It sounds terrific. Anything that creates empathy in troubled youths is valuable. But a victim should not be denied a voice in court.

Linda White found what works for her as the victim of a terrible crime. In 1986, her twenty-six-year-old daughter Cathy was abducted, raped, and murdered by two fifteen-year-old boys. Cathy, the mother of a small child and pregnant, met the boys at a gas station in eastern Texas, where they asked her for a ride. Inside her car, one of the boys pulled out a stolen handgun and ordered her to drive toward Houston, where they raped her, shot her in the leg, and then, drunk and high, killed her so she couldn't identify them. The killers were arrested, confessed, pled guilty to murder and rape, and received fifty-four and fifty-five years in prison.

Nothing brought true closure to Linda's life or to the deep sadness she felt until she began to confront the reality of what had happened to her daughter at the hands of these juvenile killers and to learn about the lives they had led. She enrolled in college and then taught inmates in Texas prisons. She became involved with the Bridges to Life program, which offers victims and inmates the chance to gather and share stories in a supportive, healing environment. In 2000, she met with one of her daughter's killers, Gary Brown, in prison. She brought along Amy, the granddaughter she'd adopted after Cathy's death. She learned that Brown had been running from abusive situations at home and in foster care and had attempted suicide at age eight.

This tragic event in Linda's life put her on a path to ending violence at all stages of life. She works in several areas of restorative justice, including victim-offender mediated dialogues, through an organization called Murder Victims' Families for Reconciliation (MVFR), of which she is a board member. Linda spoke at an event at Georgetown University Law Center, primarily to juvenile public defenders and juvenile justice professionals.

"When I had the first opportunity to talk to Gary Brown, one of my daughter Cathy's killers," she said, "I learned for the first time what my daughter's last words to them had been: 'I forgive you, and God will, too.'" Of her advocacy of juvenile justice, Linda said, "Cathy would love what I am doing."

Linda White is also a member of the Amici organization, which is made up of people who have lost family members to violent crime committed by juveniles, yet who oppose life sentences for those defendants. Angela C. Vigil, a designated public service and pro bono attorney with one of the world's largest law firms, Baker & McKenzie, and counsel of record for amici curiae in the cases of Terrance Jamar Graham and Joe Harris Sullivan versus the state of Florida, filed an amicus brief challenging life without parole for juveniles. In it, Ms. Vigil neatly summarized the beliefs and testimony of some of the victims of violent juvenile crime:

"Amici believe that children are fundamentally redeemable. The principle of rehabilitation—providing offenders a second chance at a productive, law-abiding life—has special resonance in cases involving juvenile offenders. This brief contains several accounts where amici have personally witnessed the rehabilitation of the juveniles they have come to know through tragic events."

One of those victims is Aqeela Sherrill, a one-time gang member from South Central Los Angeles who knows firsthand that change is possible. He believes that even his firstborn son's killer deserves a chance to change, as he himself did. The circumstances of Terrell Sherrill's 2004 shooting were inexplicable to Aqeela, who received a phone call telling him that his dynamic, charismatic son had been shot in the back multiple times while attending a party in an affluent neighborhood. To Aqeela, imprisoning the seventeen-year-old killer for the rest of his life was unjust punishment for someone who likely had been failed by the people most entrusted with his care: his parents.

Robert Hoelscher is a self-described "tough on crime" guy from Texas, whose father was killed by a troubled seventeen-year-old during a convenience store robbery in 1961, when he was seven. Ray Hoelscher's murder left behind a widow and six children. As the middle child, Robert withdrew into himself, unable to discuss his father's death until he began work in 2001 as a volunteer for the Innocence Project in New Orleans. The next year, he became the project's first executive director. Robert learned, decades after the murder, that his late mother had called her husband's killer's parents, expressing sorrow and forgiveness. This inspired him to focus his volunteer efforts on juvenile crime. Robert finds it illogical that the criminal justice system imposes tougher sentences on juveniles who commit serious crimes, because of some heightened sense of their level of maturity and accountability. "Wrongheaded logic," Robert calls that. "If anyone imprisoned by life deserves a second chance at life, it is those individuals whose criminal acts were committed under the misguided influence of youth."

Bill Pelke believes that all juveniles, including his grandmother Ruth's killers, can be turned around. In this case, four drunk and high teenage girls took advantage of an elderly lady's generosity by pretending interest in her free Bible lessons, when they really wanted to steal her money. One of the girls hit Ruth over the head with a vase, another stabbed her thirty-three times. They took off with only $10 and her car. Paula Cooper, the fifteen-year-old who stabbed Ruth, was sentenced to death in 1986, a year after the killing. But Bill decided that the death penalty was too severe a punishment. He collected over two million signatures calling for her sentence to be overturned. In 1989, she was given sixty years, or thirty with good behavior. Paula obtained her GED and college degree in prison and wants to help others who share her experience. Bill is president of Journey of Hope, an organization he cofounded with families of murder victims who oppose the death penalty.

Angela Vigil concluded her amicus brief by writing,

It may be contrary to our assumptions that victims of violent crime would be as forgiving as the victims who constitute amici here. But the rationale for their opinions is supported by the sometimes emotional, sometimes spiritual, and always personal journey they have traveled. For amici, this journey has led them to a place where they advocate to see the juvenile killers of their family members freed after they have paid the price for their crimes and have shown that they have been rehabilitated. Each account reflects the significant impact of successful rehabilitation on the healing of the victim's family and the way that this process of rehabilitation engenders a parallel process of forgiveness in so many victims.[2]

CHAPTER 16

Toughest Job in the Courthouse: Public Defenders in Juvenile Court

CATHRYN CRAWFORD is a four-foot-eleven, cropped-blonde, athletic, supernova combination of energy, intelligence, and wit, with a passion for juvenile justice. It's easy to see why she's been deployed across the country to train public defenders to represent their juvenile clients better.

Growing up poor in the 1970s in a collective in Dallas, Cathryn learned advocacy from her mother, a tenants' rights organizer and mother of four. She moved between Dallas and Chicago, and, after graduating from the University of Texas, followed two of her brothers back to Chicago. There she worked for the American Civil Liberties Union and moonlighted as a cocktail waitress. She cobbled together loans and scholarships so that she could attend what she calls "that fancy pants" Northwestern University Law School.

Cathryn returned to Dallas for a summer internship after her freshman year and was picked to be a juror for the trial of an eighteen-year-old involved in a homicide. He was behind the wheel of a car carrying several other teenagers, one of whom fired a gunshot in the air, hoping merely to intimidate another youth who had recently shot at him. Instead the passenger's bullet fatally struck a teenage pedestrian. The driver was charged as a principal to the crime under an "accountability" theory. Cathryn was the foreperson of the jury that convicted him.

During the sentencing phase, the jury learned that the defendant had successfully requested that he and his fourteen-year-old brother, also a passenger in the car that night, be transferred to a different school to get away from gangs. The boy volunteered at a hospital and had never been in trouble before. After deliberating the same length of time as in the guilt-or-innocence phase, Cathryn's jury recommended the minimum sentence of ten years' probation. A wealthy Dallas businessman on the jury later gave the defendant a job. Cathryn was hooked on criminal justice.

She returned to Northwestern and signed up for a criminal procedure class taught by the popular professor Thomas Geraghty, only to find that she was seventh on the waiting list. She pled her case to the professor, who telephoned the registrar and asked that the class be expanded by seven. From that day on, Cathryn was hooked on Professor Geraghty.

After graduation, she took a job with a boutique Chicago law firm specializing in personal injury and criminal defense. Cathryn fielded her share of critical depositions and jury trials but couldn't ignore the pull of the classroom. She returned to Northwestern, and her proudest moment came upon seeing her name next to Professor Geraghty's the first time they taught a clinical class together. She became a staff attorney at the Children and Family Justice Center of Northwestern's Bluhm Legal Clinic from 1998 to 2008, where she focused her practice and research on indigent youths charged in criminal and delinquency proceedings.

The National Juvenile Defender Center dispatched her to Texas, Georgia, Florida, Ohio, Montana, West Virginia, and Alabama to assess the quality of public defender representation of juveniles. Northwestern also granted her a six-month leave following Hurricane Katrina in 2005, to set up shop in New Orleans as the inaugural director of Juvenile Regional Services, providing full-service representation to delinquent kids.

Over lunch near her office in Chicago, where she was on leave from Northwestern and working on juvenile justice issues for the MacArthur Foundation, Cathryn shared some of her experiences with me. I told her that I thought public defenders representing juveniles had the toughest job in the courthouse; she nodded in agreement.

"Everywhere we went, there was a lack of resources," she said. "In New Orleans, we set up a freestanding public defender clinic. We had to change the culture. The judges were not used to so many trials for juveniles; the public defenders were not used to filing so many motions to suppress, writs of habeas corpus. We were working with huge caseloads and inexperienced lawyers who rotated too often in and out of juvenile."

Cathryn was particularly sensitive to her relationship with the juvenile judges as they decide the guilt or innocence of juveniles in most states. Only eleven states provide jury trials for delinquent kids as a matter of state law: Alaska, Kansas, Massachusetts, Michigan, Montana, New Mexico, Oklahoma, South Dakota, Texas, West Virginia, and Wyoming. Nine states provide a jury trial if kids may be subject to an adult sentence: Arkansas, Colorado, Connecticut, Idaho, Illinois, New Hampshire, Ohio, Rhode Island, and Virginia.

"We had to teach basic trial skills, like how to use leading questions on cross exam and how not to ask a witness a question if you didn't know the answer. No surprises!

"We taught them how to weave questions in direct exam into a compelling story. How to prioritize facts, link questions together to promote a theme, and, of course, how to control their client.

"We had to train the juvenile public defenders to think of advocacy as beginning at detention hearings and continuing beyond sentencing. Vertical representation, meaning having the same public defender throughout. There are so many opportunities for helpful intervention with kids at each point.

"We taught the ideal," she said, "meeting with kids in their homes, seeing the family circumstances, engaging the parents in the defense."

I interjected, "Too often, I see the parents as an obstacle to a good defense. They want the kid to plead guilty so they won't have to come back to court again. Or they maintain the kid's innocence, even when he wants to admit to the charge, because he's afraid to admit it to Mama."

"That happens," she acknowledged, "but just as often, the parents are embarrassed that their son or daughter is charged with a crime. If you sit down with them and explain possible defenses, sanctions, you earn their trust as well as your client's."

"That takes a lot of time."

"That and a lot of patience," she added, "as well as enjoying talking to kids."

As a judge, I have a front-row seat to watch juvenile public defenders in action. Over the years, I've seen the best and the worst: brilliant, passionate advocacy and sloppy, careless defense. I've seen sullen kids disrespecting their lawyers as well as the court, angry at the verdict, but I've also seen kids engaged in the process, writing notes on legal pads to their lawyers, whispering to them at the defense table, eager to tell their side of the case on the stand and offer suggestions during the sentencing. It wasn't all about guilt or innocence, winning or losing. It was about engaging the youth in the defense and showing respect. Kids have a great sense of fairness. They are far less likely to commit another crime and more likely to respect the law and accept judicial intervention if they feel they've been treated fairly. Keeping them out of the juvenile justice system is our goal.

Research supports this view. Professor Bruce Winick at the University of Miami has written that the "child's perception as to whether he or she is being listened to and whether his or her opinion is respected and counted is integral to the child's behavioral and psychological progress." The Florida Supreme Court cited Professor Winick's research in amending juvenile procedure rules in 2001.

Dwight Wolfe is a seasoned public defender who's tried murder cases, death penalty cases, rapes, and countless drug cases in our adult criminal courts. Because he loves working with kids, he rotates in and out of the juvenile division and always sharpens the skills of the younger lawyers he supervises.

"I don't see the hardness in most of the kids that I see in most adult defendants," Dwight told me. "If you show kids that you are willing to take the time to listen to them and consider what they have to say, they in return will listen to you and give you the same consideration. It's rewarding when you see many of them getting their lives on the right track. And that's not easy to do when many kids suffer from a lack of adequate structure, guidance, support, and firm but fair discipline."[1]

The juvenile public defender often fills the void created by poor parenting. That's why Cathryn Crawford's teaching is so important. She now travels the country for the MacArthur Foundation, supporting the efforts of partners working on juvenile justice reform efforts in sixteen states as part of the foundation's juvenile justice initiative, Models for Change. She still finds time to lecture and train on juvenile justice issues across the country. Northwestern professor Thomas Geraghty is one of her biggest fans:[2,3]

"During the ten years that Cathryn taught in the clinic, she proved herself to be one of the nation's top lawyers for children," he said. "I had the pleasure of co-counseling many cases with Cathryn over the years and never ceased to be impressed with her intelligence, dedication, energy, and effectiveness. I always felt that working with Cathryn made me a better lawyer because it required me to keep up with her. It's rewarding and invigorating to work with such a colleague.

"Cathryn's dedication to her clients was also evident in her efforts to support her clients outside of the legal proceedings. Cathryn would typically spend hours with her clients in the Juvenile Detention Center, in prison, and in her office. She provided counseling as well as educational and employment opportunities for her clients. Cathryn's clients always knew—and still know—where they can find their best advocate and their wisest counsel.

"All of this means that Cathryn was an outstanding role model for our students. She set the standard for skillful, vigorous, and effective advocacy."[4]

A fifteen-year-old Arizona youth named Gerald Gault indirectly paved the way for Cathryn's work.

On June 8, 1964, Gerald allegedly made an indecent telephone call to his neighbor, Mrs. Ora Cook. She reported it to the police, who traced it to Gerald's house. Gerald, already on probation for theft, was picked up by the police and arrested even though his parents were at work and weren't advised of the arrest or the charges. Two hearings were held before a juvenile judge, who declared Gerald guilty and ordered him to attend the state reform school until he turned twenty-one. The same offense, if committed by an adult, carried a mere two-month sentence.

Gerald didn't have the assistance of an attorney at the hearing, and he and his parents weren't given a copy of the charge against him. He couldn't question Mrs. Cook, because she failed to attend the hearing. The judge relied on the testimony of Gerald's probation officer.

Gerald and his parents appealed, claiming a lack of due process under the Bill of Rights to the United States Constitution, as he wasn't able to confront his accuser in court, he didn't receive assistance of counsel, and his parents weren't notified of the charges. The case eventually made its way from the state level all the way up to the U.S. Supreme Court, which rendered its decision on May 15, 1967. Judge Tom Jacobs neatly summarizes the ruling in his book *Teens Take It to Court: Young People Who Challenged the Law—and Changed Your Life:*

> The U.S. Supreme Court reviewed the sixty-year history of juvenile law in the United States. In a seven-to-two decision written by Justice Abe Fortas, the Court concluded that juvenile court procedures must be fair and follow due process guidelines. In other words, Gerald and his parents shouldn't have been kept in the dark about the charge against Gerald, and Gerald should have been given an opportunity to tell his side of the story in court, with the help of a lawyer. The Court noted that the possibility of losing one's freedom is as significant (if not more so) to a minor as to an adult. The Court further held that Gerald should have had the right to confront and cross examine his accuser, Mrs. Cook. The Court sent the case back to the trial court with an order to follow due process. Gerald spent five months at the reform school and was released.[5]

More than forty years after Gerald Gault's victory at the U.S. Supreme Court, can we look back and see that it was in some sense a pyrrhic victory for juveniles? By giving juveniles all the due process rights of adults, have we moved away from the model of a separate juvenile court focused on the family and rehabilitation begun in Chicago more than one hundred years ago? How come so many kids are being direct filed to adult court and transferred from detention centers to jails? Is it because we began to treat them as adults under *Gault v. United States,* so let's consider them adults from the onset?

Famed Miami-Dade County juvenile judge Dixie Chastain had those concerns. The first female University of Miami Law School graduate, in 1930, she was appointed to the juvenile bench in 1965 after serving as an investigative attorney for the Juvenile and Domestic Relations Court. When she died at age one hundred on October 25, 2009, the obituary in the *Miami Herald* quoted Judge Chastain as telling her great-granddaughter, "In those days, it was all informal and friendly. The judge, the child, and the parents discussed the problem and then did something about it. Legal requirements were observed; they were not emphasized."

Senior Judge Seymour Gelber, who once headed the Miami court's juvenile division, recalled how after the *Gault* decision, proceedings became more formal, which left Judge Chastain "kind of at sea. But everybody loved her, and she still had that same warm feeling for the kids, even if she was forced to follow all the rules that didn't necessarily help kids."

Tom Petersen, the first public defender to represent a child in her courtroom after the 1967 ruling, said that he "never saw her lose her temper." And daughter Dixie Lemons observed that even as juvenile crimes became more frequent as well as more violent, Chastain believed that "if you can get a child and the parents early enough," kids could be saved. "She had no ambitions beyond the juvenile bench. She found what she was meant to."[6]

Veteran juvenile judge Lester Langer of Miami knew Judge Chastain for almost forty years. "I first met Judge Chastain as a young attorney in 1972 at the old juvenile court in Miami," he recalled. "She was a charming, soft-spoken Southern lady who cared about every child and family who appeared before her. She treated everyone with respect regardless of the case or their circumstances. She was fair, compassionate, and understood the parties who appeared before her. She applied the law to the facts of each case, understanding that her decisions would have a profound impact on a young person's life. We spoke many times about that part of the job. She taught me by example that a judge should not ignore that fact. She never did. I had great respect for her. The children of Florida were very lucky to have her for a while."[7]

The children of Miami-Dade County are also very lucky to have Judge Langer. On May 14, 2010, the community designated him a Wall of Honor recipient. He joined Judge Chastain, Judge Bill Gladstone, and others who have received the highest honor in Miami-Dade County's juvenile justice world.

Judge Chastain also became a footnote in history in 1933, after would-be assassin Giuseppe Zangara tried to shoot president-elect Franklin D. Roosevelt in Miami's Bayfront Park but hit Chicago mayor Anton Cermak, who later died. Chastain, on her way to the park, rushed to the Flagler Street courthouse, where she took the shooter's confession.

Public defender offices have never received the funding that the state attorneys do, and the national financial crisis beginning in 2008 made things a lot worse, on both the adult and juvenile sides. U.S. Attorney General Eric

Holder lashed out at insufficient resources and lack of independence in public defender offices nationwide at the Brennan Center for Justice Legacy Awards Dinner in Washington, D.C., on November 16, 2009:

> Imagine with me, for a few moments, that you receive a frantic call saying that your son or daughter, niece or nephew, has been arrested and charged with a crime. I would wager that most of you would make a call and hire a great lawyer. You certainly would never allow your child to plead guilty and face the possibility of jail time without first speaking to a lawyer. You would not stand by if someone in your family was made to wait weeks, even months, before getting access to a lawyer who could fight for his or her release.
>
> But hard as it may be to believe, some of our fellow citizens suffer through circumstances like these every day.
>
> In Tennessee, a county public defender office had six attorneys handle more than ten thousand misdemeanor cases in 2006—which means lawyers could spend an average of just under an hour per case. High caseloads leave even those lawyers with the best of intentions little time to investigate, file appropriate motions, and do the basic things we assume lawyers do. Some don't even have time to go to trial.
>
> In addition to resource problems, many public defender offices have insufficient independence or oversight to ensure that the lawyers are effectively representing the interests of the accused. In some places, judges assign cases to lawyers, which can influence the representation the lawyers provide. For example, a statewide survey of Nebraska judges in 2006 raised such concerns, including concerns about judges who refused to reappoint those lawyers who requested too many trials.
>
> Perhaps most troubling, all too often we've seen similar problems in juvenile systems. In 2005, for example, the Florida Supreme Court found that in one Florida circuit, *three out of four youths* waived the right to counsel and faced charges without the guidance of counsel. What is more, such waivers sometimes occur without the opportunity to speak to counsel who might help young people understand what they are giving up.[8]

In 2007, that Florida circuit was *my* circuit, and that dismal distinction led me to become involved in the MacArthur Foundation's Juvenile Indigent Defense Action Network (JIDAN), in an effort to reduce the number of waivers of counsel in court by providing a meaningful opportunity for juveniles to confer with counsel before entering a plea. That's how I met Cathryn Crawford. Our court was used for a pilot project run by Barry University School of Law's Juvenile Justice Center.[9]

Wait a minute! Aren't there state attorneys in court prosecuting the juveniles? Yes, since the U.S. Supreme Court's decision in Gerald Gault's case, juvenile prosecutors play a significant role in investigating the case, deciding whether to prosecute, working with victims and witnesses, preparing for trial, trying the case, and making recommendations for sentencing. Enlightened juvenile prosecutors also work in the community to create prevention and diversion projects and alternatives to commitment. They are open to negotiations for reduced charges, when appropriate. They are sensitive to the impact of a criminal record, and they use their power to direct-file a youth to adult court sparingly and wisely.

Respecting the hard-working, enlightened state attorneys in our courts, Andrea Luce, Will Shopper, and others under the leadership of State Attorney Bernie McCabe, I continue to believe that public defenders representing juveniles have the toughest job in the courthouse.

Kids lie, for one thing. Not to their attorneys so often, but to their parents, and especially to Mama, who promised severe punishment if they committed a crime. This means that public defenders have to try more cases than they should, and have to listen to their clients lie on the stand, because Mama is in the front row glaring at the youth, and he doesn't dare tell the truth. (Cathryn disagrees with me here. She sees excessive plea rates, not enough cases going to trial. We agree, however, that the experience of going to trial with a well-prepared, supportive lawyer benefits the juvenile, win or lose.)

Kids mumble and talk slang. It's hard to understand them. Talking to them in court is an art form that has to be developed.

Kids can be incompetent to stand trial, for reasons of age, immaturity, or mental illness. This complicates and delays the proceedings, and the public defender is under continuing pressure from the judge, the victim, and the state to counsel the youth to become competent about court proceedings, so that he can enter a plea and get the necessary services or request a trial. Kids who continue to reoffend during this competency process bring grey hairs to the lawyers, the judge, the victim, and the family.

Kids take risks in court, as they do on the street, and it's often hard for their lawyers to rein them in to make a better decision.

Kids come before juvenile judges who often know the youth's history even before trial and may be predisposed to find guilt so as to put services in place.

Kids have personality traits that are magnified in court: The shy kid won't talk, the joker is flippant, the angry young man snarls, the promiscuous girl wears a tight T-shirt that says, "Your Boyfriend Loves My Tits."

It's a tough job. It's difficult not to get burned out.

Recently, I met a young public defender who's nearly a veteran in his office with five years' experience and who has managed to maintain his zest and enthusiasm for the work he does representing juveniles and adults charged with misdemeanors and felonies in the Brooklyn (New York) Criminal and Supreme Court.

Adam S. Heyman is a staff attorney with the Legal Aid Society, Criminal Defense Division, in Brooklyn and, as such, carries a caseload of 75 to 150 clients from arraignments through trials. He's extremely bright, having graduated magna cum laude from Georgetown University with a major in biblical studies before attending the University of Virginia School of Law, where he received his Juris Doctor degree in 2003 as well as the Pro-Bono Commitment Award for volunteer service. The law school invites him back periodically as a motivational speaker to encourage the law graduates to try public interest law.

Adam was making a lot of money for two years as a corporate associate with Akin Gump Strauss Hauer & Feld, a well-known New York law firm, when he quit and took the job with Brooklyn Legal Aid, the public defenders for the Brooklyn criminal courts. Adam's story, like Cathryn Crawford's, is important, as those two energetic, committed young lawyers have found a way to keep the toughest job in the courthouse stimulating and immensely satisfying.

I asked Adam to give me a list of tips to help juvenile and adult public defenders maintain their enthusiasm. Here are his words:

- On transcending yourself: "I get a kick out of providing free zealous advocacy to those in need. I feel like I'm doing something that is greater than myself; in other words, not doing this work for a paycheck but, rather, to help those in need. That makes me feel good."

- On high stakes: "Dealing with people's lives every day—their basic freedom of autonomy—definitely helps keep me motivated to work hard on behalf of my clients. The stakes are so heavy and real. I have people's lives in my hand. This responsibility is motivation to keep enthusiastic in and of itself."

- On variety: "Due to the nature of this work, I am always learning something new. Each case brings a whole new set of issues, parties, and facts. I have to become an expert over and over again to make sure that I am providing zealous advocacy. This variety keeps my work fresh and continuously interesting."

- On client interaction: "I love meeting new people. It's a lot of fun getting to know so many different people from diverse backgrounds. This keeps my job fresh and fun."

- On appreciation: "The appreciation that I receive from my clients always picks me up if I am feeling less than enthusiastic. Just this past holiday season, I received a number of phone calls, cards, and small gifts from current and former clients and their families telling me how appreciative they are for what I do. It really makes me feel great to hear that I have touched so many lives."

- On taking proactive steps to avoid getting burned out: "I always try to pace myself with the trial work and plan vacations in between trials to recharge the batteries."

- On his love of defending the Constitution: "When people ask me what I do, I always say two things: On the micro level, I defend poor people who are accused of crimes, and on the macro level, I defend the Fourth, Fifth, and Sixth amendments to the Constitution. These rules and rights do not exist unless they apply to everyone. As a public defender, I make sure that they apply to all people, regardless of one's financial means."

- On winning: "I love to win, whether it's on the soccer field (I was a varsity college soccer player) or in the courtroom. When I am winning based on my principles of equality, truth, and justice—that's even sweeter."

- On committing to professionalism: "I always act like I am being filmed or recorded. This way, I am always aware to be polite, respectful, and hardworking. Focusing on professionalism encourages me to stay enthusiastic."

- On inspiring people: "In my work, I have become an expert very quickly. I am starting to understand a craft and learning a lot about what works and what doesn't. As a result, I have started to teach others about being a trial lawyer. It feels good teaching and having people become better as a result of my experiences."[10,11]

In 2010, Adam accepted another challenge: running the public defender's office in Kathmandu, Nepal, through a fellowship with the International Legal Foundation, as part of a yearlong sabbatical.

He plans to go back to Brooklyn Legal Aid when he returns.

Keeping Kids Out of Court: The Annie E. Casey Foundation and Wansley Walters in Miami

TO APPRECIATE THE IMPACT of the juvenile justice reforms that Wansley Walters has brought to Miami-Dade County over the last fifteen years as director of the Juvenile Services Department, we have to look at detention issues around the country and especially the fine work of the Annie E. Casey Foundation. Wansley Walters adopted the Casey Foundation detention reform philosophy and then took it to an even earlier prevention and intervention opportunity.

Hands down, the Casey Foundation has done the most over two decades to keep kids from being locked up and to improve detention facilities for those who are detained. The foundation's Juvenile Detention Alternative Initiative (JDAI) is the most widely replicated juvenile initiative in the country, embraced by juvenile judges and entire juvenile justice systems.

To understand the value of the Casey Foundation's work, it's helpful to get a quick look at the detention process and the decisions the juvenile judge must make quickly, often with insufficient information.

Bart Lubow, director of the Casey Foundation's program for high-risk youths, is the undisputed leader in the movement to keep kids out of detention. He's not only knowledgeable about all the alternatives to detention, such as prevention and diversion programs. His passion and persuasion focus on reducing the detention population because he believes that these juvenile jails are harmful to kids.

"I don't think of detention reform as adding on additional programs," Bart told me. "Our initiative is premised on two basic notions: First, detention use is not driven by juvenile crime but by misdirected public policy and poor practice. Second, if you want to change detention use, you need to change behavior."[1]

Speaking at the University of Florida's conference "Passages, Prevention, and Intervention" in February 2010, Bart warned the audience that "we can't expect systems to behave in rational ways unless we engage in systems reform, beginning first in reducing incarceration. If we do not, in fact, address the harm that the system does through incarceration, we will find it difficult to do anything good.

"Incarceration is the system's safety net, and moral outrage becomes the fundamental problem: Let's isolate and blame the children. Until that culture is changed and diminished, I'm not sure there will be a place for these good programs of prevention and intervention."[2]

In JDAI newsletters, Bart praises the cities and counties that have achieved detention reform, such as Washington, D.C., which "has established an array of creative community-based programs, implemented significant case-processing reforms, and reduced its secure detention population by 31 percent since JDAI first began here." He urges reformers to "focus the attention of the federal government on our detention reform movement, its accomplishments, its transformative potential, and its desire for new partnerships that can strengthen our collective efforts to improve juvenile justice across the country.

"We need renewed leadership, especially in the Office of Juvenile Justice and Delinquency Prevention, so it promotes what works and stimulates best practice throughout the national, state, and local systems."

Let's look at the detention process:

Monday, my duty day, begins with detention hearings at a quarter to eight in the morning. By law, a juvenile arrested and detained has a right to be brought before a judge within twenty-four hours to determine whether there was probable cause for the arrest, whether to appoint a public defender to represent the juvenile, and whether to hold the juvenile in secure detention or release him to a parent or guardian, either outright or under house arrest. It's usually fairly easy to determine probable cause, and even easier to appoint a public defender if the parent or guardian doesn't hire a lawyer, but the sticking point is deciding whether to hold the youth in a secure detention facility.

All states now use some kind of scoring instrument that mathematically computes points based on the following factors:

- Whether the kid is on probation

- The type of underlying crime

- The nature of the new crime charged (for example, whether weapons, force, and/or violence were involved)

- An enhancement or aggravation category regarding the youth's cooperation or misbehavior in the assessment center

- The parents' concerns regarding violence or out-of-control behavior, drug use, or victim safety concerns

In the risk-assessment instrument that Florida courts use, if a youth scores 12 or more points, he or she can be held for up to twenty-one days. The youth can be released early if a probation officer authorizes it, unless he or she is put on a "judge's hold," which would require a court hearing before release. With a score under 12 points, the youth can be placed on home detention (essentially house arrest, except for attending school and/or work) or released outright to wait for the next hearing.

What's important here is that even though a juvenile is presumed innocent at this point, he is not entitled to post bail and bond out of detention, as adults can do from jail. However, the youth must be released after twenty-one days, except for extraordinary circumstances involving public safety or if other proceedings take place within that time.

From everything we've learned, being in secure detention is not usually in the child's best interest; yet, this must be balanced with the need for public safety, first, and, admittedly, the need to protect the youth from further harm to himself. Recent examples in my court include:

- Miranda, fifteen, a first-time offender charged with felony battery on a pregnant person, for throwing her shoe at her nineteen-year-old sister, with whom she shared a bedroom.

- Tyree, fourteen, on conditional release following a commitment program, for absconding from home and school, and not reporting to his probation officer.

- Lizbeth and Thomas, both seventeen, runaways from Ohio who used their Christmas money to buy bus tickets and were caught shoplifting groceries.

- Edward, fifteen, just short of being honorably discharged from probation, for throwing a rock at a moving vehicle driven by his girlfriend's new boyfriend.

Each case requires an independent decision by the judge after he or she has assessed the scoring, to determine whether (1) public safety is involved, (2) the youth is out of control, (3) the probation officer needs an opportunity to meet with the youth in a secure setting, or (4) the youth can be released on home detention (house arrest) or perhaps to a shelter for runaway, ungovernable teens. The public defenders, state attorneys, probation officers, parents, and victims all have input. In our court, our child psychologists provide valuable opinions, advise the parents, and prepare safety plans. Then the judge decides. Typically, with a full docket of kids, each case takes five to ten minutes. It can be the quickest decision a judge makes, but perhaps the most important.

Judge Jerrauld Jones from Norfolk, Virginia, and Judge Patricia Koch from Alexandria, Louisiana, presented their views regarding JDAI at the national convention of the National Council of Juvenile and Family Court Judges in Chicago in July 2009. Their enthusiasm was contagious, and they set the bar high by beginning with the principle that "juvenile delinquency court judges should ensure their systems divert cases to alternative systems whenever possible and appropriate." That means we have an obligation to keep kids from even entering our courts, these judges advocated. We don't even *want* to see them. When we do, we need to consider a diversion from further court proceedings at the earliest stage if public safety can be ensured.[3]

I buy that!

Judges Jones and Koch cited statistics showing that the average detained delinquent is fourteen years old, most likely to be an African American male, with a 60 percent likelihood of having a mental health issue, identified special-education need, and more than likely a victim of abuse. This fits my detention census to a tee. The risks associated with detention, the judges claimed, are an increased recidivism rate, high costs for detention compared to treatment, lack of investment in youths, and the creation of a more hardened criminal. Over a lifetime, they said, the value of sparing a fourteen-year-old first-time offender from further involvement with the system came to an estimated $3.2 million to $5.8 million, including savings in incarceration costs, victim losses, and the loss of a productive citizen to prison.

The judges promoted JDAI as a way to reduce reliance on secure confinement, improve public safety, reduce racial disparities and bias, save taxpayers' dollars, and stimulate overall juvenile justice reforms. They advised the judges in the audience to focus on the age of the child, the type of crime, the parental involvement, the youth's mental and physical fitness, and the level of education or IQ. They encouraged the judges to explore alternatives to detention, such as electronic monitoring, alternative guardians, and specific after-school or evening-reporting centers.

They cited a long list of model and promising programs found to be effective alternatives to detention. (Appendix A)

The Annie E. Casey Foundation statistics supporting JDAI are compelling. According to its website, each year 1.7 million kids are referred to juvenile justice systems, and 400,000 cycle through detention centers—100,000 on any given night. Of those, 13,000 have documented reports of child abuse. African Americans make up 28 percent of the arrests, although they compose only 16 percent of the population. Some 58 percent of juvenile defendants sent to adult prisons are African American. Over 200,000 youths under the age of eighteen are tried in adult court.[4]

JDAI reform has been successful in hundreds of sites across the country, including Chicago, Albuquerque, and Portland, Oregon, as well as smaller sites such as Multnomah County, Oregon, and Bernalillo County, New Mexico, reducing detention use by one-half to two-thirds.

The Casey Foundation also works hard to improve the caliber of the workforce in juvenile justice and the benefits they receive. According to the foundation, direct-care workers earn an average of $30,000 per year (far less in Florida and other states), and since the year 2000, federal funding has been cut by 60 percent.

Now, if we can keep kids out of detention, how about keeping kids from having an arrest record? Wansley Walters did just that in Miami-Dade County.

Wansley's *coup d'oeil* was to create collaboration out of chaos in Miami-Dade County through her fifteen-year effort to reduce the numbers of kids arrested. Her success has brought her fame in this country and abroad. Miami-Dade is now a national demonstration project for not burdening kids with an arrest record, while still delivering appropriate services. The civil citation initiative she helped to create now includes fifty programs and over 6,000 kids served without being arrested. With an 82 percent successful completion rate and a savings to Miami-Dade County of almost $500 per child, compared to traditional diversion, it's a great success.[5]

I met Wansley during our Florida Blueprint Commission hearings, at which my eyes would often glaze over at yet another PowerPoint presentation on juvenile justice reform. But Wansley's businesslike good looks led us commissioners into a snappy, heartwarming introduction and a short, but fact-filled, dollars-and-cents presentation that grabbed my attention like no other. Governor Charlie Crist created the Blueprint Commission in 2007 and appointed twenty-five commissioners to listen to the citizens of Florida and the experts in order to make recommendations to reform juvenile justice policies and promote program initiatives.

"Let me tell you about two little guys, ages nine and eleven, who would have been arrested for residential burglary before our program began," Wansley said. "Police found that they had used force to break into a neighbor's unoccupied house. They spent the night there huddled together until discovered. No one had reported them missing. Clearly, there was probable cause for a felony burglary arrest. Instead, however, police brought them to our Juvenile Services Department for an assessment, without an arrest. We learned that they lived with their grandmother, who had left town for the weekend, leaving them with older teenage cousins who were terrorizing them. They escaped and broke into the house to hide and stay safe. We put services in place for the boys and the grandmother, who was admonished not to use these cousins as babysitters. The whole family benefitted, the boys were not in trouble again, and they avoided having a felony burglary arrest on their record. That wouldn't have happened here in Miami before our collaboration began."

The heart of the Miami-Dade initiative is the use of a civil citation for first- and second-time misdemeanors, with services in place rather than an arrest. This avoids the negative effect of arrest records, which are public documents in Florida and elsewhere, and can affect the youth's ability to get a job, join the military, receive a student loan, or even get into college.

"How a group of community members who did not particularly even like each other much of the time became a national model in collaboration astounds me," Wansley told us in a visit she made to Pinellas County to encourage our efforts. Miami-Dade County is the fourth-largest local government in the country, with the seventh-largest population center. "In the mid-nineties," she continued, "the arrest process for juveniles was so dysfunctional that organized crime was using juveniles as a 'labor force,' coaching them on how to provide false information. Juvenile arrests in her county hit twenty thousand in 1995. There were high-profile, violent juvenile crimes that began to scare tourists away from Florida.

"In this atmosphere, we began a three-year intensive planning process, with many, many meetings. We decided that we wanted to do more than simply processing arrested juveniles, which many assessment centers in Florida do. We had to open up and work together to overcome distrust and turf protection. We had to get the buy-in and support of thirty-seven police departments in the county, which we did through the association of police chiefs.

"We made the whole process open and accountable and worked hard to get a congressional earmark, which kept the partnership enthused and expanded communication," said Wansley.

Sometimes it's the local folks who know you best.

Miami Judge Lester Langer has this to say about Wansley:

Without the passion, attention to detail, and blood, sweat, and tears that Wansley has dedicated to the Juvenile Services Department, it would not have reached or exceeded its potential. Wansley's work is not only recognized in Miami-Dade County but also nationally and internationally. People from all over the world are coming to Miami to see what we have built. The information we have gathered and the programs that have been created and the policies formulated as a result of the project would not have happened without Wansley's leadership. Because of her and her team, we are a showcase for cutting-edge progress in juvenile justice for the world.[6]

From 1998 to 2008, the Juvenile Services Department reduced arrests by 46 percent. Rearrests were down 80 percent, and as a result, Miami-Dade County should generate a $33 million gross systemic savings each year, if not billed for statewide fixed detention costs.[7]

In 2008, when the state was slashing budgets and pushing more costs onto the counties, it was those potential dollar savings to the county, as much as the service to the youths, that attracted the attention of our local officials. Joe Clark, CEO of the Eckerd Family Foundation, and a champion of civil citations and the Miami-Dade initiative, sponsored a group of us to tour Wansley's program in Miami.

Wansley, her deputy director, Morris Copeland, and her entire staff inspired our group, and we began a collaborative. After a series of planning meetings, we developed a Juvenile Arrest Avoidance Project (JAAP), modeled after the Miami-Dade program, which kicked off on April 1, 2009. Nine months later, we had saved 750 first-time misdemeanor offenders from having an arrest record, with a 90 percent completion rate of services.

Wansley said our task was more difficult, as we had over twenty separate municipalities in our county and no central point of entry like the Miami-Dade assessment center used by all municipalities there. But our collaboration worked well from the beginning, as we had strong partners supporting diversion, including our trial court administrators, Gay Inskeep and Michelle Ardibly, and Kathie Gibson from the state attorney's office. Our juvenile arbitration and teen court programs were well run, popular, and successful. The courts, police, and sheriff's department had diversion programs that simply needed to be identified and coordinated. Court administration, our child psychologists, and Michelle Jameson, our alternative sanction coordinator, added richness to the mix that even Miami-Dade lacked.

Wansley, whose roots were in police work and child advocacy, has become a well-known speaker and consultant on juvenile justice reform. She has spoken and consulted in Ireland, Thailand, Belgium, Italy, France, Mexico, and Spain, and all over the United States. She confided in me that on one of her first international visits, to Belgium, she assumed that they wanted to learn how juvenile justice was carried out in the United States. Not so, she found out. They wanted nothing to do with what they thought was an overly punitive, incarceration-oriented system. However, they'd heard about the "exception" in Miami-Dade County, which is why she'd been invited.

In addition to her international work, Wansley speaks proudly of her partnership with the Office of Juvenile Justice and Delinquency Prevention and the White House Office of National Drug Control Policy. Those two agencies hosted a juvenile justice summit in Miami in May 2008, to call attention to the success of Miami-Dade's Juvenile Services Department.

Wansley continues to inspire herself and others with a selection of motivational thoughts and writings from others that she includes on her website. Here is a fitting example: "Excellence can be attained if you care more than others think is wise, risk more than others think is safe, dream more than others think is practical, and expect more than others think is possible."

Reclaiming Futures: Substance Abuse Intervention and Collaborations That Really Work

FIFTEEN-YEAR-OLD RONALD'S first charge is a felony: stealing his stepfather's car, joyriding with a few friends, and crashing it into a fence when he tried to return it in the middle of the night. Fortunately, no one was hurt.

After Ronald admitted to the charge in my courtroom, he'd moved back in with his father. His relationship with his mother and stepfather was beyond strained. I placed Ronald on probation with a seven o'clock evening curfew and an order to attend school and family counseling, submit to random drug tests at the probation officer's discretion, and to put forth his best effort to get a part-time job to reimburse his stepfather the $1,200 in damages to the car. Two months later, Ronald appeared before me for a violation of probation, for skipping school. I ordered him to school each day and to perform twenty-five hours of community service.

Three months later, Ronald was arrested for stealing his mother's credit cards and some jewelry during a weekend visit. Because he was arrested, he was screened at our juvenile assessment center and questioned about drug and alcohol use. He readily admitted to having used marijuana regularly since age thirteen, alcohol on the weekends, painkillers from his mother's medicine cabinet, and ecstasy on two or three occasions.

"I suspected he might be using drugs," his mom said, admitting that she'd never tested him, asked him about it, or looked into counseling.

"He stole my car. That had nothing to do with drugs," his stepfather offered.

"Neither parent mentioned any drug use, so I didn't do any random testing," the probation officer volunteered.

"He's never been caught with any drugs," dad offered.

Yet, the very first time a screening and assessment officer asked Ronald about it, the teenager admitted to having had a serious drug problem for the past two years. If we'd been a Reclaiming Futures model site, Ronald would have been screened and assessed for drug treatment—and well on his way to completing the treatment—by the time that I saw him for the credit card theft. Perhaps effective treatment might have prevented the theft. Who knows?

The Reclaiming Futures Initiative, sponsored by the Robert Wood Johnson Foundation, is a substance abuse intervention for youths who've become involved in the juvenile justice system. It's fast, methodical, collaborative, evidence based, and effective. Foundation money is made available to the selected sites for up to seven years to fund systemic change and to create partners among juvenile justice agencies, treatment providers, and community groups.

None of the foundation's money is used to fund actual drug treatment. That's worth repeating: None of the foundation's money is used to fund actual drug treatment. Rather, the foundation financially supports the development of a local community response to juvenile drug use. Its goal is to withdraw support once the community effort is self-sustaining, and then go on to develop another site.

Every Reclaiming Futures site operates under a six-step model:

1. Initial screening
2. Initial assessment
3. Service coordination
4. Initiation
5. Engagement
6. Completion

All youths eligible for treatment or supervision in the community are screened, regardless of the charge. It doesn't have to be drug-related. If the youth admits to *any* drug use—and most users do if asked—a plan for drug treatment is designed to meet the needs of the youth and family. No waiting lists. Drug counseling begins within two weeks and is frequent, often twice a week. After six weeks, a team meets to design a plan to withdraw the drug treatment and engage the youth and family in community resources. The fast pace of the program is a key to success. Reclaiming Futures partners believe prolonged treatment loses its effectiveness and may worsen the problem. Rather, the goal is a fast transition to positive community activities. It's the fast, comprehensive, and effective pace that appeals to me; I wish we were a chosen Reclaiming Futures site.

Rose Golden and Dennis Reilly, the Reclaiming Futures project directors for Cook County (Chicago), Illinois, and Nassau County (Long Island), New York, respectively, couldn't be more enthusiastic ambassadors for the model. Both sites are among the original ten sites funded by the Robert Wood Johnson Foundation for up to seven years.

Rose, who's spent twenty-five years in the juvenile court's probation department, actually wrote the grant to obtain Reclaiming Futures. "It's such a nice framework to get the system to think collectively," she says. "It creates a common language for our drug treatment providers. Since Cook County is so big, our struggle was in coordinating resources and getting the service providers to work together. The foundation money is gone now, but we have a sustainable program, and we score high on collaboration."

Rose credited the Reclaiming Futures screening tool, a fifty-two-question questionnaire for kids, as largely responsible for the degree of cooperation among providers. "The providers know exactly why they are getting the referrals, and we can make different referrals for mental health issues, without a lot of lag time," she said. In Chicago, this screening takes place before the youth is sentenced or diverted on the initial charge.[1,2]

The Nassau County Reclaiming Futures Initiative's white paper concisely sums up the extent of the national problem and the honesty of the kids reporting:

Nearly two million children under age eighteen were arrested in 2006. That large number may surprise many people. Sadly, research shows there is a direct connection between young people who end up in trouble with the law and are also abusing drugs and alcohol. The National Center on Addiction and Substance Abuse at Columbia University reveals that four out of five teens in the juvenile justice system are under the influence of alcohol or drugs while committing their crimes. Further, four out of five also test positive for drugs, are arrested for committing an alcohol- or drug-related offenses, admit having substance abuse problems, or share some combination of these characteristics.

While teens in trouble come from many walks of life, they are disproportionately from low-income areas and communities of color, and often have other problems besides drug or alcohol abuse—such as coming from abusive or neglectful families. They often suffer from mental problems as well. Nearly 85 percent of youths treated for substance abuse problems also have a mental health disorder. Clearly, these young people are in need of help. Yet, many go without treatment. In 2006, more than twenty-one million people ages twelve or older needed treatment for a drug or alcohol problem and did not receive it at a specialty substance abuse facility. And even when substance abuse treatment and mental health services exist, they might not be coordinated from one provider to the next.

This lack of cooperation among service agencies often leaves teens shuffled around between fragmented services that aren't as effective as they should be. This is too bad, because researchers have found that teens who receive coordinated comprehensive services are more likely to stay out of trouble and abstain from drug and alcohol use. Plus, studies show treatment works. Research suggests that treatment can cut drug abuse in half, drastically decrease criminal activity, and significantly reduce arrests. Substance abuse among teens in trouble with crime affects all of us, and our pocketbooks, when it goes untreated, whereas treating addiction can save our communities money. For every dollar spent on addiction treatment programs, four to seven dollars are saved on drug-related crimes.

Dennis Reilly works within court innovation for the state of New York. He is quick to credit Chief Judge Judith Kaye, now retired, for beginning the problem-solving court initiative in New York back in the 1990s. "Her leadership," he said, "led to the creation of the Midtown Community Court, Brooklyn Drug Court, mental health and domestic violence courts—altogether more than two hundred specialty courts in the state. Specialty courts focus on a specific problem, such as family violence, mental health or drug abuse, and bring services into court in a holistic manner under the direction of the judge. Encouragement and incentives are offered. Fines can be waived, and sentences suspended. In dependency drug courts, parents who successfully complete the program reunite with their children more quickly.

"The Reclaiming Futures model brought drug courts into the new century," Dennis said. It provided the missing piece: community involvement. Drug courts fall into a trap, creating an insular relationship among the judge, case manager, treatment provider, and drug abuser. You'd have to look beyond that for educational, vocational, and supportive services. The treatment providers were so strapped for time and money, they couldn't fill this function.

"Reclaiming Futures recognizes that treatment alone is not enough for juveniles. You must bring in community involvement, such as prosocial activities, mentoring, 'natural helpers,' faith-based groups, bridge programs," Dennis said. "The court is the convener, the hub. Actual drug treatment is brief; all that a juvenile can stand. The community support services take over the task."

Like Rose, Dennis credited the screening tool as essential to success. It allows for specific targeting of services, necessary when treatment dollars are cut. He stressed that the initial seven sites all had strengths and remarked that the Chicago site had achieved "systems change on a broad urban scale"— much larger than Nassau County, where there were fewer than one thousand delinquency petitions filed in 2006.

Both Rose and Dennis are dedicated, enthusiastic, knowledgeable "project fellows" for Reclaiming Futures. Rose, a petite brunette, and Dennis, a tall Irishman, spent hours with me in their busy offices explaining the benefits of the Reclaiming Futures models to their communities.

Rose definitely thought the foundation's idea of designating fellows for each site helped to sustain the project past the foundation's funding. The justice, judicial, treatment, project, and community fellows meet as a group locally to coordinate services. Then each group of fellows, such as the project fellows, meets nationally to exchange ideas.

Two effective juvenile judges who lead Reclaiming Futures sites are Judge Anthony Capizzi, from Dayton, Ohio, and Judge Beth Dixon, from Salisbury, North Carolina. In a presentation made to the National Council of Juvenile and Family Court Judges, community engagement—particularly a mentoring program called Natural Helpers, which includes transportation and surrounding each teen with a circle of caring people—was touted by Judge Capizzi as the strength of his Reclaiming Futures site. Judge Dixon, from a more rural area in North Carolina, focused on the systemized screening tool, something new to her county. "Most youths," she said, "had already completed their probation before the results of drug assessments were provided to a judge." Reclaiming Futures changed that by providing a screening tool, referring every teen in the juvenile delinquency system for assessment and working to recruit more treatment providers.

Evaluations of Reclaiming Futures by the objective, evidence-based Urban Institute and Chapin Hall at the University of Chicago conducted between 2003 and 2008 suggest a promising strategy for improving interventions for youths. This is a modest appraisal of a very successful program, I believe. Most of the nineteen sites in 2009, located from Anchorage, Alaska, to the Sovereign Tribal Nation of Sicangu Lakota in Rosebud, South Dakota, to Santa Cruz, California, would agree.

One of the things I like about Reclaiming Futures is that it doesn't fund drug treatment services. Therefore, it doesn't regulate or compete with the many good drug counseling and treatment agencies that exist in the community. For example, Operation Parental Awareness of Responsibility (PAR), the primary drug treatment agency for Pinellas County, provides outstanding outpatient and residential treatment to youths. I've worked closely with Suzanne Austin in truancy court and have observed her keen ability to detect a youngster's drug problem, especially when the parent is in denial. I've seen her jump up to follow the family out of court, with a referral for services and an appointment slip in her hand. Truants and their parents need this hand-holding. Reclaiming Futures would allow us to continue to work with the good people at PAR, who not only provided drug evaluations of our youths but also full social assessments of their needs.

Another appealing feature of Reclaiming Futures is that it encourages local innovation, imagination, and support. That's what's needed to combat the ever-growing variety of harmful drugs, such as smokeable herbal blends—imitation marijuana—marketed as legal highs called Spice or K2. They act on the cannabinoid receptors of the brain to produce euphoria and are four times more potent than marijuana.

According to Calvina Fay, executive director of the Drug Free America Foundation, "K2 was invented by Dr. John Huffman at Clemson University in 1995 during medical research on the effects of cannabinoids on the brain. He found no medical benefits—only negative side effects similar to marijuana. Unfortunately, marijuana users reproduced the recipe, creating a legal alternative to marijuana.

"Although the actual company manufacturing K2 is unknown, it is legally available for purchase in the U.S. by anyone, including minors. The sale of this synthetic marijuana is banned in Britain, Germany, Poland, France, South Korea, and Russia. The U.S. should move urgently to protect the public from yet another dangerous and potentially deadly class of drugs," she says.[3]

My colleague Judge Dee Anna Farnell has reinvigorated and refashioned our adult drug court to fit her high-spirited, goal-setting, no-nonsense personality. In doing so, she has created a resource for me to use in juvenile court. When a youth admits to selling drugs, I order him to attend a session of Judge Farnell's drug court, so he can see up close the despair and destruction caused by drug addiction. Busy as she is with a crowded courtroom of drug users and their families, she takes the time for straight talk with the kids I send to her, often getting the adults in court to help make her point. It's an eye-opener for many youth who don't think they have a problem because they sell cocaine rather than use it. "So you want to be a drug dealer and ruin other peoples' lives, not to mention your own future in prison?" she asks the youth.

Reporter John Barry of the *St. Petersburg Times* wrote about the personal stamp that Judge Farnell puts on drug court as both an athlete and a demanding, but compassionate, taskmaster:

> Even in her judicial robes, Judge Dee Anna Farnell has that marathon look. She projects a lean physicality and speed, thinks and talks fast, is quick to get in close. She takes pride in staying one step ahead of a phony story.

Farnell has run thirty marathons. She ran her fourteenth Boston in April. She posts T-shirt race numbers on her courtroom wall. The numbers aren't hers. They belong to men and women recovering from addictions to everything chemical—pot, crack, prescription pills—who pile out of a Goodwill van at 6:00 a.m. three times a week to run laps in the dark.

Farnell's Pinellas County Drug Court is an alternative to criminal court, an offer of treatment instead of prison to nonviolent offenders. It's a velvet fist approach. The failures go back to criminal court. But since 2008, it's also a locker room of sorts for a running team.

Back then, Farnell heard about a running group made up of offenders she had referred to the St. Petersburg Goodwill for treatment. They ran with their counselors on the old Friendship Trail Bridge on Gandy Boulevard.

"Aha!" said Judge Farnell.

The judge encouraged other defendants to join the runners. In 2009 she offered a legal enticement. She promised runners a break on court costs and early completion of probation. The Goodwill group began running under an acronym: CLEAN—Citizens Learning to End Addiction Now.

They don't call themselves that. They say it plain, no pretenses. They're Farnell's drug court running team. They're running from rock bottom, from jail sentences, from their thousand failures and their thousand broken promises.

Running for their lives.

Most of the runners say logging miles clears their heads, gives them peace, and awakens their senses. "I could hear the birds in the trees. I saw the sun rise.... It just blew my mind," said Tony Harris, 38, after a three-mile run with the Goodwill's running group.[4]

Our juvenile drug court ended just a few months after it began, a victim of state budget cuts. I don't know if we could have achieved Judge Farnell's results, but I do know that when it's resurrected, I'll recommend a young judge with a good pair of Nikes to *run* it, as kids would thrive in that courtroom. Reclaiming Futures would applaud the approach.

CHAPTER 19

Saving Kids While Saving Money: Washington State Proves You Can Do Both

C AN YOU REDUCE the crime rate while saving taxpayers billions of dollars in criminal justice costs? That's a goal all state legislatures and the federal government should seek to achieve.

Aha! said the authors of the report made by the Washington State Institute for Public Policy. "We find that if Washington successfully implements a moderate-to-aggressive portfolio of evidence-based options, a significant level of future prison construction can be avoided, taxpayers can save about two billion dollars, and crime rates can be reduced."

This didn't come out of the blue. Washington has long relied on economic analysis of evidence-based, what-works programs, and forecasts of future spending on prisons to guide lawmakers to decide where to spend criminal justice dollars. The Institute is a non-partisan research arm of the legislature, created in 1983. In 2007, it was charged with analyzing the results of a years-long economic study of the costs and effectiveness of juvenile justice.

Florida's commissioners heard a remarkable presentation from economists in Washington: "Reducing Crime with Evidence-Based Options: *What Works*, and Benefits and Costs." I was excited to learn that an economic analysis made over a ten-year-period credited very specific programs in juvenile justice with reducing the crime rate while putting money back into taxpayers' wallets. In other words, these evidence-based programs *proved* that they worked better and cost less than incarceration. What more did we need to take to our own legislature?[1]

While the Washington analysis included programs in the adult offender system, it actually analyzed more programs for juvenile offenders. Furthermore, it identified specifically those programs that had no impact on reducing juvenile crime and, therefore, were a waste of money. In that least-effective category were regular surveillance-oriented parole, juvenile-intensive probation, and parole supervision and juvenile wilderness challenge. Juvenile boot camps used to offset institution time did nothing to reduce crime, the study found, but they did cost substantially less than incarceration. The study concluded that one drug intervention program, Scared Straight, a radical, get-tough approach to substance abuse treatment for juveniles, actually increased the crime rate, at a cost to taxpayers of $14,667 per participant.

Juvenile programs that reduced the crime rate and saved taxpayers dollars in Washington State, in descending order of their effectiveness, are listed below, followed by the percent change in crime reduction and the total dollar benefit, minus costs, to the taxpayer, per participant:

Program	Effect on Crime Reduction	Benefits Per Participant
Multidimensional treatment foster care	–22.0 percent	$77,798
Adolescent diversion for low-risk kids	–19.9 percent	$40,623
Family-integrated transitions	–13.0 percent	$40,545
Functional family therapy while on probation	–15.9 percent	$31,821
Multisystemic therapy	–10.5 percent	$18,213
Aggression replacement training	–7.3 percent	$14,660
Teen courts	–11.1 percent	$9,208
Juvenile sex offender treatment	–10.2 percent	$7,829
Restorative justice for low-risk offenders	–8.7 percent	$7,067
Interagency coordination programs	–2.5 percent	$5,186
Juvenile drug courts	–3.5 percent	$4,622

At least in Washington State, these eleven programs achieved both goals: reducing crime and saving money. The study also analyzed programs that seemed to reduce crime but lacked evidence of either economic benefit or loss. Those included counseling and psychotherapy for juvenile offenders, juvenile education programs, other family-based therapy programs, juvenile behavior modification, life skills education programs for juvenile offenders, and diversion programs with services.

Following that was a category for programs that didn't reduce crime and lacked sufficient economic analysis, such as court supervision versus simple release without services; diversion programs with services versus simple release; and juvenile intensive probation as an alternative to incarceration. The study concluded with a list of programs that needed more research: dialectical behavior therapy; increased drug testing while on parole versus minimal drug testing; juvenile curfews; juvenile day reporting; juvenile jobs programs; juvenile therapeutic communities; and mentoring in juvenile justice.

Every state needs to conduct its own analysis, as criminal justice and prison costs vary. We can all benefit from the Washington State study because the programs examined appear to be specific programs operating in the United States for a sufficient time and with enough evidence of lowered recidivism rates to give the economists the data they needed. This begs the question of why any state would implement or continue with a program that isn't evidence based, so that indeed we can determine what works. That should be a given.

The summary of the Washington State study reads as follows:

Under current long-term forecasts, Washington State faces the need to construct several new prisons in the next two decades. Since new prisons are costly, the 2005 Washington legislature directed the Washington State Institute for Public Policy to project whether there are "evidence-based" options that can:

- reduce the future need for prison beds;
- save money for state and local taxpayers;
- contribute to lower crime rates.

We conducted a systematic review of all research evidence we could locate to identify what works, if anything, to reduce crime. We found and analyzed 571 rigorous comparison-group evaluations of adult corrections, juvenile corrections, and prevention programs, most of which were conducted in the United States. We then estimated the benefits and costs of many of these evidence-based options. Finally, we projected the degree to which alternative "portfolios" of these programs could affect future prison construction needs, criminal justice costs, and crime rates in Washington.

We find that some evidence-based programs can reduce crime, but others cannot. Per dollar of spending, several of the successful programs produce favorable returns on investment. Public policies incorporating these options can yield positive outcomes for Washington.

We project the long-run effects of three example portfolios of evidence-based options: a "current level" option as well as "moderate" and "aggressive" implementation portfolios.

"We find that if Washington successfully implements a moderate-to-aggressive portfolio of evidence-based options, a significant level of future prison construction can be avoided, taxpayers can save about two billion dollars, and crime rates can be reduced.

There are many things I like about the Washington State study. It combines juvenile and adult crimes to determine crime reduction outcomes. Part of the motto of Florida's Department of Juvenile Justice is "to reduce juvenile crime." I've often argued that it's easy to reduce juvenile crime. You just lock up all the offenders. The problem comes when they are released without being rehabilitated and then commit crimes as adults. The goal should be to reduce *all* crime.

Furthermore, the Washington study validates the position many of us have taken that prevention, intervention, and diversion actually reduce crime and save money. Many of the programs mentioned in this study are written about in this book. I've been honored to meet many of the pioneers of those programs. I've seen the programs work with the kids and families I see in court. Hundreds more kids are successful in diversion programs and stay out of court. That was another interesting conclusion I drew from the

Washington State study: The more court or juvenile justice involvement the youths had, the worse the outcome. For real success, keep them out of court and out of the juvenile justice system. Away from me, or away from commitment if you can.

Florida's Redirection Initiative program does that successfully. It's an example of an evidence-based program that "redirects" youths from commitment to a community-based, family-centered alternative therapy program in the community and in the home. The types of therapy provided by Redirection are discussed more fully in chapter 21; however, since we are talking cost savings here, it's fitting to highlight those.[2,3]

Dr. Kristin Winokur, vice president of the Tallahassee consulting firm Justice Research Center, presented the irrefutable facts of cost-effectiveness at the 2010 Blueprints for Violence Prevention Conference in San Antonio, Texas. She tracked the growth of Redirection, administered by a company called Evidence-Based Associates and its president, Dr. Dan Edwards, in the role of "general contractor," from 154 youths served in 2004, to 5,142 youths served in 2010.

The bottom line, Dr. Winokur said, was that Redirection's youths had fewer rearrests and lower reconviction rates than matched samples at a cost savings to the taxpayer of $30,940—that being the difference between the average cost for completing residential commitment ($40,235) and the average cost of Redirection ($9,295).[4]

In 2009, the Office of Program Policy Analysis and Government Accountability (OPPAGA), an agency of the Florida legislature, concluded that Redirection saved Florida $36.4 million and avoided $5.2 million in recommitment and prison costs.

I've been amazed by how well Redirection works for some of the most difficult kids and families in my court. Other model programs, like Big Brothers Big Sisters (BBBS) of America, effectively run by Susan Rolston in our county, excel in the prevention side. BBBS kids were found 46 percent less likely to try drugs, drink, or become aggressive, and more likely to do well in school!

How much more proof do we need?[5,6]

CHAPTER 20

Girls Matter! The Importance of Gender-Specific Programs

S HE STOOD IN MY LIVING ROOM: tall and composed, at ease with the invited guests. Her thick auburn hair framed her expressive face. What she said, however, contradicted how she looked. "I was frightened...afraid... scared. I didn't want to be alone. I felt insecure, all the time, for the first time in my life. I felt—let's just say it—unsafe."

The women attending the benefit for PACE Center for Girls looked startled and a little uncomfortable. The speaker was Dr. Lawanda Ravoira, director of the National Council on Crime and Delinquency Center for Girls and Young Women. She is a nationally known advocate for girls, and a consultant and staff trainer for juvenile justice programs. She's testified before Congress and state legislatures. She's been a keynote speaker at national meetings. Dr. Ravoira is bold and outspoken when it comes to the needs of girls in the justice system. And yet she was afraid? She'd often told stories of the girls who touched her heart. Their fears, their hurts, their dreams. She'd never talked this way about herself.

"You see," Lawanda said, "this year I lost Jim, my husband of more than twenty years, my best friend and soul mate, to cancer. I expected to be heartbroken, lonely, and to grieve. But I never expected to feel unsafe and fearful in our home. I'd been alone lots of times in my life. It wasn't that. It was the loss. The tremendous loss I suffered that made me feel unsafe, even in my own home.

"That experience made me understand, for the first time, how important safety is to the girls in the system. This was my first major loss, but most of them have suffered many, many losses. Their parents or caregivers have died, or their rights have been terminated. They've been abused, and suffered a loss of a caring person that way. They've been victimized, beaten, raped. They've bounced around, living in chaos, changing schools and neighborhoods all the time. Each event comes with a loss, a grieving, and need for healing. When that hasn't happened, they want to feel safe most of all.

"My experience caused me to re-evaluate the priorities in girl's programming. Safety Matters is now my number-one core building block. Creating a culture that promotes physical, emotional, and psychological safety is the foundation of a gender-responsive environment. You can't do anything else without assuring safety first."

So Lawanda's "Aha!" moment arose from a personal tragedy.

Listening to her speak, I thought back to my trips to the Umatilla Academy for Girls and recognized that the cascade of negative reactions I experienced indeed involved a lack of safety. No one feels safe if the staff members hate their jobs, turnover is high, and the girls despise the staff for the mistreatment they receive. When you live in a war zone, no one cares about aesthetics like paint on the walls, books in the classrooms, doors on the bathroom. Danger rules!

Girls are the fastest-growing segment of the juvenile justice population, representing about one-third of the arrests and one-fourth of the incarcerated population. The United States incarcerates more women than any other country. In 2007, almost one-third of all U.S. female prisoners were being held in three states: California, Texas, and Florida.

Lawanda believes that gender-responsive interventions are needed in every state to reverse the escalating trend of girls entering into the system. In her work with the National Center for Women and Girls, generously funded by the Jessie Ball duPont Fund in partnership with the advocacy organization Children's Campaign, Lawanda has traveled the country providing training to direct-care staff in commitment programs for girls. She has developed a curriculum called Girl Matters, which includes evaluation, training, and assessment of gender-responsive programs for girls.[1]

Lawanda earned a national reputation for girls' issues when she served for thirteen years as president and chief executive officer of the PACE Center for Girls, a Florida not-for-profit organization that annually provides gender-specific, comprehensive educational, therapeutic, and transitional support services to 4,400 girls at risk for delinquency at twenty centers around the state. Prior to that, she served as director of program services for the National Network of Runaway and Youth Services in Washington, D.C., as an administrator with the child care agency Covenant House in Fort Lauderdale, and as a social worker for troubled inner-city youths in New York City.

Savvy to the ways of state legislatures, she worked successfully to have Florida's juvenile justice statutes amended to mandate gender-specific services. Florida now leads the nation in implementing Girl Matters in residential facilities, for which Lawanda gives a lot of credit to Florida's assistant secretary of residential services, Darryl Olson, and secretary of juvenile justice, Frank Peterman, Jr. A published author, she holds a doctorate in public administration, a master's degree in allied health, and a bachelor's degree in sociology.

In partnership with the Children's Campaign, and supported by the Florida Bar Foundation, Lawanda authored *Justice for Girls Blueprint for Action* (2006), which laid out girls' fundamental rights: fair and equitable treatment, freedom from violence and exploitation, to be valued and respected by those who interact with them, to be able to trust the system, and to have a system advocate. She urged that girls be looked at differently from boys.

Lawanda provided testimony to the Crime, Terrorism, and Homeland Security Subcommittee of the United States House Judiciary Committee on October 20, 2009, in Washington, D.C. The hearing was the first of its kind in addressing what has become the fastest-growing trend in criminal justice: the involvement and incarceration of girls in juvenile justice systems nationwide.

The Center for Girls and Young Women and the Children's Campaign encouraged federal lawmakers to hold the hearing. "We must strike the right balance," said Roy Miller, founder and president of the Children's Campaign. "We are calling for the equitable allocation of resources so that girls can be held accountable while we address the abuse and victimization underlying many of their actions and poor decisions."[2]

Lawanda writes: "The types of offenses girls commit generally do not pose the same threat to public safety as those committed by boys. Too many girls are being detained who do not pose a public safety or flight risk. Girls are more likely to be admitted to residential commitment programs for less serious offenses than are boys. There is an immediate need to review the additional charges girls are receiving while in residential placement."

After safety, the core building blocks that make up Girl Matters include communication, relationships, mental and physical health, nutrition, education, and goal setting. Lawanda proudly relates some of the specific successes she'd been told of: changed menus, with dietitian review; a sanctuary room set up with plush carpets, bean bags, and soothing colors; an advisory board developed by the girls on themes they chose; an enhanced safety plan formalized through education, coping, and self-soothing skills; and a changed intake process, with no more "ganging up" on a new girl.

Lawanda never speaks or writes without telling a girl's story, like Tamela's: "Hair that needs care, dark circles under her eyes, a few blemishes on her face, Tamela is a petite African American living in a one-room cell behind razor wire in a juvenile lockup facility. Her dad left when she was seven. No one ever talked about it when he left home. The sexual abuse started at age four. By age seven, she was shuffled from relatives to foster home placements. She started 'smoking weed' at age twelve. Weed led to cocaine, to prescription drugs, to crack. She was 'doing a lot of drugs and running away from home.' By age thirteen, she was arrested for trespassing, running away, shoplifting, and prostitution. She needed money to 'pay people' for a place to stay. She has been in and out of juvenile lockup since age thirteen."

Tamela, age seventeen, told Lawanda, "Tell adults to be there for us. Be what our parents couldn't be. Be somebody we didn't have, be a friend. Kids have no one to really talk to. That's where you can start to help us. Whether a girl is good or bad, be there to help. I have no one. And I really try to be good, but I always mess up. I need to hear that someone like me can make it."[3, 4]

Francine T. Sherman, clinical professor and director of the Juvenile Rights Advocacy Project at Boston College Law School, has written about the connections between domestic violence and girls in the juvenile justice system:

The connection between trauma and later delinquency is well established and particularly significant for girls. Recent research, building on findings from the late 1980s, confirms the link between childhood trauma and future delinquency, finding high rates of trauma and family chaos in the profiles of girls in the delinquency system. Although the connection between childhood trauma and later delinquency is present for boys as well, it is particularly striking for girls, who are more often victims of sexual abuse and who are less likely than boys to be violent in the absence of childhood trauma. Girls' experiences of trauma, including domestic violence, are predictive of involvement in health risk behaviors and delinquency.

While boys and girls in the juvenile justice system have high rates of mental illness, substantial research shows that these girls have higher rates of mental illness than their male counterparts. In particular, system-involved girls suffer from post-traumatic stress disorder, depression, and anxiety disorders.

The connection between girls' trauma and their involvement in the delinquency system has multiple levels. Trauma is related to mental health issues, for which the juvenile justice system is the system of last resort. Moreover, trauma leads girls to risk-taking behaviors, which in turn results in delinquency. An additional and sometimes overlooked part of the equation is the system responses themselves, which play a role in criminalizing girls who are trauma victims.[5]

I had seen far too many girls in commitment charged with assaulting or battering a staff member, a felony. I also began to think in terms of safety when deciding whether to acquit or find guilty a girl charged with battery in a home or school setting. Like LaPorsha.

The fifteen-year-old appeared before me charged with battery on a school resource officer, a felony. She'd just been removed from an abusive family situation and transferred to an alternative school for behavior problems. She'd just begun anger management counseling, when another girl in class tried to start a fight with her. She ran for the exit door, trying to avoid the confrontation. The teacher yelled at her to stop. "It's not your fault, LaPorsha! I can handle this without you having to leave class." LaPorsha turned to look at him, her hand on the door frame, trying to decide what to do. A school resource officer in police uniform and gun belt heard the commotion from the hallway, crept up behind LaPorsha, and, well-intentioned, "gave her a bear hug, gently, just to reassure her and keep her in the classroom." LaPorsha reacted in fear and thrust her elbow back into the officer's ribs. For this she was maced, arrested, and charged with a felony battery to the officer.

I couldn't articulate at that time what Lawanda meant in terms of safety, but I instinctively understood what LaPorsha was seeking. I acquitted her at trial, finding that her actions were an instinctive reaction to being bear-hugged unexpectedly, and not an intentional battery.

Don't touch girls who feel unsafe.

Lawanda's Girl Matters programming is in the process of being implemented in Illinois and Pennsylvania and is well advanced in Florida, especially at places such as the Desoto Dual Diagnosis Correctional Facility in central Florida.

I had visited Desoto a few years before Girl Matters was introduced, and even then I was very impressed with the girls' appearance and comfort level, the staff's level of job satisfaction, and the programming in place, including an apprentice beauty salon. Desoto is not privatized but, rather, run by the state of Florida. Its direct staff is paid substantially more than minimum wage, with a low turnover rate. And the girls looked great. They wore khaki slacks with red, blue, or green golf shirts to indicate their placement level, not the baggy grey prison suits I had seen at Umatilla. There was no disorder. They appeared engaged and focused on a schedule. Desoto was head and shoulders above most of the programs I visited. Then the staff attended a Girl Matters conference in Jacksonville and brought back additional ideas.

The Desoto staff added a grief counseling group and enlisted a volunteer to conduct weekly group sessions. Community speakers were brought in during National Women's Awareness Month, in March, speaking on the theme of "Women Taking the Lead to Save Our Planet," and representing leadership roles and high achievement to the girls. They added a 240-hour nail tech program for girls who have earned their high-school diploma or equivalent degree, leading to board certification as a nail technician. Imagine leaving a commitment program and getting a job right away as a nail tech! Girls at Desoto were rewarded for good behavior with manicures and pedicures. The Desoto staff was faithful to the training requirement of Girl Matters and formed an assessment team to evaluate progress.

The staff posted famous quotes by famous women around the Desoto campus. The girls are surrounded by the words of Eleanor Roosevelt ("No one can make you feel inferior without your consent"), Harriet Beecher Stowe ("Never give up, for that is just the place and time that the tide will turn"), Dolly Parton ("If you want the rainbow, you've got to put up with the rain"), and others. A good program was getting even better due to Girl Matters programming.[6,7]

Listen up, New York!

In an article in *The New York Times* in August, 2009, Susan Dominus reported on the brutality and humiliation experienced by girls at the Tryon Residential Center in upstate New York. According to the piece, a fourteen-year-old girl who apparently "didn't move fast enough for one staff member's satisfaction ended up pinned beneath him—all 300 pounds or so":

> I told him two times, "I can't breathe, I can't breathe," recalled the young woman, now a reed-thin 16-year-old with long, curly hair who is about to start her sophomore year at a Manhattan high school. It was only when a female coworker warned the staff member that he was violating the rules—that too much of his body was covering the girl—that he hauled himself off, the young woman said. By then, her bones and back ached, and she had the telltale red welts of rug burn across the side of her face that was rubbing against the floor.
>
> Even if his body had only partially covered hers, the counselor was violating more basic rules—like the ones in the Constitution that courts have decreed give youths in the custody of the state the right to be free from physical abuse at its hands.

The Girl Matters philosophy permeates New Beginnings, a small commitment program for delinquent girls in Bartow, Florida. I knew we'd come a long way when I saw "Dora the Explorer" and rock star bedspreads on the twin beds in the neatly kept rooms, family photos on the walls, and, even more surprising, girls knitting and crocheting colorful caps for newborns and cancer patients. I'd like to see Girl Matters programming throughout juvenile justice. Even short of commitment, girls' issues are the good news–bad news feature of juvenile court. On one hand, girls commit far fewer crimes than boys, they respond well to open communication, counseling, and relationship building, and when a few positive changes are made in their lives, they can do a turnaround that makes you dizzy. On the other hand, when relationships at home and school are bad, they fight at school, run away, and turn to older boys or men by using and selling drugs and prostituting. The pull of the streets is so powerful, they ignore the risks.[8]

Cassidy, age sixteen, gave me a letter to read aloud in court the day I released her from detention for running away, thus violating her probation. It was during a session of our Girls Mission Possible court, our alternative-sanctions-for-girls project that operates on a shoestring of volunteers, a philosophy of more carrots than sticks for rehabilitating girls, and a goal of keeping them out of commitment facilities. We encourage the girls to speak to the whole group from the witness stand, write letters expressing their feelings, perform community service, bring family members to court, and try to resolve problems peacefully, with appropriate services. Our hook is the threat of detention. They don't want to be there. Cassidy wrote:

Your Honor,

I have realized a lot while serving my time in JDC. In the past, my transgressions have gotten me into the current situation. While sitting here, I have had a lot of time to think. I know I have a past of lying to you, but I have thought a lot about what I have been doing to myself, my future, my family, and also my caseworker and father while I'm on the run. To myself, I'm ruining my life while not going to school or taking care of my health. I'm hurting my family because all they do is worry about me while I'm out on the streets. They don't even know if I'm safe. I realize I make a lot of work for my case manager and add to her stress level.

I want to inform you that if I am released early, you can do it without the worry of me running again. I just would really like to get out of JDC because I don't get along with other females. I've already served 21 days without incident, even over my birthday.

So when released, I am going back to St. Petersburg High and graduate. I will be keeping up with going to my doctor appointments. I wish to visit my little brothers and father.

Sincerely,

Cassidy

Some in the audience clapped. Dr. Adele Solazzo, our child psychologist partner in Girls Mission Possible, complimented Cassidy on her insight and concern for her father and caseworker. I wished her well and opined that the twenty-one days in detention had really matured her.

Two days after her release, Cassidy ran away from home. A week later, she was arrested for lewd and lascivious behavior and prostitution, caught performing oral sex on a customer in the parking lot of a run-down hotel. Both were arrested. Cassidy hung her head in shame during her detention hearing. A few weeks later, she was staffed for commitment; however, Operation PAR, a residential drug treatment program, agreed to give her a second chance.

The best child prostitution investigation program I've heard about began in Dallas, sparked by Detective Catherine de la Paz, a petite, energetic brunette who presented her program to the National Council of Juvenile and Family Court Judges in St. Louis in March 2008. Catherine shared figures estimating that there were 300,000 juvenile prostitutes nationally; 75 percent were runaways, and 95 percent of those were chronic runaways.

What was happening in Dallas, Catherine said, was almost unthinkable. Police had been told to give out "preprostitution citations," or warnings, to anyone, mostly women, who appeared to be prostituting. This avoided an arrest and put the person on notice that the next time around, an arrest would be made. According to Catherine, the problem was that police were giving these citations to girls, boys, and young men and women who appeared to be prostituting without bothering to check their runaway status, to bring them into custody or shelter, or to return them home. Although they had the unique status of "victim-offender," Dallas police rarely took the occasion to run their names and bring them to safety. They simply handed them a citation.

Catherine felt that these girls were caught in a "cauldron" of physical, psychological, and sexual abuse. She did enough research to know that these child prostitutes were not only runaways but "throwaways and lock-outs." They had no place to go, were often from dysfunctional homes with a history of prior physical and sexual abuse, and exhibited low self-esteem and a poor self-image. Many were exploited by pimps who first befriended them, fed them, housed them, slept with them, and then sold them into prostitution.

So, this detective's "Aha!" moment began with a desire to change policy.

Her first job was to locate the child prostitutes. To do so, she formed a squad that worked first with the older women prostitutes well known to the police. Not surprisingly, they felt maternal and protective toward these children. They told Catherine where to find the children and often the names of the pimps who sold them into prostitution.

Catherine's years of working this project provided her with a number of interviews with the child prostitutes and their pimps. She found the child victims to be mostly runaways who meet up with a pimp. At first they're seduced by affection and attention, but then they become controlled through emotional and financial security and pressured into prostitution. She found that the pimps maintained control through violence and drugs. "It's very easy to get in and hard to get out," Catherine said.

The pimps whom Catherine studied or interviewed were "expert" in human nature, manipulation, seduction, and coercion, as well as in identifying and locating their victims. Often pimps assumed a domineering father-figure role to foster complete economic dependence and psychological submission.

Catherine's unit intensified efforts to find and rescue these child victims. As a result, the number of children arrested for prostitution in Dallas declined by nearly 80 percent in three years, from 64 per month in 2005 to 12 per month in 2008. Most significantly, many of the pimps were successfully prosecuted for coercing girls into prostitution, aggravated kidnapping, and human trafficking. One of the worst offenders, named Frankie, got a seventy-five-year sentence.

And it all started with one spunky female detective who stood up for child victims.

I BELIEVE THAT AS Lawanda Ravoira's Girl Matters curriculum spreads through juvenile justice programs across the country, more girls will be empowered, fewer will run away, and, hopefully, none will turn to prostitution. The Girl Matters program can be implemented at the earliest stages of juvenile justice involvement. Our chief probation officer, Tim Niermann, has dedicated a unit to girls on probation. Girls gather to discuss anger and relationship issues with their probation officers as well as guests such as female police officers and community leaders. Tim's budget has been cut year after year, but he has imagination, flexibility, and a commitment to what works. Juvenile Probation Office Karin Popkowski works so effectively with the girls assigned to her. Our local PACE Center for Girls, an affiliate of the statewide PACE Center network, provides one-stop education, counseling, drug evaluations and discussion groups for about sixty girls, many referred by our juvenile judges. The director, Sally Zeh, a longtime colleague and admirer of Lawanda's, inspires her staff and her "spirited girls" to success by overcoming tremendous obstacles. Sally is "relationship" personified. The girls and staff have a strong bond with her, she has resources to help their families when in need, and she glows with satisfaction when she turns "stinkerbelles" into "tinkerbelles."

All these thoughts—safety, commitment programs, prostitution, building relationships—churned in my head when I visited Vanessa and Alena, two sixteen-year-old girls whom I had to recommit to another residential facility due to runaway behavior, failure to attend school, drug use, and prostitution. It's hard enough committing kids for the first time, but to send them away again...it's tough. However, a facility adjacent to the courthouse that had formerly housed a boot camp for boys began to receive boys and girls transferred from a moderate-risk program that was closing. I was skeptical at first, as I thought the facility was too small and confined; it even lacked a cafeteria or dining hall.

But when I paid a visit with our alternative-sanctions coordinator, Michelle Jameson, and Judge Raymond Gross, I couldn't have been more surprised. Adrienne Conwell, overseeing the move for the Department of Juvenile Justice, arranged for Vanessa and Alena to give us a tour. They hugged us, seemed glad to see us, and for the next hour skipped ahead of us, laughing and joking with staff, teachers, and counselors as they showed us their rooms and classrooms, introduced us to people, and then sat down to talk. Vanessa, who'd been chubby, had lost weight and was pleased about that. Alena, who had been gaunt and hollow-eyed when on the run, had gained weight and looked healthy and relaxed. They both admitted that they needed the structure of the program.

"The streets were bad," Alena said.

"I'm so sorry that my mom worried about me all the time," Vanessa said. "She visits every Sunday now, as this is close to home."

They talked about their class work, the counseling, and the good grades they were getting. Both girls agreed they had needed another cycle through a program to get straightened out.

"But the food sucks," Alena said, and Vanessa concurred, telling us how it was brought from the jail next door because their facility lacked a dining room or cafeteria. "But we get to decorate our rooms," they said, showing us walls plastered with magazine photos of rock stars. As they joked around with each other, arguing over who had the neatest room, Michelle and I smiled. It was like getting a tour of a boarding school, except for the locks on the doors.

"We go out every day for exercise," Vanessa said as we stood on the large, fenced-in yard that the boys and girls shared. "We go out right after the boys leave. Sometimes we get to look at them a little," they giggled. "We like to play red rover and kickball."

Red rover and kickball? How far can you get from the pull of the streets, drugs, and prostitution? As to the value of athletics, in reading an article about a repetitive girls basketball rivalry between two of our local high schools, I reminded myself that in nine years on the juvenile bench, I had never had a female basketball player in my delinquency court.

CHAPTER 21

Repairing the Broken Whole: Family Therapy for Juvenile Offenders

"**I**T IS EASIER TO BUILD** strong children than repair broken men," the nine-teenth-century abolitionist and orator Frederick Douglass said.

Amen.

Individual counseling based on the child's mental health needs is a must for kids involved with juvenile justice. But individual counseling loses its effect unless combined with evidence-based, what-works family therapy. If you heal a child who must continue to remain in a distressed family, you've only put a Band-Aid on a mortal wound. In other words, you can't build strong children without repairing the broken adults in their family.

The customers know what's right here. When I see Mrs. Glover standing in court next to her defiant and delinquent twins, Derek and Darrell, look-ing less tense, talking more softly, praising the in-home family therapy that's taking place, smiling at the therapist, I know I'm looking at a winner. It's not easy to allow strangers into your home. Many parents resist. When it works, it's just short of a miracle—except that its roots are based in science, proven evidence, and economic savings for taxpayers.

Three family therapy programs that I know of meet this test: the Redi-rection Initiative program run by Evidence-Based Associates; multidimen-sional family therapy, developed by Dr. Howard Liddle and administered at the University of Miami Miller School of Medicine; and Parenting With Love and Limits, a model aftercare program for parents and adolescents begun by Scott P. Sells, Ph.D.

Clay Yeager, a Pennsylvania-based consultant to Evidence-Based Associates and editor of its quarterly publication, the *EB-Advocate,* makes an interesting comparison in an article in the Spring 2010 newsletter:

> Like many of you, I've watched some of the debate raging across the country on health care reform. Regardless of one's political stripe or personal position on this polarizing national issue, I am nonetheless struck by the passion on full display by all sides...watching these gatherings does make me pause and wonder if groups would turn out in similar numbers and with similar collective passion to discuss school dropouts, teen pregnancy, juvenile crime, violence, or substance abuse. After all, health care is expensive, but the societal cost of substance abuse and crime, victims, prosecution, and incarceration are not far behind. Beyond the financial cost, lives are ruined, families destroyed, and communities ravaged.
>
> We're reminded once again of some of our (mis)guided national priorities by yet another national report and how we (mis)allocate resources to address them. The National Center on Addiction and Substance Abuse's "Shoveling It Up II: Substance Abuse and Its Impact on Federal, State, and Local Budgets" provides a clear, compelling, and even shameful description of woefully underfunded prevention efforts aimed at reducing substance abuse (less than 2 percent of a staggering $500 billion in spending) compared to the costs of "shoveling up" the mess afterward.
>
> So, now that we're in this collective national effort aimed at reform and at improving outcomes while containing costs, let's also put forth proven strategies to rethink how we respond to the high cost of juvenile delinquency, substance abuse, violence, and other social ills for which we ultimately pay a very steep price. The national health care movement now taking place will help to underscore the essential role of prevention in reducing many ailments and their associated costs.... Let's also push for a massive realignment of

resources away from costly and ineffective incarceration and toward proven and established evidence-based programs for children. If we take the same approach with kids as we do for health care—better outcomes and costs savings through prevention, early detection, and intervention—we can build a nation of strong children and fewer broken adults.

Mr. Yeager knows of what he speaks. Evidence-Based Associates's Redirection Initiative, which seeks to keep kids out of commitment by providing evidence-based, community-based treatment, including in-home therapy, is a rousing success in Florida. In the four years (2004 to 2008) that it was evaluated in Florida by the Office of Program Policy Analysis and Government Accountability (OPPAGA), Redirection saved the state $36.4 million in initial juvenile commitment costs and avoided $5.2 million in subsequent juvenile commitment and adult prison costs, while significantly lowering recidivism rates.[1]

"It's simple," says CEO Dan Edwards. "Improving public safety while reducing costs. What could be better?"

The heart of Redirection in Florida is its family therapy programs, adapted to each family's needs, with a goal of keeping the youth out of commitment. The Florida legislature in 2006 specified that Redirection provide multisystemic therapy (MST) and functional family therapy (FFT). In 2008, brief strategic family therapy (BSFT) was added to the mix because of its success with Latino and African American families.

In a nutshell, and rather unscientifically, here are the elements of these programs:

- Functional family therapy (FFT): Named by the U.S. Surgeon General as a model program, it consists of specific phases of treatment with organized interventions and targeted skill requirements. The therapist focuses on family relationships: how family members interact, who sits next to whom, who interrupts, who sneers, who cowers, and so on. For example, in the early stage, the trained therapist develops alliances and reduces negative behavior. In the next stage, the therapist emphasizes changing individual behavior and building relationships.

The final stage focuses on maintaining good relationships and connecting with community resources.

- Multisystemic family therapy (MFT): The longest and most intensive family therapy, its goal is to work with the family as part of the community and make positive changes in the family's relationship to various social systems, such as the school, juvenile justice, and peer relationships. The therapist works with the family in the home and community and is available twenty-four hours a day, seven days a week. Children are not included in parental counseling involving discipline, so as not to undermine the parent. Parents or caregivers are coached to improve their marriages or domestic relationships, as a way of reducing juvenile delinquency.

- Brief strategic family therapy (BSFT): The shortest of the interventions—eight to twenty-four sessions—is used to treat juvenile drug use or behavior problems seen as reactive to other family members' problems. Its underlying principle is that what affects one family member affects the others. BSFT is used for cultural groups who emphasize family interpersonal relationships, such as Hispanics and African Americans. The therapist identifies patterns of interaction between family members. For example, Teenager shoplifts every time Mom and Grandmother get into a fight. After identifying the pattern, the therapist works with the family to develop a prevention plan.

In our county, 243 youths were served, with a greater than 70 percent success rate, meaning reduced recidivism and families reporting improved relationships. The functional family therapy (FFT) model used was outcome driven, targeting youths between the ages of eleven and eighteen from a variety of ethnic and cultural groups who were marching toward a commitment program or otherwise out of control.

The FFT clinician worked with families for an average of twelve sessions over a period of three to four months. Services were conducted in the home, schools, and community. Regardless of the population, FFT emphasized the importance of respecting all family members on their own terms. The relationship between the therapist and the family was critical. The therapist engaged the family as people of great worth, with dignity and nobility, instead of as a family characterized by inappropriate behaviors or dysfunction. Treatment costs of this strength-based model were well below those of traditional services and other interventions.

The Henry and Rilla White Foundation, out of Jacksonville, Florida, founded to serve troubled youths and their families, funded a number of multisystemic therapy teams in northern Florida. The overall success rate was well over 80 percent. Over four years, this is how the youngsters in Redirection fared as compared to those committed to facilities:

- 48 percent less likely to be arrested
- 46 percent less likely to be convicted
- 35 percent lower recommitment rate
- 66 percent less likely to serve an adult prison sentence

In addition, over a five-year period, the Florida Redirection Initiative reduced placement costs and netted savings of more than $100 million.

A mother's testimonial follows:

I would like to express my sincere appreciation for the advice, counsel, friendship, encouragement, and guidance given to me and my family through your family intervention specialist, Alicia Peton. I have to admit, I was skeptical on how this was going to work but was pleasantly surprised by the approach taken by Ms. Peton. She was able to get both of my children to open up and talk about life with her and tell her things that they had never said to me. I was amazed. But it didn't stop there. She also instructed me on how to do the same. I also had to come to the realization that my children are going to be who they are and not my formulated image of them in my mind.

When I'm ordering Redirection or other family therapy as part of a juvenile's disposition, I've learned to talk cost savings in court, especially if the parent is resistant. To the dad who's been trying for months to have his defiant daughter committed, mainly at the urging of his wife, the girl's stepmother, I ask, "Why should the taxpayers of Florida pay fifty thousand dollars in commitment costs for your daughter, when the problems are with the family, and in-home family therapy hasn't yet been tried?"

What impressed me about multidimensional family therapy was that the therapist actually accompanied the family to court and spoke on behalf of the youth. Denise Auffant's soothing manner and constructive suggestions raised the quality of the dialog. More than a few parents praised her skillful diplomacy and resourcefulness. When the goal of sobriety was achieved, many families didn't want to see Denise end her relationship with them. That's effective family therapy!

MDFT is a "treatment system" rather than a one-size-fits-all approach. It has been named a model program by the National Registry of Evidence-Based Programs and Practices, a service of the U.S. Substance Abuse and Mental Health Services. It claims to produce superior outcomes in a clinical approach that includes extensive and ongoing training for the therapists and videotaping of clinical sessions, for training purposes.[2]

"In-home treatment is the key," Denise told me. "That's where we get the global picture of the temptations the youth has, the origin of the drug use, and the need for other community resources. If Grandma can't navigate the Social Security system, we help her. If the youth wants to establish a bank savings account, and no one in the family knows how to do it, we help him. If we discover that Uncle Jack in the attic is smoking pot daily while we're working with the youth on his substance abuse problem, we bring that to the family's attention."

Dr. Liddle and his MDFT team cite superior outcomes in comparison to other treatments and at lower costs. About 96 percent of teens completed the 120-day treatment as compared to 78 percent of youths in group therapy, at a weekly cost of $164 for MDFT versus $365 for community-based outpatient treatment. Even an intensive version of MDFT designed as an alternative to residential treatment provided superior clinical outcomes at one-third the cost: $384 per week versus $1,068.

I joined Dr. Liddle at a national drug treatment conference in Washington, D.C., to give a perspective from the bench. I learned a lot more about MDFT in the process. He reminded me that Multidimensional Family Therapy is defined as a comprehensive intervention, "since we think that's what is needed to alter lives in practical and meaningful ways.

"MDFT works with four units," he explained: "the teenager alone, the parent(s), the family as a unit—to change their interactional patterns—and the family members in relation to the outside social forces and institutions, such as juvenile justice and the schools. Programs without these four components don't obtain the same results.

"Remember also that MDFT is unique in that it has different versions of the core model that have been adapted and tested in rigorous controlled trials. The version of MDFT that you were involved in, Detention to Community: A Reintegration Program for Drug-Using Juvenile Detainees, was the first attempt to adapt an evidence-based therapy, MDFT, to the juvenile detention setting. So, we started the intervention right in the detention setting, offering individual counseling for the teen, family sessions that included the parents and kid, and HIV prevention as well. These interventions were continued postdetention for another four months after the teen's release," he concluded.

Defiant parents? It takes a lot of chutzpah for a therapist to label his program "A Model Program for Defiant Parents and Adolescents," but that's exactly what Scott Sells, does, and the program succeeds beyond expectations. I've attended at least three sessions at judicial conferences featuring Scott's presentation on Parenting with Love and Limits, including one focusing on aftercare counseling for kids coming out of commitment programs. At each presentation, I've gained another nugget in my pan, or notch on my belt, for how to deal with the parents I see in my courtroom. Scott very effectively uses videotapes of parenting experiences and coaching sessions in his presentation, so I'm a bit hampered without those visual aids. However, I'll summarize Scott's description of the innovative program he's developed, an outgrowth of his popular book *Parenting Your Out-of-Control Teenager: 7 Steps to Reestablish Authority and Reclaim Love*:

"Engaging parents of adolescents with severe behavior problems is challenging for even the most skilled practitioner," he says. "The challenge is made more difficult when one tries to engage parents in a parenting education group and/or family therapy session. In addition, even though parenting groups are widespread, there is a question about both their effectiveness and transportability. Transportability is the ease of which the average practitioner can take the concepts of a model and integrate them into the real world with real clients.

"In response to these problems, a model program called Parenting with Love and Limits (PLL) was developed after a four-year process research study. It is the first program of its kind to combine a parenting education group with family therapy into one complete package." It was Scott's "Aha!" discovery.[3,4]

Every head in the room nods in agreement when Scott begins his presentation: "Juveniles will return to future delinquent acts if their parents remain unchanged in the areas of consistent limit setting, rebuilding emotional attachments, and improved communication."

Traditional parenting groups have had three main problems, Scott found. First, parents may have learned a new skill, but no one showed them how to use it through role playing in a family therapy format. Second, some parents resent coming to group sessions, as they see their adolescents as solely to blame for their own difficulties. Third, practitioners have a difficult time "transporting" proven therapy models into the real world with real clients.

To address these problems, Parenting with Love and Limits developed from a research study to become the first evidence-based program of its kind to combine group and family therapy over a six- to seven-week period, to use the stages-of-readiness concept, a building block approach to break parental resistance, and to present step-by-step road maps for the therapist to transport the concepts into real-world practice.

In the videos we watched, we saw a mother who'd called her twin daughters "a good twin and a bad twin" apologize on her knees to the "bad twin," bringing all three family members to tears. We saw a father who could only be described as a bully hug his son for the first time in years. We saw a boy released from a commitment program try to use two techniques called "time out" and "validating each other"—which he'd learned in counseling—during a clash with his mother, who could only tell him to "shut up," that she was "the boss in this house," and that she was calling the police so that he would be recommitted. "Time out" was to remove himself from the conflict and "validating" was to repeat to his mother her concerns; however, she'd had no counseling herself, and she responded horribly to what he was doing.

The PLL model combines both group and family therapy and is designed to progress from "venting" and "button pushing" topics to "restoring lost nurturance" and "presenting a new contract to your teenager." Two group facilitators lead a small group of no more than four to six families—twelve people total—in collective sessions and separate breakout groups, for six two-hour sessions. The coaching piece uses a model called "undercurrents," to show parents how to recognize hot-button issues and use the newly acquired skills.

Here's a case study that Scott uses to demonstrate the stages-of-readiness scale in the program:

Fifteen-year-old Galvin was diagnosed with a conduct disorder and symptoms of extreme disrespect, destroying property in the home, and chronic truancy. During the first group, it was apparent that Galvin's single-parent mother, Kelly, was firmly entrenched within the precontemplative stage of readiness. She sat in the back of the room with her arms crossed and repeatedly stated that she did not see that Galvin had a problem. Galvin's probation officer previously informed Michelle (the group leader and coach) that Kelly had never lasted more than two therapy sessions before she had dropped out. Galvin's probation officer also described Kelly as angry, burnt out, and in extreme denial as to her role in helping her son misbehave.

It was not until the breakout session in the second hour of the first group that Kelly's icy veneer began to melt. A key moment came when Michelle asked the following question to Kelly and the other parents: "When I get to know you better, what qualities will I come to admire about you as a parent?" The question stunned Kelly and the other parents because they had come expecting to be judged or told what to do.

Instead the therapist was asking them to focus on strengths. Kelly's defenses were further lowered when Michelle asked for a show of hands from the other parents as to who thought Kelly was a good parent. Everyone raised their hand. At the end of the first group, the parents said they would return because they felt supported and not so alone. Kelly and many of the other parents were still stuck in precontemplation, but the walls around them were slowly weakening.

Another watershed moment occurred during the second group on button pushing. Kelly and Galvin both admitted that they pushed each other's buttons. Then they had fun putting their top buttons on Post-it notes and sticking them all over their body. Galvin picked the buttons that his mom "lectured" and "nagged," and Kelly wrote down that Galvin used "swearing" and "mumbled under his breath." Kelly began to move into "contemplation" when she saw another parent and her son role-play their last argument in front of the group and playfully push each other's buttons. Kelly liked it when another parent held up flashcards that showed the mother dropping in age as she lost control of her emotions and took her son's button pushing so personal [sic]. Kelly later said that she could "see" herself in the mother's shoes.

Kelly and the other parents were shocked that the group leader never openly discussed their teenager's charges or insinuated on any level that they had to change. Instead the group leader, Michelle, playfully provided new tools each week through video examples and fun role plays.

The defining moment came during the fourth class, when Kelly watched a parent struggle to put together their first typewritten, loophole-free contract around disrespect. As this mother struggled, Kelly was moved to tears as she watched the other parents in the outer circle move in to support and offer suggestions. For the first time, Kelly began to see how easily a teenager can exploit loopholes and how helpful it was to have both rewards and punishments. Most importantly, she began to see Galvin as not a "bad kid" but one who was extremely skillful in finding loopholes to get what he wanted. After this group, Kelly told Michelle that she would attend coaching.

Things really started to move in a positive direction when Kelly connected with another single-parent mother in the group. Kelly was alone and isolated, but this ended when the single-parent mother joined her in several of her coaching sessions for support. Galvin was stunned. For the first time in his life, Kelly became assertive but fair by using rewards instead of empty threats and punishments. During coaching, Michelle also used extensive role plays (Galvin was in the waiting room) to practice delivering the button-buster techniques she'd learned in group. After two coaching sessions, Kelly felt "battle ready" and delivered the contract to Galvin. Galvin "got worse before he got better," but the mother stood firm with the support of her friend from group. After three weeks, the extreme disrespect, destroying property, and chronic truancy ended.

If I win the lottery, I'm bringing Scott's Parenting with Love and Limits program into my truancy court for every one of the three hundred-or-so truants I see each year and their families. Before that, however, I want to convince our county school board and children's services council, the Juvenile Welfare Board, that they need to bring this program to our troubled families.

Fortunately, in 2009, Scott contracted through Redirection in Florida to bring his PLL program to our county as part of aftercare. Now, if a youth from our county is sentenced to a residential commitment program in the Tampa Bay area (not a given—kids are sent all over the state, based on bed availability and their specialized needs), a PLL therapist will work with the youth and family while the youth is in the commitment program and afterward, to provide counseling to promote a successful transition back into the community.

That's a tough nut to crack, if you think about it. The kid has been away from home for seven to ten months, on average. He is probably doing well, due to the structure of the program, focus on education, and lack of drugs or other temptations. Meanwhile, the parent(s) has had a vacation: visiting the youth, perhaps, but not living together. Upon release, the youth, eager to get home and experience freedom, expects to be welcomed and loved and can't wait to get out with his friends. The parent(s) expects that the youth has changed, that the program has "fixed" him. Without the intervention of a parenting program like Scott's, it doesn't take long for expectations to wither and animosities to revive.

It's too early to review the results of Scott's aftercare program in our county, but I'm very optimistic. After all, Scott began with the premise "You can't change the child until you change the behavior of the parent."

CHAPTER 22

Crossover Kids: Fewer Silos, More Legal Representation

D ANNY'S ROUGH LIFE actually got better when he was sentenced to a moderate-risk commitment program for boys in central Florida. He found that he liked the structure, and he thrived in the program.

As a foster kid, lean, lanky, with straight blond hair and pale blue eyes, he'd bounced from home to home, living in some group homes, running away, out of school for long periods of time. He hadn't earned a single high-school credit. His charges included two residential burglaries and possession and sale of cocaine. He needed money to survive on the street.

Now, at sixteen, for the first time in years, Danny knew where he was going to eat and sleep each night. With small classes, he was rapidly making up high school credits. He was drug free, crime free, and opening up in counseling sessions. His evaluations were terrific. He was a model inmate, earning points for a home visit during the Christmas holidays.

There was one problem: Danny had no home.

His parents' rights had been terminated, and he hadn't seen them in years. He had no relatives in Florida. His probation officer and caseworker seemed to have disappeared. His last foster placement was full. There wasn't a bed for him anywhere. So, Danny remained in custody over the holidays with a skeleton staff and a few dozen troublemakers who'd broken all the rules and hadn't earned a home visit.

Danny had no one. Involved in two systems—delinquency and dependency—he's what we call a "crossover kid."

California's experience with crossover kids mirrored that of most of the country. Dependent youths who become formal wards of the delinquency court ended up losing their social workers, attorneys, and judges from the dependency court. Services to the family were discontinued as the burden shifted from social worker to probation officer. Wards of delinquency court in foster care often stayed in the delinquency system longer, often due to probation officers' inexperience in developing permanent plans for them.

California judge Michael Nash and Shay Bilchik, director of the Center for Juvenile Justice Reform at the Georgetown University Public Policy Institute, authored a series of articles, "Child Welfare and Juvenile Justice: Two Sides of the Same Coin, Parts I and II," which was published in the fall 2008 and winter 2009 issues of *Juvenile and Family Justice Today,* a quarterly magazine published by the National Council of Juvenile and Family Court Judges.[1]

The authors focus on a project in Los Angeles that provides for joint assessments by the dependency and delinquency departments for crossover youths. That means working together for a common plan. No longer can one department simply hand the youth over to the other. "The joint assessments must include the nature of the referral, the age of the youth, the prior record of the youth's parents for child abuse, the prior record of the youth for out-of-control or delinquent behavior, the parents' cooperation with the youth's school, the nature of the youth's home environment, and the records of other agencies which have been involved with the youth and his or her family."

Assessment is only the first step, the authors suggest. Implementation is the key. So far, however, preliminary results indicate that the reports and case plans generated by the multidisciplinary team are more comprehensive. The recidivism of these youths is slightly lower as well.

In Florida, if you are a youth involved in both systems, you probably fall through the cracks, according to a project begun under the office of Governor Charlie Crist to address the needs of the 200 to 300 crossover kids who are in residential commitment programs run by the Department of Juvenile Justice.

The project's desired outcomes are to:

- design and develop high-level case management tracking options;
- harvest and distribute national research results;
- develop a strategy for a "youth voice" and participation for committed youths;
- assist in developing a directory of contacts, people, and resources; and
- assist in producing a "how-to" guide for accessing services during case management.

Governor Crist appointed Andrea Arce-Trigatti as the first "fellow" to this position. She's considered to be a full-time staff member shared by the Department of Juvenile Justice and the Department of Children and Families, and managed by senior staff. Andrea updated me on the project in late 2009. She and her interview teams planned to talk to sixty to eighty of the 184 "dually served" youths in juvenile justice commitment programs to see whether they received meaningful transitional planning prior to their release. That's an example of a specific project for an acknowledged problem that could produce results quickly, if it's not managed to death.

Andrea's second project, "Where are they now?" identified fifteen former foster kids previously released from a juvenile justice commitment program to be interviewed about their lives postcommitment. The news was not good. Of those located to date, two were in jail, and two were pregnant as teens. Andrea found huge communication problems between the local juvenile justice and child welfare agencies. "A few circuits had a liaison working between the agencies; in most, there was bickering between them or a hands-off policy."

In our court, Public Defender Bob Dillinger created a program to provide holistic representation to crossover youths. Since 2006, well over 100 of these youth have been represented by the same attorney before the same judge on both their delinquency and dependency cases.[2]

"This 'one judge, one attorney' approach provides consistency and a comfort level for the child," Bob explains. "It also ensures that professionals working with the child are more familiar with the child's specific needs. As a result, the children are better informed of the legal proceedings, more involved in their dependency case, and, through client education, better able to understand the efforts and reasoning of the professionals working on behalf of the child.

"The crossover attorneys worked to build partnerships with many different agencies on behalf of our clients. These coalition-building efforts have paid off. The crossover program partners with our local community law program to address Social Security and education issues, with our court psychologists and the guardian ad litem program."

In court, I see twelve-year-olds standing taller and looking more engaged as their attorney stands beside them in both delinquency and dependency courts. The lack of a parent seems a little less painful as their lawyer advocates for placement, school, and medication issues, as well as the trial on the delinquency charges. I see seventeen-year-olds fully prepped on independent living issues, relying on their lawyers to make sure that the child welfare agency is preparing them to leave foster care.

Here's an example of good lawyering:

Kevin, a thirteen-year-old foster youth who had bounced from home to home, tried to avoid a fight on a school bus by kicking out a panel of the bus door while trying to leave. He was charged with criminal mischief for the damage. Kevin couldn't deny that he caused the damage; however, Steve Nelson, the crossover attorney who represented him, did a fine job of proving that part of Kevin's anger management therapy included removing himself from an escalating situation. Kevin didn't intend the damage. He just wanted out of the bus, and the driver wouldn't open the door. This defense wouldn't work for everyone, but it did for a foster kid on medication for anger issues, trapped in a situation he couldn't control.

One very practical crossover project, established by Mr. Dillinger and his wife, Kay, was a "clothes closet" located in the public defender's office, where kids could shop for an entire wardrobe of clothes, shoes, and accessories to brighten their lives. I've seen many a happy kid, encouraged by a relationship with a public defender familiar with all the kid's cases, eager to do a little shopping in the courthouse.

When you see these kids sorting through racks of clothes and looking for shoes and jewelry to match, it's hard to think of them as the "most difficult kids in the system," but that's how Claudia Wright describes them as she advocates for individualized care for crossover kids. Ms. Wright was one of the founders of the Children's Advocacy Center at Florida State University College of Law, and founder and director of Gator Team Child, a multidisciplinary juvenile law clinic at the University of Florida Levin College of Law. Now working as a senior juvenile justice monitor in the Office of the Maryland Attorney General in Baltimore, she spoke frankly at a juvenile justice conference held at the University of Florida in February 2010:

> Juvenile justice is like a huge funnel, and the bottom end is prison. The huge open top end comes from disabilities, mental health, child abuse, and the child welfare system. Look at these systems and then try to keep the kids out of juvenile justice.
>
> For teachers, lawyers, and counselors, start with the hardest kids first—the crossover kids—not with the nicest, easiest kids. Match the advocates to the individual child. Put your very best, most skilled, most experienced caseworker or lawyer to the most difficult kids, the ones that everyone cringes at, and give those workers small caseloads.

Not only is this exactly what Bob Dillinger does with his "crossover kids and lawyers" program, but it is what Claudia Wright has been advocating for years as she's trained hundreds of lawyers and social workers to be better advocates for children. Her article "Rethinking Juvenile Justice: Using the IEP Concept to Create a New Juvenile Justice Paradigm" was published in the fall 2007 issue of the *Link,* the newsletter of the Juvenile Justice Division of the Child Welfare League of America.

An "IEP"? An "individualized education plan" designed for special-needs students revised to become a juvenile justice plan to meet the individual needs of these most difficult kids? How creative. How necessary. How important. How collaborative. "How soon we can get it?" most juvenile judges would ask.

CHAPTER 23

The Limits of Zero Tolerance: What We Need to Do to Improve Good Intentions

T HERE ISN'T A PARENT in the world who could enforce a "zero tolerance" approach to discipline without running afoul of the law for child abuse or abandonment. Whether you raise kids or are just around them, you simply have to "tolerate" some things. You can't toss them out or run away from them. Yet, in the name of school safety, we've expanded zero tolerance into a school disciplinary model that's thrown kids out of school and into the juvenile justice system for minor offenses or behavior problems that have nothing to do with school safety.

First, of course, I sympathize with teachers and administrators who put up with bad behavior and neglectful parents. We need to create a partnership between the schools and juvenile justice. Way too often, zero tolerance policies become zero tolerance for kids. Students suspended from school become the next truants and dropouts. These kids commit crimes and enter the school-to-prison pipeline.

The horrible events that led to zero tolerance policies—the Columbine High School shootings in Littleton, Colorado, in 1999, and shootings in Lake Worth, Florida, and other incidents involving weapons at school—were followed by all-too-familiar stories of another kind:

- In West Virginia, a seventh grader who shared a zinc cough drop with a classmate was suspended for three days pursuant to the school's anti-drug policy because the cough drop had not been cleared with the office.

- In North Carolina, a six-year-old kissed his classmate and was suspended for one day for violating the school's rule that precluded "unwarranted and unwelcome touching."

- In Louisiana, a second-grader brought his grandfather's watch to school for show-and-tell. The watch had a one-inch-long pocketknife attached. Pursuant to the school's weapons policy, the child was suspended and sent to an alternative school for a month.

- In South Carolina, an eleven-year-old who brought a knife to school in her lunch box to cut her chicken was taken away from school in a police car.

While the message is clear, and the punishment is swift, certain, and nondiscriminatory, the child who views it as unfair or extreme may be more harmed than helped. Furthermore, experts in the field contend that zero tolerance has *not* made schools safer, as complex situations require more than a knee-jerk analysis. In their 1999 journal article "Zero Tolerance for Zero Tolerance," educators Richard L. Curwin and Allen N. Mendler offer a case to illustrate the painful reality of an arbitrary reaction:[1,2]

"A young high school student was expelled after bringing a gun to school.... That morning, his father, in a drunken rage, had put a gun down the youngster's throat and, before passing out, threatened to kill him and his younger brother. The student brought the gun to school to save their lives. Before he could give it to his principal, the gun was discovered. No amount of explaining helped because of zero tolerance."

In a victory for opponents of quick-fix zero tolerance policies, the Florida legislature adopted a bill that narrowed the application of zero tolerance solely to the school safety issues originally intended—*not* to misbehavior. The new law, which became effective in July 2009, requires district school boards to review their policies involving zero tolerance to ensure that those policies do not include reporting to law enforcement agencies petty acts of misconduct and misdemeanors. Children will no longer be referred to law enforcement for minor violations at school, such as possession of plastic butter knives, drawing pictures of guns, or throwing an eraser. The bill also encouraged school districts to use alternatives to expulsions.

Mary "Dee" Richter, then the executive director of the Florida Network of Youth and Family Services, an organization responsible for putting more than twenty thousand at-risk youths back on track annually, thanked the leadership of the National Association for the Advancement of Colored People (NAACP), the Children's Campaign, and the Blueprint Commission for supporting the legislation and related reforms in a press release:

"When kids who do not need to be in a delinquency system are diverted from it, young lives are turned around and Florida taxpayer dollars are saved. Senate Bill 1540 is an example of how a well-intended law can be improved when state government, elected officials, and concerned citizens work together, and we urge the governor to sign it immediately," she said at the end of the legislative session.[3]

Although Governor Charlie Crist signed the improved zero tolerance bill into law, the debate on how to otherwise punish bad behavior in school—a huge problem for our public schools—has just begun. It's a difficult discussion. Black children are disciplined, suspended, and expelled from school more often than whites. From 2000 through 2009, African Americans made up 17 percent of public school enrollment nationwide but accounted for 34 percent of suspensions, and made up 16 percent of the overall youth population nationwide, but accounted for 45 percent of the juvenile arrests.

Pinellas County School Board member Mary Tyus Brown, one of two black members, spoke with the *St. Petersburg Times* after a school board retreat on March 22, 2009, after making a provocative comment that the district must address "the elephant in the room" when it comes to kids behaving badly.[4]

> I think the big thing about it is that unless we get high standards of appropriate behavior, you can't have high standards for learning."
>
> If you allow black children to not act appropriately, it's not good for them. We have too many black males in particular not graduating from high school and dropping out. Something is wrong. I don't know

what it is, but I do know that we can't afford to have this many young black males without jobs. Our prisons are full of them. We have got to do something about whatever is causing the problem. We have to set those standards in school. We really do. When they walk through our doors, we should have control. We should be able to tell them what is and what is not acceptable. If teachers set the standard and say, "This is the expectation," the kids will have to follow the rules.

Big kids intimidate teachers. It's with all races. I mentioned black children because they're the ones on the bottom when it comes to this learning gap. Some of our schools need more help than others. We need two things. We need strong administrators to set that standard and develop strong teams and let teachers know they're supported. Along with that, we need training for the teachers. Sometimes you can handle things right away so they won't get started. High expectations for behavior breed high expectations for learning. Without the first, you're not going to get the second.

Ms. Brown and a few other school board members have been regular fixtures in my truancy court, trying to analyze what it will take to get truants to want to attend school. Together, these educators and I lament the elimination of our OCIPS, or On Campus Intervention and Prevention Sites. Their students served suspensions at the school, were monitored, and were helped with school work and afforded behavioral counseling. OCIPS worked!

Imagine how ridiculous I feel when I order a youth to attend school, and the school suspends him, ordering him not to attend. Except for federally mandated expulsions for drugs or weapons, I think banishing kids from school should be against the law.

On March 8, 2010, U.S. Secretary of Education Arne Duncan lamented "schools that seem to suspend and discipline only young African American boys" as he pledged stronger efforts to ensure racial equality in schooling. He could have been talking about Keyshawn, age 14.

Habitually truant, nagged by his mother to attend school, the slight, five-foot-three, soft-spoken boy told his teacher, in his usual soft-spoken way, that he would "beat your ass and pound your pussy." Keyshawn got what he wanted: a ten-day suspension from school without his mother nagging him.

He'd violated his probation. Keyshawn needed a lot of help, as did his mother in her parenting skills. What better place to do this than in school?

Research suggests that heavy use of suspension does less to pacify schools than to push already troubled students toward academic failure and dropping out. A number of progressive districts have been reversing course and trying new approaches, including behavioral counseling and mediation, to reduce conflict and create safer, quieter schools, while ejecting only the worst offenders. Many cities, including Denver, Baltimore, and Cleveland, have moved away from zero tolerance and toward antibullying programs, positive-behavior feedback, and training students and teachers in conflict resolution.

Juvenile judges don't like bad behavior any more than schoolteachers or administrators do. Yet, a meeting that my colleague Judge Raymond Gross and I requested at one of our "failing" high schools shows the disconnect that exists between the courts and the schools when it comes to zero tolerance. Especially with kids on probation.

Gibbs High School, built in 1927 in south St. Petersburg, was the city's first high school for black students. Now integrated, the state had given it a solid F because of its low graduation rate, poor test scores (especially for minority students), and high truancy and school suspensions. For the juvenile judges, Gibbs raised additional problems. We received more referrals from Gibbs than any other high school in the county, mainly for kids already on probation supervision.

As we walked through the long administrative corridor for our meeting, our eyes took in the magnificent artwork hanging on the walls: oils, watercolors, charcoal drawings, clay and metal sculptures. It was an incredible mixture of color and design. Emotions leapt off the canvasses, like they do in Edvard Munch's *Scream*. Colors were as vivid as van Gogh's flowers. The details in the drawings were worthy of a Dutch master. You see, Gibbs High School was also a magnet school with a quality curriculum for students talented in the arts, including music and drama. (A few months after our visit, Gibbs student Blaine Krauss was named one of only twenty finalists in the U.S. Presidential Scholars Program for his exceptional work in musical theater.) Raymond reminded me that we almost never see a delinquent kid in court from this magnet arts program. That small part of the troubled school was doing just great. We were here to talk about the larger problem—and to offer help.

We'd both been seeing far too many kids arrested in school for probation violations that were really infractions of school policy: talking on a cell phone, leaving campus without permission, being tardy or unexcused from class. Often they spent the night in our detention facility, as they were scored on the risk assessment instrument by the nature of the underlying charge, regardless of how minor the violation. We wanted to see whether we could help reduce the bad behavior. Perhaps we could conduct a school assembly or bring some actual hearings or delinquency trials to the schools to educate the students. Tim Niermann, our chief probation officer, and Michelle Jameson, our alternative-sanctions coordinator, joined us.

Kevin Gordon, the new principal, looked composed and in charge as he welcomed us into a conference room and introduced us to School Resource Officer Kenneth Jamison, a member of the St. Petersburg Police Department. It had been a really bad day for both men, full of multiple discipline problems and three students taken into custody to be "Baker Acted." The Baker Act is a Florida law that permits mentally ill people to be involuntarily committed to a psychiatric facility for seventy-two hours.

Principal Gordon, who'd attended Gibbs himself, starring in track and basketball, has a stellar reputation as an educator. The school board had assigned him to the high school a year earlier to restore order and to raise its state ranking. Tough job!

Before Raymond or I could express our concerns about excessive arrests or offer to help in some constructive fashion, Officer Jamison took control, proudly showing us a small notebook he kept up to date with the names of all the Gibbs students currently on probation. He looked formidable in his police uniform, a big, beefy African American man who would fit in on a SWAT team. "I watch them extra closely," he said. "I'm ready to file a violation of probation if they get out of line."

Our heads drooped. That overzealous attitude was exactly the problem we'd come to discuss. It seemed to us so unfair to give one kid a referral or write-up for using a cell phone in class, while arresting another kid for the same offense, just because he's on probation. The Department of Juvenile Justice's probation officer, who knows the youngster best, should be filing violations of probation when necessary. Not the school resource officer, who should be there as a true *resource,* ensuring safety and order on campus.

Officer Jamison was unhappy with us. He couldn't understand why we didn't act on his arrests by detaining more kids for longer periods of time. He's a good man. I felt his pain. His policies resulted from his frustration with student misbehavior. We understood that and wanted to help. But his strategy wasn't working, because the kids returning to school from a detention facility had fallen further behind in their schoolwork. They felt defeated and singled out for unfair treatment, with huge chips on their shoulders and a real axe to grind with the school resource officer. To them, he had morphed from a resource officer to a probation officer, with a "gotcha!" goal.

PARENTS AND ELECTED OFFICIALS alike find absurdity in broadly interpreted, strictly enforced zero tolerance policies as well as the financial costs involved in locking up kids. A recent high-profile case involved Zachary Christie, a six-year-old from Delaware who was suspended for five days and then reassigned to an alternative school for forty-five days, for bringing to school a camping utensil that contained a knife, fork, and spoon.

"I think it's crazy that they don't use common sense," complained Debbie Christie, Zachary's mother and the school's PTA copresident. "It's almost like taking a jaywalker and throwing him into a maximum-security prison," said Fred Hink of Katy, Texas, who founded Texas Zero Tolerance, a parents group that urges school administrators to use common sense in disciplinary cases.

Yet David Resler, vice president of the Delaware school board, which eventually reduced Zachary's sentence to a three- to five-day suspension, defended the policy classifying the camping tool as a dangerous weapon. "I'm sure we've got many other devious kids in the district who are trying to figure out how to duct-tape a spoon and fork to their switchblades right now," he said.

Zachary was six years old when suspended. Shouldn't age be taken into account?

When misbehavior and technology combine in schools, it's hard to keep up with new crimes. A 2009 survey for the National Center for Missing and Exploited Children found that 19 percent of teenagers had sent, received, or forwarded nude or partially nude photos through phone messaging, email, or social networking sites.[5] "Sexting," as it is called, meets the definition of child pornography in Florida and many states, and may bring criminal charges. Bullying has become a group sport that in its meanest form includes verbal attacks (increasingly spread online) and physical attacks, as exemplified by the charges filed in 2010 against nine teenagers from South Hadley, Massachusetts, after the suicide of fifteen-year-old freshman Phoebe Prince, who had recently moved there from Ireland and had been bullied mercilessly.

In our county, arrests suddenly skyrocketed to upward of eighty at John Hopkins Middle School in St. Petersburg—whose student newspaper was named the best in the nation three years in a row—when school officials failed to recognize and prepare for the disruptions and fights between rival neighborhood gang members recently admitted to the school. On March 18, 2010, the student newspaper featured this editorial, titled "J. Hop's Fate Up to Us":

> In the old days, John Hopkins used to be recognized for our award-winning newspaper; superior music programs, outstanding artwork, and Broadway-bound drama students. Lately, we have been known for the outbreak of fights and high number of arrests.
>
> The media and community view us as "bad kids." But the truth is only a few "bad" students are weighing down the good.
>
> It's up to us if we want to save our reputation. It's now or never.
>
> At the beginning of March, J. Hop was in and on the news for five days in a row. This made school life rough for students and staff.
>
> "If you think that camera from Bay News 9 likes you, here's the truth. They like you to act a fool and give them stories," sixth grader Kenyon Ford wrote in a letter to the *J. Hop Times* editor. "I for one am tired of this drama and the state looking at us like we're a bunch of dumb, ignorant, violent vandals. If we come together now, we can be better…"
>
> To get to that point, we've got a long way to go.
>
> Because of our current reputation, parents are having second thoughts about sending their children to J. Hop. According to the school district, last year 1,020 parents applied for our magnet programs. This year 570 applied.

But when it comes to quality, some things haven't changed. Just this year:

- The drama students scored superior ratings;

- Art students received Gold Key awards;

- Eleven eighth grade students competed in the county History Fair;

- Foreign language students got 22 superior ribbons in World Language Day competitions;

- The school orchestra earned the highest ratings possible in the MPAs (The Musical FCAT); and

- The girls' basketball team was south county champs. Again.

Though there are many positives, we can't ignore the negative things going on.

The students here need to step it up. Let's get our reputation back by doing the little things that can make a big difference. That means getting to class on time, helping staff, being more civilized, and stopping arguing with each other.

Every student has the potential to make this happen. Now is the time to clean up our act. If we want to change this campus, we are going to need a lot of help; but it starts with me and you.

Maybe it's a coincidence, but arrests diminished when the students became engaged.

Misbehavior is a terrible problem in our public schools, particularly middle schools. The whole community needs to help: parents most especially and the judges, too. Bring the judges into the schools to hold assemblies; hold youth court hearings in the schools when transgressions occur; use community service and school "cleanup" days; provide intensive drug education on campus, like the Face It program, which allows even a kid with a drug charge to remain in school if he undergoes on-site drug counseling. But don't lock up kids or transfer them to alternative schools, except in the most egregious cases involving danger to the school.

I keep thinking of the art on the walls at Gibbs High; the display of awesome talent, done by kids who were engaged in school. Or the Presidential Scholar who wanted to be there. These kids weren't truants or under suspension. The next chapter shows some ways to get there.

CHAPTER 24

Truancy: Where Most Behavior Problems Begin

"**R**EADY, WILLING, AND UNABLE TO SERVE**" is a shocking report prepared by a group of more than sixty retired generals, admirals, and civilian military leaders. They call attention to the fact that, according to the Pentagon, 75 percent of young people ages seventeen to twenty-four are unable to enlist in the military. Some 30 percent are high-school dropouts, 30 percent can't pass the written tests, 10 percent are physically unfit, and 5 percent have felony records.

These military leaders elevate school failure to a national security issue and conclude: "The most proven investment for kids who need help graduating from high school starts early: high-quality early education. It also helps kids stay away from crime and succeed in life." It goes without saying that kids have to be present in school to get the education.[1]

As the truancy judge for our county, I place the blame for school failure squarely on the back of chronic truancy—significant unexcused school absences that begin as early as elementary school. Every high-school dropout was, at some time, a truant.

When I was asked to preside over truancy court, I felt a bit insulted. High crimes and misdemeanors, yes. Significant child abuse cases, yes. But presiding over kids who were skipping school? In Florida? Near the beach? I didn't consider that much of an assignment. Nine years later, I know I couldn't have been more wrong. Truancy reduction and dropout prevention is the most significant intervention I can make for kids and the community. Almost all misbehavior and crime in juvenile court begins with issues of truancy.

"Attendance, Attachment, Achievement," the motto of our "education court," was borrowed from Ken Seeley, executive director of the National Center for School Engagement, a Denver-based think tank for truancy reduction and dropout prevention. It's even inscribed on bookmarks handed out in court. I see about fifty kids twice a month in truancy court: new cases and status hearings on unexcused absences ranging from fifteen to twenty days in the fall to upward of one hundred days absent by late spring. That's more than half the school year lost.

Our court is a true partnership with Family Resources, a local agency providing counseling for troubled youth and their families, as well as the schools, the state attorney, law enforcement, and drug counselors. We "graduate" many successful turnaround students to cheers and a round of applause. We discharge many others, sadly, who drop out of school at age sixteen or who rack up delinquency charges, so that truancy issues are handled in delinquency court. My partners, Patti Kohler, Jerri Evans, Barbara Jacobs, Esq., Betty Turner, Laurie Dart, Esq., Angela Simmons and others, including school attendance specialists and social workers and the many Family Resources case managers, mourn each loss but celebrate each success.

We also operate a highly successful truancy magistrate program modeled after the Rhode Island initiative described below and administered by Debra Leiman, our Unified Family Court director. The lawyer-magistrates, Carmen Follis and Sharon Gallagher, conduct hearings for truants and their parents in twelve middle schools, supported by attendance specialists, social workers, guidance counselors, and teachers.

Chronic truancy precedes or accompanies every other significant social and justice system problem. Truants often commit crimes, use drugs, or suffer from untreated mental illness, low self-esteem, or uncontrolled anger. Many are physically unfit, abused, and impoverished, with unstable housing and nonexistent parenting. Truancy is a class issue, a public school issue. While I could write an entire book about the devastation caused by chronic truancy, it is valuable to look at just a few effective programs that address the problem.

The National Truancy Prevention Association (NTPA) is made up of educators, lawyers, judges, researchers, and court and school personnel. It promotes, educates, and trains communities to improve school attendance. Inspired by Rhode Island Chief Family Court Judge Jeremiah S. Jeremiah's groundbreaking truancy magistrate program, I joined the organization.

Rhode Island's size and population of just over one million were so similar to Pinellas County that we decided to replicate that state's truancy magistrate program. It's been a rousing success, popular with teachers and parents, as the cases are heard weekly in the middle schools—not in court. The Rhode Island program has been in existence for ten years. During its first year of operation, attendance rates nearly doubled among middle-school students, from 49 percent to 89 percent. Ron Pagliarini, Judge Jeremiah's right-hand administrator and NTPA president, aggressively pursues federal and foundation grant money to expand the reach of NTPA programs.[2]

I joined two other NTPA officers, Tifny Iacona and Stacey Jamieson in Baltimore in August 2009, to present our truancy-reduction programs to a conference of the federal government's Office of Safe and Drug Free Schools. Although we were scheduled dead last in the two-day program, our audience was enthusiastic, as we were *the only* truancy program on the program. Imagine our glee when Associate Attorney General Thomas Perelli prioritized truancy reduction in his keynote speech and spoke of a Philadelphia study that tracked chronic truants and dropouts back to third-grade attendance and discipline problems. Then Tifny and Stacey presented their progress.[3]

Tifny Iacona's enthusiasm for truancy intervention work at the Granite Education Center in Salt Lake City, Utah, begins in elementary school. The first "habitual truancy letter" is sent to parents after just five unexcused absences, followed by interventions and home visits. Parent involvement increases. Parents or guardians become part of the solution. Resources are put in place well before any court hearings, and truancy is nipped in the bud.

In Brooklyn and within the New York City subway system, Stacey Jamieson and her district attorney colleague, Mary Hughes, under the leadership of Kings County district attorney Charles J. Hynes, created and administered TRACK, a program to combat truancy while reducing daytime crime and youth victimization. The most important goal of TRACK is to make parents aware of the issue of truancy and get them involved in their children's education.

TRACK began in 1998 with a small truancy center located in a subway station. It has grown to six centers throughout Brooklyn. At TRACK centers, students meet with the district attorney's social workers who connect them to services through referrals to community agencies. Since its inception, 83,865 students have been brought to a Brooklyn TRACK center, and 77,239 parents or guardians have been contacted by TRACK. Significantly, because of the collaborative efforts of TRACK, 428 missing children have been recovered and returned home.

It began with truancy reduction; it saved missing and exploited children. In January 2000, then mayor Rudolph Giuliani recognized the success of the TRACK program in his State of the City address, expanding it citywide so that truancy reduction is now in place in four of New York City's five boroughs.[4,5]

In East Harlem, Judge Eileen Koretz presides over one of New York's newest courts, attendance court, using a problem-solving approach and "a very strict face" to coax kids to go to school. Such courts are intended to "take aim at chronic truancy, so often a precursor to serious delinquency," Mayor Michael R. Bloomberg said in his State of the City address in 2007. Truancy courts, he added, would help by "holding children and their families accountable for school attendance."

What does it take to find missing and exploited kids, truants, and kids committing crimes during school hours? It takes the mobilization of the entire business community, says Harry Shorstein, former state attorney from Jacksonville, Florida. His push within the business community encouraged shopkeepers and customers to look for truants during school hours, to refuse them service, and to call the police. Like TRACK, intervention at a community level paid off.

How punitive can you get? I didn't think I'd like the presentation of Texas truancy judge John Sholden, who presides over 135,000 students in a large suburb of Dallas County. The description of his presentation to the National Council of Juvenile and Family Court Judges in July 2009 implied draconian measures to get kids to attend school. It wasn't the way we operated, I thought. Once again I was mistaken, and I learned a lot.

The Texas legislature gave the truancy judge certain tools that most states lack: the imposition of $500 fines for truancy, revocation of driver's licenses, and possible jail sentences for willful noncompliance. But it's a carrot-and-stick approach throughout. Start going to school regularly, and you can earn back the $500 fine. Get your high-school diploma or GED—and Texas will allow you to attend public school past age nineteen to accomplish this—and you earn back your driver's license, fine waived. Texas has achieved leverage that Florida and most states lack. Judge Sholden demonstrated a shrewd, yet compassionate, side when telling us how he gave jigsaw puzzles to the kids and parents. "I ordered them to complete it together and to take a photograph of it to show me. Sometimes it was the only activity a parent and child did together; the only cooperation between them. It was amazing how many completed the project and how proud they were of the pictures they brought to truancy court."

Truancy reduction is indeed a matter of leverage. We have to find ways to make kids want to go to school: carrot, stick, or both.

Sometimes it's a bureaucratic fix. Philadelphia recently established an Education Support Center to track the educational progress of students in out-of-home care, responding to a study that showed that one-third of the city's dropouts had been in foster care or juvenile justice facilities. "When you try to get two really large institutions to work together at a kid level, it's really difficult," said Lori Shorr, Mayor Michael Nutter's chief education advisor. "It's going to take close to eight hundred thousand dollars to bring these agencies together to serve up to five hundred children in the next two years, coordinating placement and school and intervention decisions. That's significant money that should produce a significant result."

For children who can and want to be in school, nothing is impossible. Look to Chicago in 2010. As reported by the *Chicago Tribune*, "The entire senior class at Chicago's only public all-male, all–African American high school has been accepted to four-year colleges. At last count, the 107 seniors had earned spots at 72 schools across the nation.

"Mayor Richard Daley and the Chicago Public Schools Chief Ron Huberman surprised students at an all-school assembly at Urban Prep Academy for Young Men in Englewood this morning to congratulate them. It's the first graduating class at Urban Prep since it opened its doors in 2006.

"Huberman applauded the seniors for making the CPS shine.

"'All of you in the senior class have shown that what matters is perseverance, what matters is focus, what matters is having a dream and following that dream,' Huberman said.

"The school enforces a strict uniform of black blazers, khaki pants, and red ties—with one exception. After a student receives the news he was accepted into college, he swaps his red tie for a red and gold one at an assembly."

Wow.

Geoffrey Canada does something similar with his Promise Academy charter school and Harlem Children's Zone (HCZ) in New York City. HCZ and the academy are the culmination of his nearly twenty-year effort to prove that even the poorest of Harlem's children and families can succeed if those children are given a quality education and meaningful after-school programs. Speaking to juvenile justice professionals at the University of Florida in February 2010, he emphasized again and again the importance of school engagement and education in reducing juvenile crime:

> There are 580,000 black males in prison now and just 40,000 graduating with college degrees. How does that work as an investment? Give me $5,000 a year, and I will guarantee a kid will graduate from college, instead of $50,000 to lock him up.
>
> We have a certain population that isn't being considered good for anything except jail or prison. At the same time, we're experiencing a fundamental shift in the global economy that most Americans aren't aware of, don't have a clue. Highly educated, graduate-level people all over the globe speak perfect English and will work for so much less. More people in India speak perfect English than in America.
>
> They're going to beat us on the low end—willing to work for low wages—and on the high end with highly educated college graduates. We have a shift of who is going to produce the most efficient work force of engineers, scientists, and teachers.[5]

We can't educate them if we can't keep them in school. Truancy prevention matters.

CHAPTER 25

Two Janes: Helping Children and Families in Need of Services

IF I'D BEEN ONE OF THOSE juvenile judges appointed in Chicago in 1899, when juvenile courts first began, I would have begged for an introduction to Jane Addams, one of the founders of Hull House in Chicago, the first settlement house in the United States. Founded in 1889 with the $50,000 estate Jane inherited from her father, Hull House at its busiest was visited by about two thousand people a week. As a true settlement house, it provided various community services to a large city population. Its facilities included a night school for adults, kindergarten classes, clubs for older children, a public kitchen, art gallery, coffeehouse, gymnasium, girls club, bathhouse, book bindery, music school, drama group, library, and social worker training centers.

What an incredible resource for the earliest juvenile courts! Is there a better way to keep at-risk kids out of the system?

Hull House served the many European ethnic groups migrating to Chicago around the turn of the century. It eventually became a thirteen-building settlement that included a playground and a summer camp. Jane Addams progressed from social work to political reforms and to befriending the early members of the Chicago School of Sociology. She worked on juvenile court law, women's rights, and workers' compensation. Her projects included a Juvenile Psychopathic Clinic. She was a charter member of the NAACP and a controversial pacifist during World War I. In 1931 she became the first American woman to win the Nobel Peace Prize, in recognition of her "expression of an essentially American democracy."[1]

Today, in my work as a juvenile judge, I have the invaluable assistance of another Jane: Jane Harper, the president and CEO of Family Resources. With a national reputation in the field, she is also chairman of the board of directors of the National Network for Youth, an organization made up of Family Resources and 234 other agencies from all over the country that provide services for runaway and homeless youths. Known as CINS/FINS providers (Children in Need of Services/Families in Need of Services), the centers operate to keep kids out of the juvenile justice system by providing a safe place to be, wholesome activities, a respite from domestic violence in the home, and individual and family counseling.

"I have no control over him."

"He won't go to school. He's flunking all his classes."

"She comes and goes as she pleases and hangs out with older boys."

"She steals money from her father and me. She's totally disrespectful."

"He hangs out with a bad bunch; won't stay away from them."

"I'm afraid he's on drugs."

"I need help, but I don't want to get him arrested."

I hear these complaints so often in delinquency court, usually about the younger siblings not yet "in the system," or in dependency or truancy court, or even out in the community. "Isn't there something we can do, before he gets arrested?" the exasperated parent asks. Fortunately, there are programs, shelters, and counseling for runaways, truants, and ungovernables, a category created by the federal Office of Juvenile Justice and Delinquency Prevention when it was created in 1974.

As Jane Harper explains, "These are kids, for the most part, who are not committing a crime and often are reacting to things happening in their lives, such as abuse or domestic violence at home." Jane began her career in social work at a domestic violence shelter in St. Petersburg. "It was like *Dragnet*," she says, referring to the 1950s TV crime series. "The names and faces changed, but the stories remained the same."[2]

She found her real passion working with kids when she was hired by Roy Miller, now the president of the Children's Campaign, when he was running Family Resources. Since Jane became the CEO in 1988, Family Resources has grown in size, creativity, and responsiveness to the needs of the community. Its menu of counseling includes groups for parents to learn from one another, for kids charged with domestic violence to meet with their parents, for young girls learning social relationships, and for individual kids with all sorts of problems. Youth Arts Corps, an after-school program, appeals to the artistic side of kids.

Shelters are the top priority for Jane and her 140 full- and part-time Family Resources employees. Each shelter group home has a maximum of twenty beds, 24-7 "awake supervision," individual and group counseling, and—amazing for a large county—an arrangement with school transportation officials to provide busing to the child's school .

I visited one of the shelters soon after becoming a juvenile judge. The cozy, neat atmosphere I experienced carried over to the kids I talked to, most of whom had never known structure, mealtime without TV, lights out, and help with homework. They appreciated the routine. Some didn't want to leave. But the shelters are funded only for temporary stays while families are engaged to help resolve the conflict.

Jane observes that kids are growing more complicated each year. "Over fifty percent of the kids in our shelters are on psychotropic medication," she says. "The mental health needs of the kids are severe. Many have been diagnosed with a learning disability or mental illness; most report being depressed and having used illicit drugs. Some have been physically aggressive to family."

Jane is up to the task of adjusting her policies, programs, and funding sources to meet the needs of more complicated kids. She has received local, state, and national awards for her service, beginning with a Susan B. Anthony NOW Award in 1983, a Florida Network of Youth and Family Services Board Member of the Year Award in 1998, and an Executive Leadership Award of Excellence from the National Network for Youth in 2003.

New York, California, and Florida serve the largest numbers of homeless and runaway youths. "Our first obligation," Jane says, "is to get them back home. However, we often deal with lockouts and throwaways as well as runaways. The parents don't want these kids, or at least not at this time. We get referrals from the schools, from law enforcement, and, because we've been in business so long, we get referrals from some of the kids whose relatives we sheltered years ago as teens. It's generational. Family Resources employees staff our juvenile assessment center, looking for status offenders to keep from further juvenile justice involvement."[3]

What do the kids and caregivers say about these shelters?

"Devin and I moved to Florida a few years ago," said Judy, the grandmother of the child her son abandoned. "His mother has abused alcohol and drugs for as long as I've known her. She surrendered his custody to me. I purchased a mobile home with my savings, and together Devin and I fixed it up. Unfortunately, I've been plagued by illness over the past several years. I have a nervous system disorder and osteoporosis. It has weakened me to the point where I have broken thirteen bones in the past nine years. I would love to be working and self-sufficient again, but it is not a reality until I can recover.

"Several months ago, our world began to fall apart. Devin and I were forced to live on one hundred eighty dollars a month. My mobile home was foreclosed upon, and most of our possessions were stolen. We lived with friends and in my car until we came upon the kind folks at Family Resources. Devin was placed in their SafePlace2B shelter," a short-term residence for children between the ages of ten and seventeen. "That's when we found out about the Family Resources Kinship Care program. The counselors at Kinship Care became advocates for us. They've helped me find an affordable apartment, and they have worked tirelessly to help us receive benefits, medical care, and legal assistance. I don't know what we would have done without them.… Had it not been for Family Resources, I might have lost Devin to the foster care system."

Fifteen-year-old Jasmine had a different take. Placed in the shelter by her father for repeatedly breaking her curfew, she told the counselor:

Sometimes I wish I never came here, sometimes I wish I wouldn't have betrayed my dad's trust. But if I didn't come here, then I wouldn't have found out how much I really need my mom. Being here made me realize that I shouldn't take my mom for granted. Some of the people that came here didn't have moms, and here I have one, but

I'm choosing not to speak to her. I listen to their stories about how they wish their moms were still here and what they would do to be able to tell their moms that they love them. Some of the stories the girls told me made me laugh and some made me cry. When they were exchanging stories, I sat back and listened because I felt really bad, 'cause here I am with a mom that I'm choosing not to speak to, and these girls don't have a mom.

I realized that I should spend all the time I can with my mom before she is gone permanently. I'm not gonna forget what she did to me, but I'm gonna try to forgive her and make the best of it. I haven't spoken to her in almost two years until the other day when I called her. Being here made me come to my senses. I'm not gonna take my mom for granted. Some young women don't have their moms to talk to or whatever. I'm glad that I came here, 'cause now I have my mom back in my life.

And Michael, age seventeen, who sought Family Resources on his own:

I'm going to explain to you how the shelter and counseling have changed my life. There are three examples that I can give you. The first example is that the shelter has helped me to be social, because I was very antisocial when I came here. The second example that I'll give you in the shelter, through counseling, is my anger management. The last example is the shelter has taught me to act as a team member in the chores, room, and all the group activities, to get them completed in an orderly and neat manner. The reasons I have for becoming social are: sleeping and living with two other roommates, and coexisting with nine other people, not including the counselors and youth care workers. Other reasons are groups such as life skills group, hobby hour group, and goals group. There are also a couple of reasons for me controlling my anger. These reasons include counseling, individual therapy, group therapy, etc. All these reasons have helped change my life in many different ways. I hope that by reading this, other people with the same problems can get the help they need to change.[4]

Jane has obtained federal grants to fund group homes for older foster kids; those transitioning into independent living arrangements. Most "graduate" into long-term stable housing, and a number actively enrolled in school receive monthly "Road to Independence" scholarships to college. Her agency also works with Alpha House, another local agency, to provide housing for pregnant teens. In addition, she's looking to purchase some foreclosed apartments to house kids who need or deserve to be emancipated prior to turning eighteen. "Some kids are more mature than their parents," Jane says. "They shouldn't have to live in a chaotic or abusive home."

Jane runs a street outreach program to find runaways. Staff members drive vans equipped with food and hygiene supplies, looking for homeless youths. They've been successful at taking them to Laundromats, where they can start a conversation over washing and folding their laundry. Many of these kids are prostituting, Jane says. "The pull of the street, the money, the drugs, is hard to fight."

Florida's approach to these children is one of the broadest in the country, winning recognition and praise. The nearly 30,000 referrals per year come from concerned individuals and family members, the schools, law enforcement, juvenile justice, and other community sources. Nearly 10 percent of the youths refer themselves.[5]

The services in Florida operate much like a hospital emergency room for troubled families and their children. The shelters provide short-term services, open seven days a week, twenty-four hours a day, for children and families in crisis. The primary goals are preserving and strengthening families; identifying critical needs that are not being met; providing referrals to specialized services; keeping youths off the streets and in school; improving school attendance, behavior, and performance; and keeping families and youths out of expensive government care if safety is not an issue.

A typical kid in need of these services is failing in school, likely years behind, and with significant truancy or behavioral issues in school. Learning disabilities and mental health issues are prevalent. Parents and family members have often given up on them; indeed, many of the parents have significant substance abuse and criminal justice issues themselves. The triage approach taken by the shelter counselors is just what these kids need.

CINS/FINS prevention and early intervention services have over a twenty-year track record of consistent positive outcomes of helping vulnerable youths and families. Florida TaxWatch, our state's preeminent budget watchdog organization, studied these services and found that CINS/FINS saves taxpayers millions of dollars each year because youths are diverted from the much more costly juvenile justice and dependency systems. Funding these services is a wise investment for any state.

Florida's network of CINS/FINS programs has received national recognition. The Office of Juvenile Delinquency and Delinquency Prevention within the U.S. Department of Justice has listed it as a "best-practice program model of care." The American Bar Association calls it a "national program model for the delivery of services to status offenders." The Vera Institute of Justice, a nonprofit organization, cites "exemplar" family-focused services, "making court a last resort."

Family Resources is partially funded by the Juvenile Welfare Board—Children's Services Council of Pinellas County, our taxing authority for programs for kids and families. As a juvenile judge, I'm a member of that board, along with our school superintendent, public defender, state attorney, a county commissioner, and six volunteers with strong records of community service. Jane appears before us in good times and bad, constantly adjusting her staff and programs to fit our community priorities and with a keen eye on which services are essential for both the youths' survival as well as improving their quality of life. Jane is always composed, flexible, and grateful for any support—a true leader and example for others to follow.

Just as Jane Addams was in her day.

CHAPTER 26

Youth Courts:
Turning Crisis into Opportunity
With Positive Peer Pressure

A JURY EQUIPPED WITH insight and power can make a real difference in an adolescent's life.

Kaylee liked cosmetics so much she couldn't wait to save the money to pay for them. Twice she was charged with shoplifting.

Tyrone set off a cherry bomb in a dry, forested area of northern California.

David and Alex spray painted graffiti on the walls of a homeless shelter.

All were found guilty by a jury. No surprise. It was the sentencing phases that were remarkable.

Kaylee's mother testified at her trial. The jury, quickly sensing the animosity between mother and daughter, recommended family counseling for the two of them, as well as restitution to the store for the unrecovered cosmetics.

In Tyrone's case, the jury recommended that he tour a local munitions facility to learn the dangers of incendiary devices. The judge helped set up the tour, and the jurors were invited to join.

David and Alex testified at their trial, and it didn't take the jury long to suspect illegal drug use. The jury recommended drug counseling and one hundred hours of community service at the homeless shelter the pair had spray painted.

Turnaround is fair play. A few months later, Kaylee, Tyrone, David, and Alex served as jurors in the same court. None of them was old enough to drive alone, vote, join the military, or buy a beer. This is youth court, one of the fastest-growing programs in juvenile justice and a shining example of restorative justice. All the jurors are teenagers. The offenders return to serve on the jury.

In her keynote speech to the National Council of Juvenile and Family Court Judges in Chicago in July 2009, Judge Judith S. Kaye advocated for "off-ramps" to keep at-risk adolescents from descending further into the juvenile justice system. Her first suggestion was to give youth courts "a twenty-first-century facelift, really starch them up, because they can be significant on several fronts.

"Youth courts," she explained, "are teen-led tribunals where young people trained in the justice system—which alone is a great benefit—actually hear low-level criminal cases involving their peers. In a typical youth court case, a young person arrested for a minor offense such as shoplifting or vandalism receives a sentence that is both punitive and restorative but avoids that first criminal conviction, which is a lifetime scar. In that sense, youth court offers a genuine second chance. Sanctions include restitution, community service, letters of apology, and links to services like tutoring and anger management workshops.

"And we're hoping to add a mentoring connection as well. No one said it better than a young woman at the Staten Island Youth Court graduation: 'Youth courts help us all realize that actions have consequences.'

"The structure of youth courts, of course, varies considerably across and even within the states, but the basic principle is the same: If peer pressure can lead young people into delinquency, then it can also keep them out of delinquency. These collaborative programs have been shown to reduce recidivism among adolescents charged with minor law violations. They're certainly worth a try."

Hundreds of judges and other juvenile justice professionals at the Chicago conference heard Judge Kaye give one of her first speeches since retiring as the chief justice of New York State. In addition to her focus on youth courts, she advocated for diverting kids short of an arrest, reworking zero tolerance, creating specialty courts, and the importance of paying attention to reentry and aftercare.[1]

I was in the audience that clapped, cheered, and gave this delightful, insightful, warm, and intelligent judge a standing ovation. I also had a special interest in youth courts, as we had one of our own, run well by Martha "Marty" Fogle and Tom Toy.

Katie Self, an elfin bundle of energy, wit, and ideas from a county just south of us, is a national youth court leader and a great help to us. Katie answered the call of the Sarasota Junior League over twenty years ago, left her stay-at-home-mom job, and grew her own career in youth court administration as the "mother" of youth courts. She and friends worked the halls of the Florida legislature and the governor's office until then governor Lawton Chiles signed a bill authorizing funding for youth courts through a fee assessment on certain traffic violations and court costs. Katie then presided over the creation of a statewide association of thirty-seven youth court programs in Florida, and in 2007 she became the first president of the National Association of Youth Courts (NAYC). By then, more than 1,000 youth court programs were operating throughout the United States, almost all of which follow her prescribed model of the youthful offender returning to sit as a juror.[2]

I didn't really understand the value and untapped potential of youth courts until I talked to Katie as well as to the two current officers of the national organization: Judge Richard Couzens and Karen Green, both of whom are from Placer County, California. Judge Couzens, who serves as president of the California Association of Youth Courts and chairman of NAYC, told me that they'd started the local program in 1990 based on a perception by many that "we just weren't getting through to first-level offenders." This is critical. Many less-informed people regard youth courts as a "soft on crime" approach. Judge Couzens, like Wansley Walters in Miami, wanted *more* accountability for misdemeanants, not just a slap on the wrist. Youth courts filled that void.

"What captured my imagination," he said, "was the opportunity for the offender to come in as a juror. That relieves the participant from feeling picked upon. The kids as jurors are amazingly perceptive. They come up with recommendations I wouldn't have thought of. Karen Green, our peer court program coordinator, becomes the defendant youth's 'probation officer' for a short period of time to make sure the sanctions are followed.

"Our recidivism rate," he noted proudly, "is less than three percent."

Although peer court participants are usually first-time misdemeanants, Judge Couzens offered an example of how even a deadly felony could be handled appropriately. The juvenile defendant, a young woman, was charged with vehicular manslaughter after the car she was driving drifted across the centerline and crashed head-on into an oncoming car, killing the other driver. She admitted she was looking at her radio and was distracted. Drugs or alcohol were not involved. The state declined to prosecute. The victim's family agreed to peer court proceedings, as they wanted closure. The defendant felt some need to exhibit remorse. The jury recommended that the defendant visit high schools to talk about the consequences of driver distraction.

A Placer County judge or volunteer lawyer presides over peer court. Members of the court serve as attorneys in a mock trial process. Victims are always included, and restitution is discussed. In the case of shoplifting, for instance, the merchants see it as more effective than the usual slap on the wrist. Program coordinator Karen Green (who, incidentally, preceded Judge Couzens as chairman of NAYC) is adept at creating meaningful community service activities that meet the county's needs, such as clearing brush from the homes of the elderly during critical fire seasons.

Both Couzens and Green spoke highly of the value of the national organization. Karen has been an educator all her life and still operates a part-time counseling service that assists high-school seniors in preparing for and selecting the right college. She has a bachelor's degree from the University of California-Davis and a master's degree from the University of La Verne and is skilled at analyzing learning disabilities and alternative ways of learning. She wrote the curriculum for the Placer County Peer Court and remained as the coordinator for years. Karen estimates that in 2008 she heard four hundred cases at an average cost of $400 per case.

Both Karen and Judge Couzens have been involved with the national organization since its founding, when Katie Self served as its charter president. With the financial support of a grant from the Office of Juvenile Justice and Delinquency Prevention and assistance from both the U.S. Department of Education and the Corporation for National and Community Service, a federal agency supporting volunteering, its membership has grown from a handful of courts to now over three hundred. It is currently striving to capture the involvement and formal membership of the approximately 1,050 youth courts in the nation.[3,4,5]

Working cooperatively with state-based youth court associations, NAYC provides technical support and training for new youth courts, enhances the quality of existing youth court operations, and seeks a greater national identity and role in creating juvenile justice policy, much as Judge Kaye recommended in her keynote speech in Chicago. One priority is upgrading communications through the www.youthcourt.net website to include more testimonials from family members, court leaders, community partners, and the young people themselves.

In early 2009, NAYC sought the expertise of Jack Levine, one of the country's best-known advocates for children. Before founding Advocacy Resources, a strategic planning consultancy, he served for twenty-five years as president of Voices for Florida's Children, a statewide advocacy organization, and helped found Voices for America's Children in the early 1980s.

Jack praised the goals and leadership of NAYC. "These folks are not at all shy about facing the reality of young people getting into trouble. They see it as their business to turn lives around, which requires rules and consequences. Above all, they understand that it's all about the legal process and accountability.

"The relationships they have built with prosecution and law enforcement are so important," he observed. "You can't send the message that this is 'kiddie court.' They don't."

Jack has worked closely with Judge Couzens, Karen Green, and their board colleagues in promoting the next stage of NAYC's achievement. "Karen Green is extremely businesslike, sticks to an agenda, and is so well balanced between strict and sensitive. Dick Couzens is very much the judge with a long gavel. If the conversation goes on too long, he'll bring down the gavel. They are terrific leaders and truly inspire the organization's members."

As a consultant, Jack worked with the organization's twenty-four-member board to develop a strategy to bring it into the national arena of juvenile justice policy making. "Good intentions do not ensure an organization's long life," said Jack. "What does is an achievable, practical strategy, grown up from the community level, and developing strong and sustaining national partnerships."[6]

Jack shared these important observations:

- Prevention is the best medicine in the youth behavior arena. A community that has the power to punish has the obligation to prevent. When it comes to youths, it's not whether we pay, it's when. Why pay for failure in deeper-end incarceration when we can invest more wisely in the success of early intervention?

- Youth courts address behaviors at the outset that, if not attended to, could eventually harm the youths, their families, or others in the community.

- Youth courts provide the first-step safety net to respond to the earliest transgression. Balance and attention to patterns of behavior are the keys.

- The peer model is the heart of youth court effectiveness. Young people are judging young people. Administrators have roles, but not as the decision makers. The model is predicated on evoking a core respect for the law. Therefore, the single most effective "buy-in" is to have the youths participate at every facet of proceedings.

- It's absolutely essential for a youthful offender to be invited back. It should almost be a mandatory aspect, as it brings the youth full circle.

- Youth courts are community driven and shaped. This is not a "cookie-cutter" concept. It's astonishing how different the courts are. As long as they adhere to basic standards, the success rate mirrors the uniqueness of the community and diversity of the youths and families.

- The salient lesson learned is that peer pressure does not always have to be negative. If it's true that practice makes perfect, you can practice to be bad or good. Youth courts give young people the opportunity to embrace and practice positive peer pressure.

Jack recently shared a podium with retired U.S. Supreme Court Justice Sandra Day O'Connor at an Arizona Youth Court Summit in Tempe. In her keynote address to an audience of 450 youths and some three dozen adults, Justice O'Connor shared her perspectives on the importance of civic engagement and her personal exposure to youth court.

"I'll tell you how I know this works," she declared with a bright smile. "My dear granddaughter served as a youth court volunteer at nearby South Mountain High School. She learned so much about how the law works and felt like she was contributing to the community in a big way. She's my trusted source to tell you keep up the great work, and I'll be glad to help in any way possible!"

And help she has, in a big way. Justice O'Connor is deeply involved in the web-based civics education organization called iCivics (www.ourcourts.org). In her travels, she's delivering the youth-empowerment messages wherever she can so that our next generation of leaders can understand the value and vitality of our three-pronged system of government. In addition, she advocates that all states adopt a formal civics education curriculum, so that all states impart knowledge of government and the importance of lifelong civic involvement. Concerned about statistics showing that 71 percent of Florida youth could not pass a basic civics test, the Florida legislature in 2010 passed the "Justice Sandra Day O'Connor Civics Education Act," thus upgrading the quantity and quality of civics education beginning in elementary school and including post-semester tests as a pre-requisite to promotion.

As Judge Judith Kaye says, youth courts teach civics as well as provide alternative sanctions. They are flexible and equipped to handle twenty-first-century youth problems. I can only imagine their bright future.

CHAPTER 27

Public Safety:
Why We Lock Up Kids,
and What Are Our Alternatives?

PICTURE THE SCALES OF JUSTICE sitting on the bench in juvenile court. Stacked on the left scale is a bunch of blocks, sacks, or bars of gold, with labels that say: "Teenage Brain," "Victim of Abuse," "Can't Control the Situation," "Acting in Self-Defense," "Failing in School," "Influenced by Bad Adults," "Untreated Mental Illness," "Uncontrolled Anger," or, simply, "A Child." On the right side is one huge block, sack, or bar of gold that says in big black letters: "Public Safety."

Absolutely, it is my duty to commit a youth to a locked-down, secure, residential facility if there is no other way to protect the public from the crimes the youth is committing. Public safety concerns trump social, psychological, and parental concerns for the child. A juvenile judge has the same obligation as an adult criminal judge to protect the public's safety. That's the first order of business. It makes sense. A community held hostage by juveniles committing crimes is not going to be interested in rehabilitating those kids.

What if the decision to commit a kid is made for the kid's own good? That's a more difficult decision, and almost never the focus in adult court. But there's not a juvenile judge in the country who hasn't used that rationale. I've done it many times, when it has seemed there was no alternative, and we have to keep them safe. "Personal safety," you might say, and it's in small type and whispered rather than shouted.

Over the years, I've come to think of commitment programs as part of a continuum beginning with probation and ending in aftercare, when the youth is released back to the community. The program itself is a chunk, albeit a large chunk, of the continuum. The work of the probation officer begins with probation supervision, continues while the youth is committed, and is critical in preparing the youth for release and aftercare. This continuum is no yellow brick road. It's a ride over a mountain road strewn with potholes, detours, sidetracks, and disinformation. Yet, if we treat probation, commitment, and aftercare separately—as individual railcars on a train track pulled by the engine that is juvenile justice—we often derail.

Probation is the easiest part for me, as I believe that I work with the finest juvenile probation officers in Florida. Chief Tim Niermann has consistently set a standard of dignity and respect for all, humane and compassionate treatment of kids, very hard work, strict enforcement of the rules, attention to detail, and innovation—even under the pressure of dwindling dollars and staff shortages. If we need a juvenile probation officer just for girls or crossover kids, he finds one. He and his special projects coordinator, Jill Gould, find the time and money for training. As a result, our probation officers don't have a "gotcha" attitude. They want the youths to succeed on probation. Karin Popkowski, Troi Owens, Shirley Darling, Pierre Connor, Jon Justison, David Remmington, Joyce Clay, Susan Hobbs, Loretta Harvey, Candy Jaynes—I could go on and on. These are just some of the fine probation officers I work with every day.

But then I went to Chicago and learned what an infusion of cash could do to enhance probation services.

HECTOR ESCALERA GREW UP in a rough Hispanic neighborhood in Humboldt Park, Chicago, running away from a chaotic home and frequently in trouble with the law. He saw his probation officers as "the enemy" until he met juvenile probation officer Carmen Casas, who kept Hector out of the Department of Corrections. Officer Casas found a family in the community to provide a stable home for Hector. He brought in community agencies for added support. "I hadn't had many people I could trust in my life," Hector reflected. "Officer Casas and the family I lived with made all the difference."

Hector graduated from the University of Illinois at Chicago as part of Project Lifeline, a scholarship program for juveniles on probation. Originally it was named for Harold Marx, a highly regarded probation officer who died in a car crash, and was administered by the Harold and Rosemarie Marx Foundation. The scholarship program is now a separate entity, Project Lifeline, for kids succeeding on probation. Hector interned with the department and was hired as a juvenile probation officer. He became the kind of officer who was "checking up on the kid to support him, not to catch him doing something wrong."

When the Robert Wood Johnson Foundation's Reclaiming Futures Initiative came to Chicago as a drug treatment model, Hector saw an opportunity. "We leveraged the funding and the community coordination that Reclaiming Futures required to get more prosocial activities for our kids. We had the money now to catch a movie with our kids, take them for dinner, a baseball game, and start a mentor program. Reclaiming Futures was a humongous jump start for these enhancements.

"Part of the relationship the probation officer should have with the kid is having fun," Hector emphasized. "There's no policy that says we shouldn't have fun. Prosocial activities like these really do produce behavior changes. It's like social work. Our partnerships encouraged the youths to build relationships in the community. We try not to meet them in the courthouse but in the community."

Hector worked with twenty-five to thirty kids in South Lawndale, a predominately Hispanic neighborhood on Chicago's West Side. "Little Village," as it's better known, is ridden with gangs and drug activity. "Until Reclaiming Futures came, there was no drug treatment in Little Village," he recalled, "and the youths would have to cross gang boundaries to get treatment. We met in small groups at churches to work on cease fire, gang prevention, drug education, and treatment. We also went out to eat a lot and to White Sox games. We worked on building a positive relationship with positive events so the kid doesn't shut down but sees the better ways of life.

"We taught them how to live in an urban setting. Our classes were always relevant to their daily lives; short—no more than twenty minutes—and powerful, using graphics, PowerPoints, blackboard illustrations. We started a Junior Advisory Council for kids on probation. Reclaiming Futures brought the resources to allow us to be creative on probation. It made all the difference," Hector said.[1]

For the youth unsuccessful on probation, commitment is the next step.

I asked Adrienne Conwell, our area's fine troubleshooter and quality-control specialist for Department of Juvenile Justice commitment programs, to provide me with a description of an ideal commitment program. Here's what she wrote:

Putting funding aside, I think we need a three-tier commitment.

The first phase would be the residential commitment where the youth would receive all the wraparound services that he/she needs. This would include the skills needed for self-sufficiency. The youth would be required to continue with his/her education to include college courses or vocational skills. An important aspect would be to wrap a service around that youth that has something to do with the youth's strength/interest. For example, if the youth likes acting, get him/her involved with something at Tampa Bay Performing Arts Center or Ruth Eckerd Hall.

The second phase would be transition, which would be located in a different living environment; a transition home. Here the youth would be required to give back to his/her community by volunteering in some aspect and repairing the harm that was caused. In addition, the youth would use the skills learned in the first phase by looking for and obtaining a job. Education would also be continued in this phase, including college or vocational programming. The youth must have a job before moving on to the third phase. All pending court-ordered sanctions can be completed in this phase.

The third phase would be independent living; a different living environment from the two above. The youth would live there, continue in school and employment, and be required to pay court-ordered restitution. He/she would also be required to save a percentage of his/her paycheck. Additionally, he/she will continue volunteering. For some youths, going home may not be an option, as that is where we lose most of our kids, back into the life of delinquency. For those youths, this phase will assist them to find an apartment for self-sufficiency.

That's an ideal commitment model. I've visited commitment programs ranging from outright dangerous and deplorable to well run, well staffed, well
furnished, and providing a good education. But I'm still disappointed with
the lack of long-range, comprehensive planning that goes into release and
aftercare.[2]

"LET'S STOP GOING TO MISSOURI," Judge Judith Kaye begged a crowd of juvenile and family court judges in Chicago in July 2009. Many people clapped
and laughed because they knew exactly what those five words meant. It
wasn't a cry to boycott Missouri but, rather, a need to bring Missouri's fine
model for residential commitment programs home to our states. "It's about
time," Judge Kaye continued. "We know *what works*, and we sure do know
what *does not* work. It's time we started to do it right at home instead of
traveling to Missouri."[3]

The results achieved by Missouri in the area of residential services for
youths are such a cliché in the industry that I feel unimaginative writing
about them; yet, no book on juvenile justice reforms would be complete
without talking about Missouri.

ABC News's *Primetime: Crime* put reporter Chris Cuomo into residences
with some of Missouri's toughest juvenile inmates. Rachel, fifteen, stole
nearly a quarter of a million dollars. A girl named Tye, seventeen, began selling prescription pills and using the drug methamphetamine at age ten, and
was first locked up at eleven years of age. In the show, Cuomo reported on
how society's so-called bad kids and juvenile predators may actually be some
of its most damaged. He heard "stunning allegations of abuse" as the kids
came to terms with their crimes and what may have led to them. So, we know
from this that Missouri isn't dealing with less criminal, less damaged kids.[4]

What is Missouri doing so right?

First, the commitment programs are nothing like prisons. I visited the
Hogan Street Regional Youth Center for high-risk boys in St. Louis, a lock-
down program run in a former Catholic school in the middle of the city.
Once we were inside the double locked doors, the facility had the atmosphere
of a boarding school—except that the boys couldn't leave. That day, twenty-
five of them were lined up on the inside stairwell to shake hands and greet us.

The boys wore their own clothes: neat jeans or slacks during the day, shorts or sweats after school; their own shirts, shoes, undergarments. In fact, laundry duty was a must unless their families brought fresh clothes during weekend visits. All were from St. Louis, so families could visit without a long drive. Engaging activities were planned for them. The boys lived in dorm rooms with bunk beds, not cells, and received instructions on how to build a "circle of peace" and diffuse arguments or escalating situations, or to call a counselor. Peer pressure seemed to work. Rewards were used to encourage good behavior: field trips, basketball competitions, and more freedom within the home. We discussed all this with them in a great room filled with books and board games.[5]

The Missouri programs are small and generally located in the youth's community. In Cuomo's report, he quoted a fourteen-year-old boy, Chris, who'd been "sentenced to the Waverly Youth Center, one of Missouri's thirty-two juvenile jails and a last-chance stop for twenty-two boys already embarked on a life of crime":

> "In my town, I was labeled the troublemaker," Chris said. "I was doing drugs and drinking every day, and I was also stealing cars."
>
> Chris says the Waverly Youth Center is nothing like a prison. "Staff are here to help you and to push you to do right," he said. "Here, everybody cares for you."
>
> The juveniles here are encouraged to solve problems with words instead of force. If one person calls a "circle," everyone must stop to discuss the issue.
>
> Only 10 percent of the kids in Missouri's juvenile jails end up in adult prison, according to Missouri Division of Youth Services. In other states, that number is as high as 40 percent.
>
> Last month, the Justice Department said inmates in New York were routinely subjected to excessive force. But in Missouri, without using confinement or prison tactics, children in the juvenile system are four times less likely to be assaulted by other inmates than in other juvenile detention programs, according to the Annie E. Casey Foundation. Additionally, they are almost never assaulted by guards or staff members.

These children also get something else not often seen in prison: hugs.

"Some of these kids come from an environment where they've never been hugged," said Kim Orear, a group leader at Waverly. "We will never replace the parent that never paid attention to them, but what we do is show them they are worthy of hugs."

The *Primetime: Crime* report was so compelling, it bears excerpting in its entirety:

The cost per child in Missouri is $50,000 a year, half the national average of other traditional juvenile programs.

"Other programs put their money into fences and isolation, cells and security hardware," said Tim Decker, director of the Missouri Division of Youth Services. "We put our money into surrounding these young people with caring adults who help them learn the kinds of skills that they're going to need to be successful."

The staff makes sure the children have daily routines of school and chores.

"You go to school, come back, do your details," said Dylan, sixteen. "If you can do it in here, then you can do it out there."

Tye, seventeen, has been in and out of detention centers and foster homes since she was two years old. She has committed multiple felonies, and was nine years old when she was arrested for the first time. "At the age of seven, I first smoked pot," Tye said. "After my father died, I was sneaking into my mother's prescription drugs... when I was in fourth grade because we didn't have hardly any food in the house...I would sell the pills. At the age of ten...that was the first time I ever shot meth, smoked meth, and did cocaine."

For Tye, who was sentenced to the Rosa Parks Center in Fulton, Missouri, this is her first stable environment.

"My past is all I have," Tye said. "Until I cannot hold onto the past anymore, is when I can start being happy."

Although the Missouri system may not appear to be "tough on crime," Decker argues it is. "This approach is much tougher than young people spending their time sitting in a cell," Decker said. "This is far more rigorous, and for a young person to complete this program takes a good deal of effort on their part."

Ultimately, staff members say the goal of the system is to give the children the tools they need to be successful.

"It's their choice whether they want to make those changes and implement them on the outside," Orear said.

The giant steps to the Missouri process, as told to us at Hogan Street, were state reforms and a shift in philosophy, regionalization, an array of services, program planning from within as a group, education, and training. A change from correctional to rehabilitative, and engaging the community.

The results are compelling: 87 percent received a satisfactory discharge; the recommitment rate was only 7.3 percent; 20 percent of the inmates achieved a GED or diploma prior to discharge (this seemed low to me); 70 percent progressed faster than their public school peers in core subjects; 70 percent were successful three years out of a program—meaning that they did not enter the adult system—and only 26 percent sustained an injury during their three years in the programs.

The lessons learned, Tim Decker and his staff told us, were invaluable. To change a system, you must change the culture.

Recently, some states have accepted the challenge, and they are seeking to reform somewhat along the Missouri model. California's effort to overhaul juvenile corrections gained steam in 2002 when a class action suit was filed "charging that the state's youth facilities were 'deplorable' and 'draconian,'" according to a *Wall Street Journal* report of October 12, 2009:

Facing the possibility of stiff penalties and of having to pay high costs for facility upgrades, the state settled the case in 2004 and agreed to hire new staff, adhere to certain standards, and allow inspectors to monitor progress in all state facilities.

Since California in 2007 began rolling out its efforts to shift more low-level juvenile prisoners to counties, the state has closed two of its largest youth-inmate facilities and cut its juvenile-inmate count to about 1,600 from about 3,000, the Division of Juvenile Justice said. The move has saved the state more than $100 million....

A recent report by the nonprofit Center on Juvenile and Criminal Justice also found that the changes resulted in many youthful inmates having better living conditions, increased behavioral counseling, and improved access to their families.

Overall, the recidivism rate for juvenile offenders in California communities that track such statistics has fallen to 25 percent from nearly 35 percent since 2007, according to the Chief Probation Officers of California, an industry association. California's juvenile crime rate also declined between 2007 and 2008, with violent offenses committed by juveniles falling 3 percent in that period, the state Department of Justice reported.[6]

Juvenile justice leaders in Ohio have studied the Missouri system and have pointed out a few pitfalls: The Missouri model focuses half of its resources on lower-risk youths, doesn't accept youths over the age of sixteen, and provides services in the community and in smaller facilities, limiting the ability to provide specialized services to a larger population farther from home.

Texas revamped its entire criminal justice system because it couldn't afford to build more prisons. The state added substance abuse and mental health beds, short-term residential and outpatient programs, and programs to reduce probation violation, combat recidivism, and parole more eligible prisoners. (Florida abolished parole for crimes committed after 1983, a "tough on crime" move.) The Texas experiment may be instructive for juvenile and adult corrections nationwide.

Florida reforms are hard to analyze and haphazard, with large programs closing—perhaps to save money—some children being moved closer to home, and Girl Matters programming more prevalent, but with no clear statement yet on adopting a more progressive model.

New York and Florida have been in the news recently for investigations of some of their residential commitment programs. At the Lansing Residential Center, Louis Gossett Jr. Residential Center, Tryon Residential Center, and Tryon Girls Secure Center, all located in New York State, violations were found by the U.S. Department of Justice in areas such as overuse of restraints, abuse by staff, and insufficient mental health treatment and behavioral management services. On August 14, 2009, a thirty-one-page report prepared by Acting Assistant Attorney General Loretta King was sent to Governor David A. Paterson.[7]

In Florida, the *St. Petersburg Times* ran a series of articles in 2009 detailing the abuses that took place at the Dozier School for Boys fifty years ago—charges brought by men who called themselves the White House Boys. The men wanted assurance that the facility had put an end to the abuse they had endured, which included beatings that left them bloody and kids gone missing without explanation; abuse they said ruined their sleep, wrecked their marriages, and destroyed their lives. The investigation revealed an ongoing pattern of abuse for the 130 boys housed at Dozier—not as violent as what the White House Boys had experienced, but still intolerable. Boys were still threatened by guards who then left them unsupervised and feeling unsafe. The program was short on nurses and trained staff.

Governor Charlie Crist called the failure to keep the boys safe "inexcusable." The superintendent resigned amid an editorial outcry to clean up the facility or shut it down. I was shocked to learn that the program cost the taxpayers $100,00 per youth committed. What I wouldn't give to have *half* that $100,000 per boy to implement prevention, diversion, education, and recreation services.[8, 9, 10, 11, 12, 13, 14, 15]

In 1975, Kenneth Wooden wrote the landmark expose of America's incarcerated children, *Weeping in the Playtime of Others*. The foreword to the second edition, published in 2000, was written by Kathleen M. Heide, a criminology professor at the University of South Florida and an expert on juveniles who commit homicides. In the foreword, Dr. Heide said that the book, "unlike any other I have assigned in two decades of teaching, has moved my students to compassion."

> When I tell them the conditions that Wooden wrote about still exist, they struggle against believing me. I quote from a November 1998 investigative report issued by Amnesty International. This report, entitled *United States of America: Rights for All—Betraying the Young*, echoed Wooden's observations in the early 1970s.

Even within the juvenile justice system, children's well-being is often placed at risk rather than being protected. Thousands of children are placed in custody when other action could or should have been taken—a ten-year-old boy handcuffed, arrested and locked up for allegedly kicking his mother; a thirteen-year-old girl detained on suspicion of possessing marijuana, which turned out to be oregano. Many facilities are seriously overcrowded and unable to provide adequate mental health and other important services that children need and to which they are entitled. Staff has subjected children in custody to brute physical force and punishments, including placing them in isolation for lengthy periods. In one case reported to Amnesty International, a boy was held in isolation for over a year.

In the last chapter of *Weeping in the Playtime of Others,* Wooden provides a blueprint for change. He sets out thirteen objectives for making juvenile corrections what its founders envisioned a century before—an organizational structure designed to help misguided, troubled, victimized, and neglected youths become decent, law-abiding, and contributing members of society. He proposes a Bill of Rights for Children to ensure a basic level of care so that the number who make poor choices is drastically reduced. As we enter the millennium, it is time to heed Wooden's call and embrace what the Child Savers of the twentieth century knew to be true. Children are our hope and our future.[16]

In the preface to his book, Ken Wooden quoted a poem written in 1951 by the African American writer Langston Hughes. It burned into my conscience as I look at committed kids:

What happens to a dream deferred?
Does it dry up
Like a raisin in the sun?
Does it fester like a sore—
And then run?
Or does it explode?

I asked Ken Wooden what he would recommend today. He referred me to a *New York Times* editorial of April 9, 2009, calling on Congress to fix the problems in juvenile facilities that were supposed to have been eliminated in 1974, like locking up "status offenders" such as truants and runaways, who hadn't committed crimes. He also congratulated Congress for introducing legislation to resurrect the White House Conference on Children and Youth.

"The conference had been held since 1910, until the Carter administration postponed it, and the Reagan administration cancelled it in 1980, instructing agency employees to use the official stationery for scrap paper. We've had thirty years of nonpresidential leadership for children's justice. It's time that changed."

Ken and his daughters now travel as consultants, trying to reduce the incidence of sexual crimes against youth. Their sex-lures and teen-lures prevention programs have been introduced in middle schools and high schools and to educators in their home state of Vermont and throughout the country. They address timely issues such as peer-to-peer abuse, cyber bullying, self-exploitive sexting, and Internet luring, as well as how to educate adults on how to educate children to resist the lures of sex predators.[17, 18]

AFTERCARE IS THE LAST PART of the continuum that begins with probation and moves through commitment. This is an exciting area, because one state—Pennsylvania—gets it absolutely right. In 2009, Joe Clark, CEO of the Eckerd Family Foundation, and I attended a juvenile justice seminar put on by Shay Bilchik at Georgetown University, and we were both wide-eyed at the presentation made by juvenile justice leaders from Pennsylvania.

In a nutshell, Pennsylvania's elected officials, from the top down, and the agencies that work with children have committed to a statewide collaborative effort to identify and plan for aftercare from the moment the youth is committed. All counties in Pennsylvania have signed on to the collaborative, which essentially is a giant "staffing" of the youth's educational, medical, psychological, psychiatric, and social needs, upon entry into the program and upon release—a smooth transition back into the community with a full assessment of what needs to be done for a successful outcome.

In April 2008, Candace Putter was appointed director of the Pennsylvania Academic and Career/Technical Training Alliance (PACTT), an initiative of the Pennsylvania Council of Chief Juvenile Probation Officers. She has considerable experience in policy and program design for work with delinquent youths. She managed the collaborative effort to improve the continuum of services for youths returning to the community from delinquent residential placement. She has also worked at the local and state levels to implement balanced and restorative justice into aftercare.

This effort by Pennsylvania to accept "ownership" and responsibility for a youth from commitment through aftercare, and to plan accordingly, is very different from what happens in most states. For example, probation typically drives the plan. "Probation is the bus," says Ms. Putter. This is a "radical transformation," says Bob Schwartz, executive director of the Juvenile Law Center. "One probation officer does both, like a case manager, planning at the beginning of commitment for aftercare." Tremendous emphasis is put on high-quality, appropriate education in the program, which is followed up upon reentry in collaboration with the schools. It is too soon to evaluate success, calculate costs, or analyze recidivism. Juvenile justice reformers all over the country will be watching Pennsylvania's results.[17]

Indianapolis has a fine reentry program that targets "the dangerous first three months."

Washington, D.C., began an aftercare program smaller in scale than the Pennsylvania model but very successful. Youths released from commitment enter an afterschool program that provides counseling, tutoring, computer labs, drug testing, and recreation in central locations away from their neighborhoods or schools. After school, program counselors pick up the youths in vans to transport them to aftercare. They are kept busy, fed, counseled, and encouraged to stay crime free.

Recreation. That was the solution Mark Friedman found for so many problems with at-risk youths, as he recommends in his book *Trying Hard Is Not Good Enough*. Certainly, in aftercare, that's a winner.

Crossover killer Leo Boatman's journey as a juvenile across the continuum of foster care, commitment, and aftercare highlights the abject failures of the system. He was never given a meaningful opportunity of probation and thus never had the guidance of a probation officer, even at age twelve. His residential commitment experiences consisted mainly of warfare between Leo and the staff, while his aftercare program was minimal: He was given a handshake and $20 by the chaplain, who left him outside his sister Rosie's apartment. Nevertheless, he had obtained a high-school diploma in commitment. And, for a short period of time, he took part in a brand-new program for foster kids aging out of state care that paid for college courses and provided a stipend.

I wonder whether a good aftercare program could have prevented the tragedy that took place in the Ocala National Forest.

CHAPTER 28

Solving the DMC Problem: A Case Study in Florida

DISPROPORTIONATE MINORITY contact is the overrepresentation of minority youths in the juvenile justice system, higher than their percentage of the population.

How do we fix this? The honest answer is that I don't know. We haven't done it yet.

In the nine years that I've been a juvenile judge, our court, schools, local juvenile justice officials, and county have partnered in many respects. We've brought an effective truancy magistrate program into the middle schools; developed a protocol and effective counseling for children and parents with domestic violence issues; enhanced opportunities for foster care youths and provided better legal representation; diverted hundreds of first-time offenders from having an arrest record; dedicated probation units to girls and to foster children; implemented a Girls Mission Possible calendar for alternative sanctions for girls; and provided continued support to our fine Behavioral Evaluations program and the three dedicated child psychologists assisting the judges.

Yet, we haven't made a dent in the numbers of young black males, ages thirteen to seventeen, who appear before me. On any given day, if you sit in my court, well more than half the cases involve black male teenagers charged with stealing cars; burglarizing houses; snatching purses, iPods, and cell phones; using and selling drugs; carrying firearms; and being involved with

236 · RAISED BY THE COURTS

gangs. The school-to-prison pipeline is as bad for them as it was nine years ago for the night swimmers you read about in chapter 1.

Just last week in court, I faced fifteen black boys, half of whom were in custody, the others with family or relatives. Two girls appeared on minor matters. None of the children was white. I've been called a racist for incarcerating so many black youths, and "Judge Hug-a-Thug" for failing to incarcerate black youths.

I'm saddened and feel a sense of failure.

We discussed the disproportionate minority contact issue a lot during Blueprint Commission hearings. Later I joined a DMC task force established by the Department of Juvenile Justice. I attended meetings in Tallahassee and locally, organized by the department's very capable Rhyna Jefferson, and heard speakers such as the eloquent DMC expert Dr. Randy Nelson and the passionate Dale Landry, NAACP chairman in Tallahassee. We kept asking and asking and asking why there are so many young black men in the system.[1]

"Adoration of the question," I learned it was called. Asking and asking and asking. We never really made any changes. And it's still very difficult to talk about race.[2]

During Blueprint Commission hearings, I quickly gained respect for Barbara Cheives from West Palm Beach, a diversity trainer and consultant on DMC and other personnel issues with Converge & Associates Consulting. She is extremely active in community affairs and has been honored many times for her civic involvement. Shrewd, astute, diplomatic, and articulate, Barbara seemed to be someone we could count on to deliver a true picture of the depth of the DMC problem and what it would take to fix it.[3]

She wasn't afraid to tell stories about herself, the commission found out the day of its meeting in Jacksonville. Barbara shared with us an experience she'd had that morning, when she walked into a nearby diner for breakfast. It was the morning after Atlanta Falcons football player Michael Vick had been sentenced to prison for his role in a dog-fighting ring.

Barbara was the only woman and the only black person in the diner. When she sat down at the counter, a man with a newspaper in hand said to her, loud enough to include all the other men in the diner, "So what do you think of Michael Vick now?"

"Do I look like a football player?" Barbara asked us as she retold the story. "A person who runs dog fights? A man? No. The only thing I have in common with Michael Vick is that we both are black. That's why he asked me that question."

Barbara's story made me think a lot, as did my work with the fine people on the Blueprint Commission. My eyes had been opened a little more. But I still didn't have anything close to an answer to the DMC problem to include in this important chapter. So I turned again to Barbara. I asked her to simply "rant" about the DMC issue in any way she saw fit, as if we were having a conversation over coffee or a glass of wine. She sent me an email that I found remarkable in its insight, honesty, frustration, and angst. It's a gem. She allowed me to share it, just as she wrote it.

Until I sat on the Blueprint Commission, I wondered why *they* couldn't do something to keep our young men, particularly young men of color, from committing crimes and out of the system. So often, or most often, those crimes are against other people of color. Now I've spent a year on the Blueprint and over a year doing DMC training around the state. I train law enforcement officers in cultural competency. I am the new chair of the Palm Beach County Criminal Justice Commission. I now realize that *I* am *they* and I have no idea what to do. [*This was Barbara's "Aha!" moment.*]

As a cultural-competency and race-relations professional, I was once publicly chastised for referring to young black men in the black community as *my* community. The person felt that I was being separatist. I, however, feel a need to take ownership. Because of that, my comments may be specific to African American children, but most of it crosses over to other children of color. I never had children, but I know that parents do the best they can. Unfortunately, many black parents of today *can't.*

My church is the oldest black Baptist church in West Palm Beach and sits in the heart of the "hood." Of course, like in most cities, that hood was once a very respectable black community. Black professionals have moved to areas where they were unable to live back in the day, and the old community is now low income, crime ridden, "blighted," and long the subject of unfinished revitalization efforts. This is part of the community targeted for our version of the Harlem Children's Zone. I really believe that until the government, law enforcement, civic organizations, the education system, and the church join forces, things will never change. Each of these entities has to accept a portion of the responsibility, and they have to offer much more than lip service and perfunctory motions. We have to collectively mean it.

"Where are the parents?" That's the first comment folks make. Well, the parents are too young, too poor, too uneducated to make a difference. They have grandmas raising many of the kids, while moms are unable because they are working or on drugs or in jail along with the dads. Or only gave birth so that they'd have someone to love them and then quickly got bored with the whole motherhood thing when they realized it was cramping their party style. And the grandmas weren't ready or able back when they had their kids, and they still aren't.

Role Models or lack thereof:

- 6 percent of the doctors in America are black.
- Less than 4 percent of the lawyers in America are black—what must that say about the judges?
- The percentage of black police officers rarely mirrors the community's population.

To what do they aspire?

Well, there's sports, as 61 percent of NCAA (National Collegiate Athletic Association) Division I college basketball players are black! Of course, we know that black basketball and football players far outnumber white players even in the pros. But how many young people will actually be selected as one of the fifteen players on a professional basketball team or the fifty-three on an NFL team? And of the ones that don't make it, how many actually got an education while they were in school? Not making the team is often their first big life failure, and they have nothing to fall back on.

And then there's music—or rap, *if* that's music. It often appears that we are taking steps backward. The images on TV and the lyrics to the music are certainly not helping. I would love to have BET television and the NBA players fund our local efforts to reduce disproportionate minority contact.

There are the rare cases of a cop or teacher or neighbor who became a mentor and saved the child from the streets. The biggest problem with that is that the child still goes home to the threats and temptations of the neighborhood. Of course, I believe that prevention is the answer, but given our current state, we have to up the prevention efforts to save the ones who have not committed crimes *and* make enormous strides with the youth and families already in trouble. If we don't, they will never get out of trouble and will go deeper into the system.

I have several very Utopian solutions. One is a version of our Palm Beach County Sheriff's Office Eagle Academy. This is a military boot camp–style alternative for at-risk kids. It's voluntary; we must have agreement from kids and parents. I say a *version*, because this is a short stay—six months, generally, with three months after-care. I'd love to see this program model expanded and have it be a four- to six-year military school. I imagine an amazing sense of pride among the students. It would also need to open to kids whose families may not be willing to participate.

The other dream I have is family-to-family mentoring. My church is actually just beginning to look at this: having successful families work with problem families or families that just have no clue how to parent. We also need job training for parents (and most folks really do want to work) and guaranteed employment, especially for offenders. Tutoring for the kids. Bankers training them in finances. Here's where it becomes a dream; many people just can't change in their current environments. We renovate neighborhoods, try scattered site revitalization, and build new "projects." It hasn't worked. I submit that we have to move the entire family out of the community and give them constant mentoring and support for as long as it takes. It's a dream, because how many of us can devote the time and resources?

But we have to have radical solutions to make a dent, and it has to be one family and one child at a time.

There also has to be a way to meet them where they are. If music is their thing, can we put lesson plans to music? Can community service mean that you have to learn a skill? Can we update the "scared straight" methods, using ex-offenders as mentors?

There was the hope that an Obama presidency would make all the difference. Well, the White House is *so* out of reach for the folks we're talking about that it has no meaning. They need to see the folks that found a way out coming back to tell them and *show* them how they did it before they can aspire to things that may seem way out of reach.

We *must* keep kids in school and get them to college or to technical training. A path to potentially high-paying jobs is the only way to stop the street methods of getting paid.

We *must* close the digital divide.

We *must* deglamorize the "thug life."

We *must* stop these young girls from having more babies.

We *must* get these kids and their families to work.

And somehow we *must* get *us* to reinvest in our "hoods." We, as black people, have to remember that but for the grace of God, we could be where these families are, and our kids could be in the system. Many of us have the ability to hire, train, mentor, tutor, and encourage, and it is incumbent upon us to do just that.

White America, on the other hand, has to realize that I am not talking about *all* black youths. Police officers, teachers, and potential employers have to recognize that a young man with dreads might just be making a fashion statement. They have to let go of the fear that young black men will steal, and the doubt that they can succeed and even excel. This is all a function of training and exposure. I am working on a project in Pahokee to have a retreat with kids and deputies to demystify the perceptions they have about one another.

The discrimination factor...Haitian and Hispanic youth have made their own serious inroads into the system. Asian and Middle Eastern kids are not far behind. There is another piece that we need to look at. When a group of people is made fun of, ostracized, marginalized, and generally discriminated against, they develop myriad defense mechanisms. For the young folks, it's acting out, which often leads to criminal behavior. I would be remiss if I didn't add that we have to work to understand racial ethnic issues, behaviors, and norms in order to help the kids. There is no "one size fits all" in juvenile justice any more than there is in diet, clothing size, or housing.

Thank you, Barbara. Not only couldn't I have said it better, I couldn't have even said it.

IN FEBRUARY 2010, I was invited to be a commentator on a DMC panel organized by the University of Florida. The academic credentials and intellectual approach of the panel were outstanding. Professor Kenneth B. Nunn, from the University of Florida's Levin College of Law, argued that the "features of group oppression lead to crime areas, community instability, poverty, and family dysfunction." Professor James Forman from Georgetown Law School, and a scholar in residence at New York University Law School from 2009 to 2010, focused on what happens when African Americans are in charge, such as in Washington, D.C. It's not much different politically than when controlled by white folks, he concluded, as the black middle class is equally skilled at oppressing those living in poverty. In fact, under black political leadership, and blacks dominating law enforcement and the courts, sentences handed down to black defendants are twice the national average.[4]

Professor Theresa Glennon from the Beasley School of Law at Temple University in Philadelphia hit the nail on the head when she referred to African American boys as "the canaries in the mines of the public school systems. Public school fails to graduate thirty percent of their students and almost one-half of African American male students." She argued that zero tolerance and No Child Left Behind policies have widened the racial divide by prioritizing high-stakes testing above other teaching methods, leaving behind millions and "widening the racial divide" by ignoring kids who can't take the high-stakes test pressure due to poverty, family dysfunction, or special needs.

My friend Dr. Randy Nelson was the last panelist, and I wasn't surprised to hear his gloomy assessment of the failure of so many black boys in their teens. He narrowed Florida's delinquency problem to 75 percent males, most of them black and most raised by single parents, usually moms. We haven't found the answer, Dr. Nelson said. He and I agree that we need to move from asking why to looking for solutions.

On the next panel, Khary Lazarre-White did just that. As executive director and cofounder of the Brotherhood/Sister Sol program in New York City's Harlem neighborhood, Khary moved beyond the "What causes this?" question to a practical, evidence-based solution. He and his team "work on prevention every day," he explains. "We are seeking to prevent the negative outcomes of black youth by holistic intervention. We're trying to stop them from entering the criminal justice system, or if it happens, to make sure it happens only once."

The statistics tell what they were up against. In 1995, for example, when his program began, most of the prison population in New York State came from seven neighborhoods in New York City, including Jamaica, the South Bronx, and Harlem. Khary and his team created "not an afterschool program but a way of life for black and Latino youth who are surrounded by poverty, drugs, violence, racism, classism, and miseducation." He talks directly about the fact that "ninety-three percent of the drugs in New York City move through a one-mile square radius in West Harlem. In that area, the average income for a family of four is twenty-four thousand dollars. The male high-school graduation rate is about thirty-three percent; the dropout rate for all kids is fifty-eight percent. Some eighty percent of the kids are from single-parent homes, three-fourths black and one-fourth Latino. Everyone fears the police, as a half million stops were made, with only six percent arrested."

Khary's program intervenes with "long-term support, love, and guidance, for as many as ten years, 24-7. It includes college tours beginning in seventh grade, international study, employment interviews, sex education, and an emphasis on personal responsibility.

"It's a way of life," he says. "No parental interview, no fee, gang members welcome as well as the straight and narrow." The program is funded by major national foundations and has been recognized by the *New York Times*, the New York State Education Department, and the Ford Foundation for "changing the world."

Evidence-based outcomes? Yes, 88 percent of Brotherhood/Sister Sol alumni graduated from high school, and fewer than 2 percent had a child before graduating. No alumni are incarcerated, and fewer than 1 percent are on parole. Some 95 percent are working full-time or are in college, and not one is addicted to drugs.

When questioned about the program's $7,000 annual cost per kid, Khary asks, "Is it worth it to spend $7,000 to replicate the program and get these outcomes, or $100,000 per year to go through the juvenile justice system and incarcerate a kid?"

In December 2009, I attended the practitioner's institute at the Harlem Children's Zone with others from our Juvenile Welfare Board, our local children's services council. Under the strong and progressive leadership of our executive director, Gay Lancaster, we are looking to create a children's initiative in our county using some of the extraordinary programs created by Geoffrey Canada and the Harlem Children's Zone.

In his book *Reaching Up for Manhood: Transforming the Lives of Boys in America,* Canada explores the adolescent boy's state of mind:

> More and more, I have become concerned with what boys think they should be, with what they believe it means to be a man. Our beliefs about maleness, the mythology that surrounds being male, has led many boys to ruin. The image of male as strong is mixed with the image of male as violent. Male as virile gets confused with male as promiscuous. Male as adventurous equals male as reckless. Male as intelligent often gets mixed with male as arrogant, racist, and sexist. If we look around and see too many men in jail, on drugs, abandoning their families, acting without compassion, or even violently, we as a society must shoulder the blame and take responsibility for change. Boys find themselves pulled and tugged by forces beyond their control as they make the confusing and sometimes perilous trip to manhood. Some lose their way. While reaching up for manhood, they tumble over a moral and ethical precipice, and many can never scale their way back up. We must all spend more time trying

to understand what happens to boys—and how we can shape them into better men.[5]

Canada, delivering the keynote address at the University of Florida conference, asserted, "Poor children fail because adults let them fail. You have to rebuild a community. You can't have people living in places that are terrible for kids. They might survive through rodents or street shootings, but they won't have an education or a job."

His message crosses racial lines. He speaks about instilling hope in disadvantaged, at-risk youths: hope that they will get out of the ghetto, hope that they will find a job, hope that they will go to college, hope that they won't see another drive-by shooting or be killed in a drug deal.

Kids without hope commit crimes. Kids with hope can grow up to be anything—even president of the United States.

Closing Argument:
Members of the Jury

N EARLY A CENTURY AGO, on November 26, 1924, the League of Nations adopted this Declaration of the Rights of the Child:

1. The child must be given the means requisite for its normal development, both materially and spiritually.

2. The child that is hungry must be fed, the child that is sick must be nursed, the child that is backward must be helped, the delinquent child must be reclaimed, and the orphan and the waif must be sheltered and succored.

3. The child must be the first to receive relief in times of distress.

4. The child must be put in a position to earn a livelihood, and must be protected against every form of exploitation.

5. The child must be brought up in the consciousness that its talents must be devoted to the service of its fellow men.

Over fifty years ago, on November 20, 1959, the United Nations General Assembly adopted a much-expanded version as its own Declaration of the Rights of the Child, with ten principles in place of the original five. This date has been observed as the Universal Children's Day.[1]

Are these principles as important, relevant, and necessary today as they were a century ago?

To help you decide, I gathered a focus group of five nationally recognized juvenile justice experts for a conference call recorded by Stetson University College of Law. You've met them all: Barbara Cheives of Converge

& Associates Consulting; Joe Clark, president of the Eckerd Family Foundation; Jack Levine, who's been involved in children's policy for more than thirty years; Roy Miller, head of the Children's Campaign; and Dr. Scott Sells, founder of Parenting with Love and Limits (PLL). I invite you to listen in:[2]

Roy Miller: "I thought maybe at the beginning, before getting down in the weeds—and I don't say that derogatorily—maybe we should start at a high level, focusing on the state of advocacy, what is going on in the state legislatures, the halls of Congress, what we need to do to accomplish our mission. How does that relate to public policy, Jack?

Jack Levine: "What I've learned over the decades is that those who are most in the conversation have a stake in the conversation. We have to bring in other voices, including businesses and philanthropy. Joe, you are a prime example, but there aren't enough Joe Clarks, and there aren't enough Eckerd Family Foundations. There is influence and power among the business coalitions and philanthropists. I haven't heard many business voices talking about the cost-ineffectiveness of unnecessary incarceration. I have not seen sustained efforts to build the base of support for juvenile justice reform among community opinion leaders who are affiliated with business organizations."

Joe Clark: "I agree wholeheartedly with Jack, and I learned so much when Roy and I worked together and went around the state with the Blueprint Commission. We really heard the same thing. Everyone knew what the problem was. We were able to articulate sources that no one could really disagree with, but nothing happened, or it happens very slowly. Why is that? Why is it so difficult to promote change? Clearly, we don't have the right voices yet. Business is a very important voice to add. I'm encouraged that Barney Bishop spoke at a conference in Tampa. As CEO of Associated Industries of Florida, he said that prison building is not producing good results and is negatively impacting our workforce. This is the kind of message we need to influence our policy makers. There are principles that business understands that we have to incorporate into our juvenile justice systems if we are going to see the kind of change we want to have happen."

Barbara Cheives: "Two things jump out at me. Palm Beach County has worked hard with the Florida Department of Corrections and its secretary, Walter McNeil, to be a model reentry site for prisoners returning to the community. The toughest piece of that is introducing to the business community the need to employ folks coming out of prison. They are federally funded to serve, and the community still doesn't get it. Palm Beach County sends 1,200 to 1,400 people to prison each year, and we get them back, although one of our mayors says, 'We aren't inviting them back, are we?' Also, about fifteen years ago, our state attorneys began direct-filing the first generation of kids to adult court and prison. They are in their thirties now, soon due to be released—a returning workforce the business community needs to address. It's a huge issue."

Dr. Scott Sells: "In my background as a social worker and family therapist, I began to see juvenile justice as a stuck system, like I see when working with a stuck family. There are so many parallel processes. You have to work with the juvenile justice system just as you have to work with the family. You have to help both see every aspect of resources, overcoming barriers and resistance. You have to be a partner and say, 'Let's think about this as a wraparound piece. How are we going to get funding? How are we going to treat this more like a business? What have we done that has not worked?' When you go the extra mile, just like you did with the family, and you meet with the stakeholders and the partnership, the whole system begins to change."

Roy: "It sounds as if we need a mental health professional for every part of the juvenile justice system. I'm wondering if we are in a stalemate. It seems like in juvenile justice, we have very powerful forces, because it is so tied up with the courts, and there are balance-of-power issues between the executive, legislative, and judicial branches. Even within the courts, you have balance-of-power issues between public defenders, state attorneys, and judges. At some point, someone has to give up a little power or allow some change to take place. Do you all see this? Is it a balance-of-power issue? Is that a stumbling block?"

Joe: "I think it is, but it is also a question of leadership. Leaders are the ones who know the right ingredients and stir the pot to make change happen. Where we've had success, we've had leadership. Two entrenchment issues we have are these: Why would you consistently fund a program that is ranked least effective, most expensive, year after year? It's because somebody is going to be hurt if that changes. Then, as I've learned in spades when Roy and I worked together, most of the time we are not talking about a juvenile justice problem but, rather, a community health problem that we are going to have to solve through juvenile justice."

Jack: "The sociological indicators are real and well documented. Of course, family structure is important in terms of supervision. Positive male role models affect both boys and girls. But let's not forget there is an industry called corrections. If anyone attends, as I have, the American Correctional Association convention, and visits their exhibitions hall, you'll see extraordinary displays of expensive high-tech security going into the prison system. These people don't want to empty prisons...in fact, they want more built to buy their wares. They are very well-heeled in terms of political contributions to both parties. I don't want to be negative, but I don't want to be naive either. We need to look at the reality that feeding young people into the corrections system is very profitable for some. Despite all of the research on cost-effective alternatives for youth, we need to take those powerful industry forces into account."

Barbara: "When we talk about the business community, those are the same people supporting the prison system and writing campaign checks to those who are turning their backs on the local community; because it's not their kids. Perhaps we need a revolution."

A revolution? A revolution framed by the principles of a Declaration of the Rights of the Child? What are we seeking in that revolution? What have we learned *that works* to help reclaim the delinquent child? What have our ingenuity and generous foundations put into place that we have to incorporate in public policy and government funding?

I suggest ten non-negotiable principles:

1. Adolescents with significant mental health problems should be treated in mental health facilities and not juvenile jails.

2. Every effort should be made to divert young kids and minimal offenders from the juvenile justice system into prevention, diversion, and appropriate referral services.

3. Adolescent boys and girls have extremely different needs and should receive gender-specific services.

4. At-risk kids and families should be identified as early as possible and given community services and assistance. Chronic truancy in elementary and middle school is a significant warning sign and should be addressed seriously.

5. Foster kids are especially vulnerable. The whole community needs to take ownership of them until they are adopted.

6. The schools shouldn't use juvenile justice as a dumping ground; nor can the juvenile justice system ignore the real plight of the schools in controlling misbehaving students. They must work in partnership.

7. The anger that results from exposure to violence can't be ignored and must be taken into account by all who work with juveniles. Intensive therapy must begin.

8. Kids are not short adults. Maturity levels and brain development must be considered in holding them accountable for their acts.

9. After-school activities, Big Brothers Big Sisters, Boys and Girls Clubs, Police Athletic Leagues, youth volunteerism, sports, tutoring, and mentors provide the biggest return on investment in kids. Monies must be re-directed there and away from juvenile prisons.

10. We know what works, what costs less in the long term, and what's better for kids. We don't have to experiment, speculate, or gamble. We just need the will to implement.

While writing this closing chapter, I had the pleasure of attending the Claire Flom Memorial Lecture given by Judge Judith Kaye on the education and well-being of children, sponsored by the Feerick Center for Social Justice at Fordham University School of Law in New York City.[3]

"We can't afford to continue to squander our nation's most precious resource," she said, urging a true partnership between the schools and juvenile justice and a common focus on prevention and early intervention. Then, quoting Albert Schweitzer, she added, "Success is not the key to happiness. Happiness is the key to success."

My cousin from Norway, Kjerstie Hylland, a child welfare case manager, joined me in New York. She was pleased to hear that our Florida Supreme Court had recently banned the use of handcuffs and leg restraints on children in court except for those known to be flight risks. We enjoyed the Broadway revival of *West Side Story*. While she learned about gangs—the Sharks and the Jets—I enjoyed the lyrics of "Gee, Officer Krupke," music that told us how little things have changed in fifty years:

Dear kindly Sergeant Krupke,
You gotta understand,
It's just our bringin' up-ke
That gets us out of hand.
Our mothers all are junkies,
Our fathers all are drunks.
Golly Moses, natcherly we're punks.
Gee, Officer Krupke, we're very upset.
We've never had the love that ev'ry child oughta get.
We ain't no delinquents,
We're misunderstood.
Deep down inside us there is good.
Dear kindly Judge, Your Honor
My parents treat me rough.
With all their marijuana
They won't give me a puff
They didn't wanna have me,
But somehow I was had.
Leapin' lizards! That's why I'm so bad![4]

I firmly believe that deep down inside of the kids I see in court, there is good. I firmly believe that if we can't give them the love and guidance denied to them by their parents, and if they have to create their own opportunities, we can at least replace their hopelessness with hope: perhaps poet Emily Dickenson's hope (the "thing with feathers that perches in the soul") or U.S. poet laureate Kay Ryan's hope ("the almost-twin of making-do, the isotope of going on").

In closing, ladies and gentlemen of the jury, I thank you very much, and it's been my pleasure. I'm sure we agree that all children need good families, all families need good communities, and all communities need good schools. Imagine, then they wouldn't need a juvenile judge!

ACKNOWLEDGMENTS

MY PERSONAL AND PROFESSIONAL dedication to the cause of children and their needs for justice has been influenced by many. First, many thanks to my trusted, loyal, efficient and knowledgeable judicial assistant, Jerri Evans, who spent nights, weekends, and vacations assisting me with this project. I couldn't have done it without her—not the book, nor the job.

I'm confident that it's the kids in this book and the visionary adults who've helped them, who tell this story. I became friends with many, and thank them for their service. Each of them adds so much to the goal of creating a smart juvenile justice system that keeps kids from going into prison when they become adults. To those named in the book, and others who struggle every day with juvenile justice issues, I give a major shout-out. To the kids themselves, my hat is off to you for your resilience, your good nature, and your charm, under sometimes dire circumstances.

Jennifer Parker, general counsel at the Florida Department of Juvenile Justice, suggested my name to Governor Crist for appointment to the Blueprint Commission to make recommendations to reform juvenile justice. I'm grateful, Jennifer, as that experience was enlightening and opened my eyes to the vast number of programs across the country that provide solutions for at-risk kids.

This book began with a proposal and a search for an agent. I'm grateful for the manuscript review provided by editorial consultants Gloria Kempton and Marcela Landress as well as the encouragement of my Wordsmitten.com buddies, Kate Sullivan and Denise McCabe.

After a number of rejections, I'm grateful that literary agent Claire Gerus found merit in my project. She zeroed in on Kaplan Publishing, and I've been pleased to work with my editor, Kate Lopaze, my publicist, Tim Brazier, and an incredible copyeditor, Phil Bashe, whose skills and curiosity kept me hopping trying to answer his many questions.

When you reach a certain age and have authored your first book, there are literally thousands of people to thank who've been inspirations through a lifetime: My parents, Mae and Harold Hyland; my aunt, May Butler; my brother Norman and his wife, Patti; my children, Mary Kelly, Pat and Andy; my grandchildren, Austin, Jordan, Shealyn, Andrew, and Maya; my daughters-in-law, Missy and Jennifer, and their extended De La Fuente, Heckman, and Padgett relatives, as well as the boisterous Sullivan/Ramey/Connelly clan ("proud of all the Irish blood that's in me!").

My law partners at Harris, Barrett, Mann and Dew (particularly Evelyn, D'arcy, Ken, John, Mike and Caryl) were my other family for twenty-two years, and I grew with them. My fellow judges from the Sixth Circuit Court of Florida became a new family for me twelve years ago. I learned so much from them, particularly Judges Farnell, Gross, and Quesada, who are stars in the book.

From childhood on, I've been blessed with circles of friends who've really had my back and have stayed in touch: Kristine Dahlen-Gemmill in eighth-grade confirmation class; high-school friends Phyllis, Linda, Sharon, Nancy, and Suzanne; college friends Mary, Linda, Julie, Peggy, Brack, Griff, Terry, Paula, and Dorrit; friends from early married life, like Sue, Susan, Nancy, Karen, Joy, Sharon, and Mary I; political and medical friends, such as Sandy and Maureen, a/k/a "grass and roots," as well as Krisy and Cecilia; marathon buddy Audrey; long-time St. Pete friends Sara, Judy, Mary Alice, Lynne, Meg, Ellen, Rosemary, Jeanne, Adelia, Ruth, Oona, Jane, Elaine, and Anthea; book lovers from the Bayou Book Club; and my special Colorado skiing and hiking guide, Judge Bob Nix.

Then, to Jack Levine of Advocacy Resources, my good friend and ally in advocacy, very special thanks. Jack was my muse, teacher, guide, and dedicated promoter; invaluable for his knowledge of children's issues and his connections to passionate people who work in that diverse and life-changing field.

But really, this book would not have happened without Don Sullivan and Maureen and Dermot O'Connor, who gave me the opportunity to spend half a lifetime in the wonderful, wacky state of Florida. Special love and thanks to them.

—Irene Sullivan

APPENDIX A:
PROGRAMS THAT WORK

PROGRAMS THAT WORK, as cited by Judges Jerrauld Jones and Patricia Koch in Chapter 17:

- Athletes Training and Learning to Avoid Steroids: www.preventionaction. org/reference/athletes-training-and-learning-avoid-steroids
- BASICS (Brief Alcohol and Intervention of College Students): https:// casat.unr.edu/bestpractices/view.php?program=132
- Big Brothers Big Sisters of America: www.bbbs.org
- Brief Strategic Family Therapy: www.strengtheningfamilies.org/html/ programs_1999/09_BSFT.html
- Can Problem Solve: www.sharingsuccess.org/code/eptw/profiles/es68. htm
- CASA START: casastart.org/default.aspx
- Functional Family Therapy: www.fftinc.com
- Good Behavior Game: evidencebasedprograms.org/wordpress/?page_ id=81
- Guiding Good Choices: www.channing-bete.com/prevention-programs/ guiding-good-choices
- The Incredible Years: Parent, Teacher and Child Training Series: www. incredibleyears.com
- Life Skills Training: www.lifeskillstraining.com

- Linking the Interests of Parents and Teachers: www.colorado.edu/cspv/blueprints/promisingprograms/BPP09.html

- Midwestern Prevention Project: https://casat.unr.edu/bestpractices/view.php?program=92

- Multidimensional Treatment in Foster Care: www.mtfc.com

- Multisystemic Therapy: www.mstservices.com

- Nurse-Family Partnership: www.nursefamilypartnership.org

- Olweus Bullying Prevention Program: www.clemson.edu/olweus

- Perry Preschool Project: www.highscope.org/content.asp?contentid=219

- Preventive Treatment Program: www.healthysanbernardinocounty.org/modules.php?op=modload&name=PromisePractice&file=promisePractice&pid=953

- Project Alert: www.projectalert.com

- Project Towards No Drug Abuse: tnd.usc.edu

- SAAF (Strong African American Families): www.cfr.uga.edu/projects

- Seattle Social Development Project: depts.washington.edu/ssdp

- STEP (School Transitional Environmental Program): www.ncset.org/publications/essentialtools/dropout/part3.3.09.asp

- Strengthening Families Program for Parents and Youth: www.strengtheningfamilies.org/html/programs_1999/14_SFP10-14.html

APPENDIX B:
ONLINE RESOURCES

FOR MORE INFORMATION on various organizations cited in this book and other important juvenile justice resources, please visit the following websites.

- America's Promise Alliance: www.americaspromise.org
- American Bar Association Commission on Youth At-Risk: www.abanet. org/youthatrisk
- Associated Industries of Florida: www.aif.com/home.shtm
- Barry University School of Law's Juvenile Justice Center: www.barry. edu/JJC
- Big Brothers Big Sisters of America: www.bbbs.org
- Boys and Girls Clubs of America: *www.bgca.org*
- Brotherhood-SisterSol Program in NYC's Harlem: www.brotherhood-sistersol.org
- California Youth Court Association: www.courtinfo.ca.gov/programs/collab/peeryouth.htm
- Center for Children's Law and Policy: www.cclp.org
- Center for Court Innovation: www.courtinnovation.org
- Center for Juvenile Justice Reform at Georgetown University: www. cjjr.georgetown.edu
- Center for Prevention and Early Intervention Policy at Florida State University: www.cpeip.fsu.edu

- Center on Juvenile and Criminal Justice: www.cjcj.org
- Chautauqua Institution: www.ciweb.org/about-chautauqua
- Child Lures Prevention/Teen Lures Prevention: www.childlurespreven tion.com and www.teeneluresprevention.com
- Child Welfare League of America's Juvenile Justice Division: www.cwla. org/programs/juvenilejustice/default.htm
- Coalition for Juvenile Justice: www.juvjustice.org
- Collins Center: www.collinscenter.org
- Converge & Associates Consulting: www.convergeandassociates.com
- Corporation for National and Community Service: www.cns.gov
- Drug Free America Foundation, Inc.: www.dfaf.org
- Eckerd Family Foundation: www.eckerdfamilyfoundation.org
- Evidence-Based Associates: www.evidencebasedassociates.com
- Family Resources: www.family-resources.org
- Feerick Center for Social Justice, Fordham Law School, NYC: www. law. fordham.edu/feerick-center/feerickcenter.htm
- Florida Blueprint Commission: www.djj.state.fl.us/blueprint/index.html
- Florida Department of Juvenile Justice: www.djj.state.fl.us
- Florida Legislature's OPPAGA: Office of Program Analysis of Government Accountability: www.oppaga.state.fl.us
- Florida Network of Youth and Family Services: www.floridanetwork. org
- Forum for Youth Investment: www.forumforyouthinvestment.org
- Gator Team Child: www.law.ufl.edu/centers/juvenile
- Granite Education Center, Salt Lake City, Utah: www.graniteeducation foundation.org/gef/site/default.asp
- Harlem Children's Zone: www.hcz.org
- Healthy Families Florida: www.healthyfamiliesflorida.org
- Howling Husky Homestead: www.drlindachamberlain.com

- Hull House: Chicago: www.hullhouse.org
- i Civics: www.ourcourts.org
- International Legal Foundation: www.theilf.org
- Jessie Ball DuPont Fund: www.dupontfund.org
- John D. and Catherine T. MacArthur Foundation's JIDAN Network: www.modelsforchange.net/index.html
- Justice Research Center: www.thejrc.com
- Justice Policy Institute and Annie E. Casey Foundation's JDAI Initiative: www.aecf.org/majorinitiativesjuveniledetentionalternatives initiative.aspx
- Juvenile Law Center: Philadelphia: www.jlc.org
- Juvenile Rights Advocacy Project at Boston College Law School: www. bc.edu/schools/law/jrap
- Juvenile Welfare Board of Pinellas County: www.jwbpinellas.org
- Kids Count Network (Annie E. Casey Foundation): www.kidscount. org
- Linda Ray Intervention Center: www.lindaraycenter.miami.edu/Home. html
- Miami-Dade County's Juvenile Services Department: www.miamidade. gov/jsd/releases/Juvenile_Justice_Summit.asp
- Missouri Division of Youth Services: www.dss.mo.gov/dys
- National Association of Chiefs of Police: www.aphf.org/nacop.html
- National Association of Counties: www.naco.org
- National Association of Youth Courts: www.youthcourt.net
- National Center on Addiction and Substance Abuse: www.casacolumbia. org
- National Center for Mental Health and Juvenile Justice: www.ncmhjj. com
- National Center for Missing and Exploited Children: www.missing kids.com

- National Center for School Engagement: www.truancyprevention.org
- National Child Traumatic Stress Network IC: www.nctsnet.org
- National Conference of State Legislatures: www.ncsl.org
- National Council on Crime and Delinquency: www.nccd-crc.org
- National Council on Crime and Delinquency's Center for Girls and Young Women: www.justiceforallgirls.org
- National Council of Juvenile and Family Court Judges: www.ncjfcj.org
- National Criminal Justice Reference Service: www.justicepolicy.org
- National Human Services Assembly: www.nassembly.org
- National Juvenile Court Services Association: www.njcsa.org
- National Juvenile Defender Center: www.njdc.info
- National Juvenile Justice Network: www.njjn.org
- National League of Cities: Institute for Youth, Education and Families: www.ncsl.org
- National Network for Youth: www.nn4youth.org
- National Network of Runaway and Youth Services: www.nn4youth.org
- National Sheriff's Association: www.sheriffs.org
- National Truancy Prevention Association: www.truancycourt.org
- Ocala National Forest: www.fs.fed.us/r8/florida/ocala
- Ounce of Prevention Fund of Florida: www.ounce.org
- PACE Center for Girls: www.pacecenter.org
- Palm Beach County Criminal Justice Commission: www.pbcgov.com/criminaljustice
- Palm Beach County Sheriff's Office Eagle Academy:www.pbso.org/index.cfm?fa=eagleacademy
- Parenting with Love and Limits: www.gopll.com
- Pennsylvania Academic Career/Technical Training Alliance (PACT): www.pacttalliance.org
- Ready, Willing and Unable to Serve: www.missionreadiness.org

- Reclaiming Futures Initiative Sponsored by Robert Wood Johnson Foundation: www.rwjf.org/newsroom/product.jsp?id=54769

- Suncoast Voices for Children: www.suncoastchildren.org

- Teen in Jail: www.teeninjail.com

- The Children's Advocacy Center at Florida State University College of Law: www.law.fsu.edu/academic_programs/jd_program/cac/index. html

- The Children's Campaign, Inc.: www.iamforkids.org

- The Fiscal Policy Studies Institute: www.resultsaccountability.com

- The Future of Children: www.futureofchildren.org

- The Henry and Rilla White Foundation: www.hrwhite.org

- TRACK Program of King's County (Brooklyn) District Attorney: www. brooklynda.org/track/track.htm

- Urban Institute and Chapin Hall at the University of Chicago: www. chapinhall.com

- U.S. Department of Justice: Office of Juvenile Justice and Delinquency Prevention: www.ojjdp.ncjrs.gov

- Voices for America's Children: www.voices.org

- Washington State Institute for Public Policy: www.wsipp.wa.gov

- White House Office of National Drug Control Policy: www.whitehouse drugpolicy.gov

- Youth Advocate Programs, Inc.: www.yapinc.org

- Youth Today (News Journal): www.youthtoday.org

SOURCES

OPENING STATEMENT

[1]Pew Center on the States, *1 in 31 U.S. Adults are Behind Bars, on Parole or on Probation* press release, March 2, 2009.

[2]Butts, Jeffrey A. "Whose Problem? A View from the United States." *Debating Youth Justice: From Punishment to Problem Solving.* www.kcl.ac.uk/ccjss.

[3]Hall, John. "Troubling Trends Threaten Florida's Well-Being." Florida Center for Fiscal and Economic Policy press release, July 14, 2009.

[4]Pew Center on the States. *One in 31: The Long Reach of American Corrections,* report, March 2009.

[5]*St. Petersburg Times.* "1 in 100 behind bars." Feburary 28, 2009, 4A.

[6]Guder, Petra. "European Juvenile Justice: A Brief Overview." *Juvenile and Family Justice Today,* (Summer 2009): 12.

[7]*New York Times.* "California Is Failing the Prison Test." August 27, 2009.

[8]Kaye, Judith S. "A 'New Beginning' For Adolescents in Our Criminal Justice System." *Fordham Urban Law Journal* XXXVI (June 2009).

[9]Brainy Quote. "Sandra Day O'Connor." www.brainyquote.com/quotes/authors/s/sandra_day_oconnor.html.

CHAPTER 1
The Night Swimmers

[1]Cameron-Wedding, Rita. "Disproportionate Minority Contact." Presentation to the National Council of Juvenile and Family Court Judges, St. Louis, MO, March 2008.

[2]Dyson, Michael Eric, April 14, 1968: *Martin Luther King's Death and How It Changed America,* Perseus Books Group, 2008, and *Debating Race,* Perseus Books Group, 2007.

Nelson, Randy. "Overview of Florida's DMC Data" report. 21st Century Research and Evaluations, Inc.

Palm Beach Post. "Officials Seek Ways to Cut Number of Minority Juveniles Going to Jail." February 1, 2009.

CHAPTER 2
Umatilla

[1]WFTV Orlando. "Video Shows Employee Dragging Girl Down Hallway." News segment broadcast January 6, 2006.

[2]*Orlando Sentinel.* "State to Shut Troubled Girls' Facility: Umatilla High-Security Home Racked Up Rocky Record, Officials Say." August 18, 2006.

[3]*St. Petersburg Times.* "State to Shut Down Girls' Facility." August 19, 2006.

[4]*Orlando Sentinel.* "Juvenile Justice Officials Turn Attention to Girls." June 20, 2007.

Chapman, Kathleen. "State Has Tighter Grip Than Firms on Juvenile Justice Centers, Ratings Show." *Palm Beach Post*, April 15, 2007.

CHAPTER 3
Crossover Killer

[1]Various newspaper articles from the *Ocala Star Banner*, the *Orlando News*, and the *St. Petersburg Times* beginning January 2006.

[2]"The Case For Mitigation Against the Death Penalty" in *State of Florida v. Leo Boatman*, prepared by the Office of the Public Defender, Fifth Judicial Circuit.

[3]Boatman, Leo. Correspondence to author, from March 2009 to present.

[4]Boatman, Leo and Steve Schick. Notes from meetings with author in 2009 and 2010.

[5]Marion County Sheriff's Office Media Release, August 29, 2006.

[6]Associated Press story in the *Independent Florida Alligator*, January 12, 2006.

www.stateparks.com website.

www.firstcoastnews.com website.

"Florida Department of Corrections Inmate Population Information Detail." March 4, 2009.

CHAPTER 4
No Peace at Home: Violence and Juvenile Court

[1]Action statements prepared by Child Protective Investigators, Pinellas County, Florida.

[2]National Child Traumatic Stress Network. "The Effects of Trauma on Children and Youth." www.NCTSN.org.

[3]Pynoos, Robert S. and Bessel A. Van der Kolk. "Proposal to Include a Developmental Trauma Disorder Diagnosis for Children and Adolescents in DSM-V." February 2, 2009.

[4]Sapolsky, Robert M. *Why Zebras Don't Get Ulcers.* Third Edition. New York: Henry Holt and Company, 2004.

Cooney, Elizabeth. "A lingering cloud: A study that began more than 30 years ago in Quincy shows that family arguing leaves a long-lasting imprint on children." *Boston Globe*, April 27, 2009.

National Council of Juvenile and Family Court Judges and the Office of Juvenile Justice and Delinquency Prevention. "A Judicial Checklist for Children and Youth Exposed to Violence."

Pinellas County Domestic Violence Task Force. "Fatality Review Team 2009 Annual Report." www.dvtf.org.

St. Petersburg Times. "Runaway Teenager Slain." January 10, 2009.

CHAPTER 5
Amateur Psychologists: Juvenile Judges and Mental Health Issues

[1]Solazzo, Adele. Summary of evaluations of "Rachael."

[2]National Child Traumatic Stress Network Juvenile Justice Working Group. "Trauma-Focused Interventions for Youth in the Juvenile Justice System." www.NCTSNet.org.

[3]National Child Traumatic Stress Network Juvenile Justice Working Group. "Assessing Exposure to Psychological Trauma and Post-Traumatic Stress in the Juvenile Justice Population." www.NCTSNet.org.

Binard, Joey (Ed.). "Enhancing the Mental Health and Well-Being of Infants, Children and Youth in the Juvenile and Family Courts: A Judicial Challenge." *Juvenile and Family Court Journal* (Fall 2000), 47.

CHAPTER 6
The Teen Brain: They're Still Just Kids

[1]Burgess Chamberlain, Linda. "The Amazing Teen Brain: What Every Child Advocate Needs to Know." *Child Law Practice* newsletter, 28:2 (April 2009): 17.

[2]Burgess Chamberlain, Linda. Email response. *Child Law Practice* newsletter, vol. 49, no. 4, 7.

[3]Articles in the *St. Petersburg Times*: "An accident or something much worse?" "Tampa boy stands trial in Ga.," "Tampa boy not guilty of murdering baby," and "Boy, 12, Is Given Probation for Death of Infant" over the summer of 2009.

[4]Email correspondence from Dan Myers, M.D., Dallas, Texas, May, 2010.

[5]Peters, Ruth A. E-mail correspondence to author, September 9, 2009.

Fox, Sanford J. "A Contribution to the History of the American Juvenile Court." *Juvenile and Family Court Journal* (Fall 1998).

Training and Research Institute, Inc. "The Developing Brain." www.trainingandresearch.com.

Training and Research Insitute, Inc. "The Neurobiology of Child Abuse." www.trainingandresearch.com.

CHAPTER 7
Connect the Dots: Gangs and Guns in the Juvenile Court

[1]Paris Whitehead-Hamilton's funeral program from April 11, 2009 and remarks made at that funeral by Elder Tony Bradley and elected officials.

[2]Numerous *St. Petersburg Times* news articles detailing the slaying of Paris Whitehead-Hamilton, the search for her killer and the weapons used, her funeral, and the aftermath of drug raids, arrests, beginning 04/06/2009.

[3]Carlton, Sue. "A Girl's Life Is Wasted; How Will We Answer?" *St. Petersburg Times*, April 8, 2009.

[4]Krueger, Curtis and Jamal Thalji. "Intimidation Charged in Pinellas Murder Case." *St. Petersburg Times*, December 23, 2009.

[5]Wyrich, Dr. Phelan, presentation on gangs to Conference of Safe and Drug Free Schools, Baltimore, August, 2009.

[6]Braden, Theodore. "Teen in Jail" blog, www.teeninjail.blogspot.com.

[7]Sims, Bryan M. "Overview of Criminal Street Gangs." Presented at the Epicenter, St. Petersburg College, 2009.

Garry, Stephanie and Abhi Raghunathan. "A Mom's Quest for Justice." *St. Petersburg Times*, March 2, 2009.

Maxwell, Bill. "Breaking the Silence at Last." *St. Petersburg Times*, April 12, 2009.

National Child Traumatic Stress Network. "Trauma in the Lives of Gang-Involved Youth: Tips for Volunteers and Community Organizations." www.NCTSN.org.

St. Petersburg Times. "Two Sides of St. Petersburg" editorial, April 7, 2008.

St. Petersburg Times. "Chicago Could Have Long, Mean Summer." April 23, 2008.

Tampa Bay Online. "Sarasota Police Statistics Show Teens Are Committing More Murders." October 4, 2009.

Thalji, Jamal. "Did Paris Have to Die?" *St. Petersburg Times*, October 4, 2009.

CHAPTER 8
Who Is My Father Today? Fatherless Children in Juvenile Court

[1] Cosby, Bill and Alvin F. Poussaint. Presentation at the Essence Music Festival in New Orleans in July 2009.

[2] Cosby, Bill and Alvin F. Poussaint. *Come On People: On The Path From Victims to Victors.* Nashville, TN: Thomas Nelson Press, 2007, 58–59; 134, 148–49.

CHAPTER 9
Crossover Kids: Lost in Both Systems

Various judicial reviews and delinquency hearings for dependent kids must remain anonymous.

CHAPTER 10
Recreational, Reactive, and Really Bad Crimes:
Uncovering the Role of Sex and Drugs in Juvenile Court

[1] Fay, Calvina. "The 'High' Way to Truancy Court." Unpublished.

[2] Jacobs, Edward A. "Marijuana and Adolescents." *Practice*, vol. 1, Issue 1 (2007).

[3] True Compassion Campaign. "About Marijuana." CD-ROM.

[4] Dyson, Michael Eric. *Know What I Mean? Reflections on Hip Hop.* New York: Civitas Books, 2007.

CHAPTER 11
The Deuces: Disproportionate Minority Contact and Juvenile Court.

[1] Peck, Rosalie and Jon Wilson. *St. Petersburg's Historic 22nd Street South.* Charleston, SC: The History Press, 2006.

[2] Juvenile Welfare Board of Pinellas County. "Hotline Abuse Investigations, CCC Provider Sites, and NFCs with Two-Mile Buffer." Jan. 2007–Mar. 2008.

[3] Perez, Luis. "Midtown gets its first financial establishment." by Luis Perez, *St. Petersburg Times*, Section C, page 3 of the business section, September 2, 2009.

[4] Samuels, Robert. "Rouson Targets Head Shops." *St. Petersburg Times*, April 12, 2010.

[5] Perkins Elementary School discipline referral, May 19, 2009.

CHAPTER 12
What Works in Juvenile Justice? A Dynamic Duo and Napoleon Show the Way

[1] Duggan, William. *Strategic Intuition: The Creative Spark in Human Achievement.* New York: Columbia University Press, 2007, 53–64.

[2] Ellsworth, Lynn. "A Portrait of Florida's Juvenile Justice System." Presentation at the Conference of Circuit Judges in Naples, FL, August 2007.

[3] Friedman, Mark. *Trying Hard Is Not Good Enough.* Santa Fe, NM: Fiscal Policy Studies Institute, 2005.

CHAPTER 13
Healthy Families: How Preventing Child Abuse Prevents Delinquency

[1] National Child Traumatic Stress Network. "Judges and Child Trauma: Findings from the National Child Traumatic Stress Network/National Council of Juvenile and Family Court Judges Focus Groups" brief, National Child Traumatic Stress Network, vol. 2 no. 2 (August 2008). www.NCTSN.org.

[2] National Child Traumatic Stress Network. "Children and Trauma in America" 2004. www.NCTSNet.org.

[3] Lederman, Cindy S. Correspondence to author, November 4, 2009.

[4] Katz, Lynn, Cindy S. Lederman, and Joy D. Osofsky. "When the Bough Breaks, the Cradle Will Fall: Promoting the Health and Well-Being of Infants and Toddlers in Juvenile Court." *Juvenile and Family Court Journal* (Fall 2001), 33.

[5] Shonkoff, Jack P. "The Neuroscience of Nurturing Neurons." *Children of the Code: A Social Education Project,* www.childrenofthecode.org.

[6] Ounce of Prevention Fund of Florida. "Estimated Costs Associated with Child Maltreatment in Florida (Children 0–3 Years of Age) for 2008–2009." Report, 2008.

[7] Sessions, Doug. Email correspondence to author.

[8] Prevent Child Abuse America. "Jim Hmurovich President & CEO of Prevent Child Abuse America Appears on the CBS Evening News with Katie Couric." Press release February 5, 2010.

[9] Sessions, Doug. Email correspondence to Ounce of Prevention board members, April 30, 2010.

Florida Children's Services Council. "Early Childhood Caucus Focuses on Investments in Children." press release, November 4, 2009, www.floridacsc.org.

St. Petersburg Times. "Boy, 10, accused of killing dad." August 31, 2009.

Training and Research Institute, Inc. "The Developing Brain." www.trainingandresearch.com.

Training and Research Insitute, Inc. "The Neurobiology of Child Abuse." www.trainingandresearch.com.

CHAPTER 14
"Among the Worst Offenders":
The Supreme Court Bans Life Without Parole for Many Young Offenders

[1] *St. Petersburg Times.* "For Life Prisoners, Hope." May 18, 2010, 1A.

[2] *St. Petersburg Times.* "Court Takes Stand for Humane Justice." May 19, 2010, 10A.

[3] Program from the post-argument panel and *Sullivan v. Florida & Graham v. Florida*, at the Georgetown University Law Center Hart Auditorium, November 9, 2009.

[4] Various Associated Press articles from Philly.com, anything and everything philly, re: Juvenile Judges taking kickbacks for sentencing, January 27–30, 2009.

[5] *Philadelphia Inquirer.* "Judges Sentenced: Kids for Cash." January 28, 2009.

[6] Jones, Ashby. "New Lawsuits Try to Pierce Shield of Judicial Immunity." *Wall Street Journal,* November 12, 2009.

[7] NJDC. "Victory in Sullivan and Graham." email sent by jidan-bounces@lists on behalf of NJDC, May 17, 2010.

[8] Stetson University College of Law. Program from Scholarship Dinner, November 5, 2009.

[9] Jones, Maggie. "The Case of the Juvenile Sex Offender." *New York Times Magazine,* July 22, 2007.

[10] Jaggi, Christine. Email and various correspondence to the author.

[11] Rosen, Erin G. "The Adam Walsh Act and Ohio's Implementation." Presentation at the conference of the National Council of Juvenile and Family Court Judges and National District Attorney's Association, St. Louis, MO, March 2008.

Fagan, Jeffrey and Franklin E. Zimring. "Myths of Get-Tough Law." *St. Peterburg Times*, Opinion section, November 2, 1009.

Franklin, Karen. "New Findings on Juvenile Sex Offending." www.feedblitz.com.

Lakeland Ledger. "Florida Stands Apart in Sentencing of Juveniles." August 10, 2009.

Myers, Amanda Lee. "Experts: Abuse Often Behind Kids Killing Parents." Associated Press, December 2008.

News articles from the *St. Petersburg Times* beginning with "Police say girl, 11, plotted to get rid of mother," page 1A, on December 30, 2009, and continuing on December 31, 2009, January 1, 2010, and March 25, 2010.

St. Petersburg Times. "Life in Prison for Teen in Rapes." March 11, 2010.

St. Petersburg Times. "State Locks Up More Kids in Adult Jails." November 12, 2009.

St. Petersburg Times. "Teen Gets Rare Life Sentence for Two Rapes." December 22, 2009.

CHAPTER 15
Curses and Compassion: Victims' Responses to Juvenile Crime

[1] Henning, Kristin. "What's Wrong with Victim's Rights in Juvenile Court?: Retributive Versus Rehabilitative Systems of Justice." *California Law Review* (2009), 1107–1121.

[2] Supreme Court of the United States, brief filed in the matter of *Graham v. Florida* and *Sullivan v. Florida*, brief of *Amici Curiae* of the Mothers Against Murderers Association, Robert Hoelscher, Ruth Johnson, Azim Khamisa, Bill Pelke, Aqeela Sherrills, Tammi Smith, and Linda White in Support of Petitioners, by Angela C. Vigil, counsel of record, and others, Baker & McKenzie, LLP, Miami.

CHAPTER 16
Toughest Job in the Courthouse: Public Defenders in Juvenile Court

[1] Wolf, Dwight. Memo regarding work as a juvenile public defender.

[2] John D. and Catherine T. MacArthur Foundation. "Toward Developmentally Appropriate Practice: A Juvenile Court Training Curriculum." www.macfound.org.

[3] John D. and Catherine T. MacArthur Foundation. "Overview, Models for Change, Systems Reform in Juvenile Justice." www.macfound.org.

[4] Geraghty, Tom. Email correspondence to author.

[5] Jacobs, Thomas A. *Teens Take It to Court: Young People Who Challenged the Law—and Changed Your Life.* Minneapolis, MN: Free Spirit Publishing, 2006, 162–170.

[6] Brecher, Elinor J. "Pioneer in Law School, On Bench." *Miami Herald*, November 5, 2009.

[7] Langer, Lester. Email correspondence to author, January 5, 2010.

[8] Holder, Eric. "Remarks as Prepared for Delivery by Attorney General Eric Holder at the Brennan Center for Justice Legacy Awards Dinner in Washington, D.C." PRNewswire-USNewswire, November 16, 2009.

[9] Lee, Carrie. Email correspondence to author.

[10] Heyman, Adam. Interview with author, January 2010.

[11] Heyman, Adam. Email correspondence to author, January 2010.

Burrell, Sue. "Perspective: Juvenile Defense Attorneys Speak Out." January 15, 2010.

Clark, Joe. "Too Many Kids Coming into the Juvenile Justice System for the Wrong Reason!" Message, January 2010.

Fox, Sanford J. "A Contribution to the History of the American Juvenile Court." National Council of Juvenile and Family Court Judges *Juvenile and Family Court Journal* vol. 49, no. 4 (Fall 1998), 7.

CHAPTER 17
Keeping Kids Out of Court:
The Annie E. Casey Foundation and Wansley Walters in Miami.

[1] Lubow, Bart. Interview with author.

[2] Lubow, Bart. Presentation to the University of Florida's Passages and Prevention Conference, Gainesville, FL, February 2010.

[3] Jones, Jerrauld and Patricia Koch. Presentation to the Conference of the National Council of Juvenile and Family Court Judges, Chicago, IL, July 2010.

[4] Annie E. Casey Foundation. "Two Decades of JDAI, A Progress Report, From Demonstration Project to National Standard." Report, 2009.

[5] Walters, Wansley. Interview with author.

[6] Langer, Lester. Email correspondence with author.

[7] *St. Petersburg Times*. "$280 a Day to Jail a Kid." January 21, 2010.

CHAPTER 18
Reclaiming Futures:
Substance Abuse Interventions and Collaborations That Really Work

[1] Circuit Court of Cook County. "Summary of Juvenile Probation and Court Services Programs And Initiatives 2009." Report, 50-51.

[2] Wojcik, Lawrence et al. *About The Chicago Signature Project in Juvenile Justice, An Overview by DLA Piper*. DLA Piper, 2008.

[3] Fay, Calvina. "'K2' Poses Risks and Should Be Illegal." CNN.com, March 2, 2010.

[4] *St. Petersburg Times*. "Feet To The Fire." January 3, 2010.

Simkim, Deborah R. "Neurobiology of Addiction and the Adolescent Brain." *Journal of Global Drug Policy and Practice*, vol. 2, issue 2 (Summer 2008).

CHAPTER 19
Saving Kids While Saving Money: Washington State Proves You Can Do Both

[1] Aos, Steve, Marna Miller, and Elizabeth Drake. "Evidence-Based Public Policy Options to Reduce Future Prison Construction, Criminal Justice Costs, and Crime Rates." Washington State Institute for Public Policy, October 2006.

[2] EB-Advocate. "Blueprints for Violence Prevention: Model Programs." *EB-Advocate Newsletter*, March 2008, 4.

[2] EB-Advocate. "Justice Research Center: Once Again, EBA's Redirection Programs Reduce Serious Crime, Save Millions." *EB-Advocate Newsletter*, Spring 2010, 5.

[3]Justice Policy Institute. "The Costs of Confinement: Why Good Juvenile Justice Policies Make Good Fiscal Sense." *Justice Policy Institute Newsletter*, May 2009.

[4]Justice Policy Institute. "Pruning Prisons: How Cutting Corrections Can Save Money and Protect Public Safety." *Justice Policy Institute Newsletter*, May 2009, 1.

Cohen, Mark A. and Alex R. Piquero. "New Evidence on the Monetary Value of Saving a High-Risk Youth," John Jay College of Criminal Justice & City University of New York Graduate Center, December 2007.

"Redirection Youth: Florida's Success Story." Presentation to the Blueprints Conference, San Antonio, TX, April 8, 2010.

CHAPTER 20
Girls Matter! The Importance of Gender-Specific Programs

[1]Ravoira, Lawanda. Webinar on Girl Matters, June 15, 2009.

[2]Children's Campaign, Inc. "Advocates Seek Federal Involvement in Justice for Girls." Press release, October 19, 2009.

[3]Ravoira, Lawanda. "Girl Matters." Presentation, Jacksonville, FL.

[4]National Council on Crime and Delinquency. "Tamela's Story." *Perspectives* (August 2008), 1.

[5]Sherman, Francine. "Reframing the Response: Girls in the Juvenile Justice System and Domestic Violence." *Today* (Winter 2009): 16.

[6]"Famous Quotes by Famous Women." Source unknown.

[7]Florida Department of Juvenile Justice. "Girls' Health." *Florida Department of Juvenile Justice's Health Services Manual* (draft), July 2006, 1-5.

[8]Sutton, Debbie. Email correspondence to author, September 1, 2009.

Children's Campaign, Inc. "Justice for Girls: Blueprint for Action." Report and presentation to the FJJA/FADAA Conference, 2008.

Coordinating Council on Juvenile Justice and Delinquency Prevention. "Lawanda Ravoira biography, October 24, 2009.

De La Paz, Cathy. "Child Prostitution" presentation to the National Conference of Juvenile and Family Court Judges and National District Attorneys Association annual meeting. St. Louis, MO, March 2008.

Dominus, Susan. "Big City: Girls in Trouble, Humiliated and Injured at the Hands of the State." *New York Times*, August 29, 2009.

Guthrie, Barbara J. "Restorative Health: An Evidence-Based Model for Ensuring Quality Health Care for Youth Within Juvenile Justice System." Presentation to Florida's Blueprint Commission, 2007.

Miller, Roy W. Email correspondence to author, January 23, 2010.

National Child Traumatic Stress Network. "Trauma among Girls in the Juvenile Justice System." www.NCTSNNET.org.

University of Miami Legal Research Center. "Facilitating Adolescent Offenders' Reintegration From Juvenile Detention to Community." *Corrections* Courts* Treatment* Law** vol. 1, no. 2 (March/April 2006): 17-32.

Wicker, Vanessa. Email correspondence on "Girl Matters" and implementation plan, to Romona Salazar, August 31, 2009.

CHAPTER 21
Repairing the Broken Whole: Family Therapy for Juvenile Offenders

[1]EB-Advocate. "Florida Gets It Right." *EB-Advocate Newsletter* (May 2009).

[2]NREPP Samhsa. "Multidimensional Family Therapy (MDFT)." National Registry of Evidence-Based Programs and Practices (November 16, 2009): 1-22.

[3]Sells, Scott. "Parenting With Love and Limits (PLL): A Model Program for Defiant Parents and Adolescents." www.gopll.com.

[4]Sells, Scott. Correspondence to author, December 28, 2009.

Center for Treatment Research on Adolescent Drug Use. "Multidimensional Family Therapy." University of Miami Miller School of Medicine, www.med.miami.edu/ctrada.

Criminal Justice/Drug Abuse Treatment Studies."Facilitating Adolescent Offenders' Reintegration From Juvenile Detention to Community" Report published in *Offender Substance Abuse Report*, VI:2 (March/April 2006): 17.

Rhen, Rob. Email correspondence to author. January 5, 2010.

CHAPTER 22
Crossover Kids: Fewer Silos, More Legal Representation

[1]Nash, Michael and Shay Bilchik. "Child Welfare and Juvenile Justice—Two Sides of the Same Coin, Part II." *Juvenile and Family Justice Today* (Winter 2009).

[2]Dillinger, Bob et al. "The Sixth Judicial Circuit Public Defender's Office Juvenile Crossover Children's Program FY 2007-2008 Status Report."

CHAPTER 23
The Limits of Zero Tolerance:
What We Need to Do to Improve Good Intentions

[1]Mission: Readiness. "Ready, Willing, And Unable To Serve." www.MissionReadiness.org.

[2]Jeremiah, Jeremiah S. et al. Rhode Island Family Court Truancy Court Mission Statement and related documents.

[3]Iaconia, Tifny, Stacey Jameison, and Irene Sullivan. "Connecting the Dots." Presentation to Safe and Drug-Free Schools annual conference, August 4, 2009.

[4]Jamieson, Stacey and Mary Hughes. "Brooklyn District Attorney's Truancy Program: Truancy Reduction Alliance to Contact Kids (TRACK)" summary.

[5]National Center for Missing and Exploited Children. Posters downloaded from www.cybertipline.com.

Canada, Geoffrey. "Passages, Preventions and Interventions." Keynote speech at the Juvenile Justice Conference, University of Florida College of Law, February 14, 2010.

Chicago Tribune. "Urban College Prep." March 5, 2010.

Glaberson, William. "Lessons in Tough Love at a Court for Truants." *New York Times*, February 27, 2010.

Perrelli, Thomas. Presentation at the Safe and Drug-Free Schools conference, August 4, 2009.

Philadelphia Inquirer. "Two News Programs to Help Philadelphia Truancy." March 30, 2010.

Sholden, John. Presentation to the National Council of Juvenile and Family Court Judges annual conference, Chicago, IL, July 2009.

CHAPTER 24
Truancy: Where Most Behavior Problems Begin

[1]The-Eggman.com. "Zero Tolerance Laws: What We Need Is a Zero Tolerance Law Against Abject Stupidity!" November 28, 2009, www.the-eggman.com/writings/zerostu.html.

[2]Cassingham, Randy. "Losing My Tolerance for "Zero Tolerance." *This Is True Since 1994*, December 29, 2009, www.thisistrue.com/zt.html.

[3]Richter, Dee. "Florida Legislature Adopts New Bill Addressing Zero Tolerance Policies." Press release of the Florida Network of Youth and Family Services, May 11, 2009.

[4]Winchester, Donna. "Good Behavior Will Breed Better Learning, Board Member Says." *St. Petersburg Times*, March 22, 2009.

Associated Press. "ACLU: Michigan's Zero-Tolerance Law Unfair to Students." Syndicated, December 29, 2009.

Bazemore, Gordon, Nancy Riestenberg, and Jeanne B. Stinchcomb. "Beyond Zero Tolerance: Restoring Justice in Secondary Schools." *Youth Violence and Juvenile Justice*. Thousand Oaks, CA: Sage Publications, 2006.

Dorell, Oren. "Schools' Zero-Tolerance Policies Tested." *USA Today*, November 2, 2009.

Eckholm, Erik. "School Suspensions Lead to Legal Challenge." *New York Times*, March 8, 2010.

Florida Department of Juvenile Justice, Office of Program Accountability, Research and Planning. "Delinquency in Florida Schools: A Three-Year Analysis." Report issued for fiscal years 2004–05 through 2006–07, www.djj.state.fl.us.

Florida State Conference NAACP Advancement Project, NAACP Legal Defense and Educational Fund, Inc. "Arresting Development: Addressing the School Discipline Crisis in Florida." Report, spring 2006.

Lospennato, Ronald. "School-to-Prison Reform Project." www.splcenter.org.

Matus, Ron. "Schools Vow Help for Black Students." *St. Petersburg Times*, July 15, 2009.

Meyer, Jeremy. "Schools' New Approach to Discipline." *Denver Post*, September 18, 2007.

National Council on Crime and Delinquency. "Zero Tolerance Policies." www.nccd.crc.org.

Pinellas County Schools. "5,000 Role Models of Excellence Project." Brochure published by school district.

St. Petersburg Times. "Decriminalize 'Sexting' by Minors." March 30, 2010.

St. Petersburg Times. "Nine Teens Charged in Girl's Suicide in Mass." March 30, 2010.

CHAPTER 25
Two Janes: Helping Children and Families in Need of Services

[1]Wikipedia. "Jane Addams." www.wikipedia.org/wiki/Jane_Addams#Biography.

[2]Harper, Jane L. Email correspondence and interview with author.

[3]Florida Network of Youth & Family Services, Inc. "Serving and Understanding Children Who Commit Status Offenses." PowerPoint presentation, www.floridanetwork.org.

[4]Family Resources, Inc. *Letters from the Heart* newsletter.

[5]Eckholm, Erik. "Florida Steps in Early, and Troubled Teenagers Respond." *New York Times*, December 5, 2008.

CHAPTER 26
Youth Courts: Turning Crisis into Opportunity With Positive Peer Pressure

[1] Kaye, Judith S. "Youth Court Helps Mold Law-Abiding Citizens." *Staten Island Sunday Advance*, June 28, 2009.

[2] Self, Katie. Interview with author.

[3] Green, Karen. Correspondence and interviews with author.

[4] Placer County Peer Court Board of Directors. "Juvenile Justice Handbook 2008" Brochure, published online at www.peercourt.com.

[5] Couzens, Richard. Interview with author.

[6] Levine, Jack. Interview with author.

CHAPTER 27
Public Safety: Why We Lock Up Kids, and What Are Our Alternatives?

[1] Escalera, Hector. Interview with author, October 2009.

[2] Conwell, Adrienne. Email correspondence to author, November 24, 2009.

[3] Kaye, Judith S. Keynote speech at the National Council of Juvenile and Family Court Judges conference, Chicago, IL, July 2009.

[4] Cuomo, Chris, Joseph Diaz, and Kate McCarthy. "Missouri's New Take on Juvenile Justice." First aired on *Good Morning America* on September 8, 2009.

[5] Decker, Tim. Interviews with author, March 2008.

[6] Justice Policy Institute. "The Costs of Confinement: Why Good Juvenile Justice Policies Make Good Fiscal Sense." *www.justicepolicy.org.*

[7] King, Loretta. "Investigation of the Lansing Residential Center, Louis Gossett, Jr. Residential Center, Tryon Residential Center, and Tryon Girls Center." Report issued on behalf of the U.S. Department of Justice, Civil Rights Division to New York Governor David A. Paterson, August 14, 2009.

[8] *St. Petersburg Times.* "100 Years Later and It's Still Hell." October 11, 2009.

[9] *St. Petersburg Times.* "Reform School Flunks Review." December 30, 2009.

[10] *St. Petersburg Times.* "Legislators Look West for Prison Solution." November 17, 2009.

[11] *St. Petersburg Times.* "Either Fix It or Close It." October 13, 2009.

[12] *St. Petersburg Times.* "Dozier: Recent Abuses at Boy's School." September 24, 2009.

[13] *St. Petersburg Times.* "Put a Stop to Horrors at School for Boys." September 24, 2009.

[14] Wooden, Kenneth. Email correspondence to author, January 8, 2010.

[15] *St. Petersburg Times.* "For Their Own Good: A Roster of the Lost." December 6, 2009.

[16] *St. Petersburg Times.* "Dozier's Failings Demand Solution." December 27, 2009.

[17] Wooden, Kenneth. *Weeping in the Playtime of Others,* Second Edition. Columbus, OH: Ohio University Press, 2000.

[18] Wooden, Kenneth and Rosemary Wooden Webb. Presentation at the 2010 Annual Child Abuse Prevention Conference Largo, FL, April 15, 2010.

[19] Putter, Candace. "Academic and Career/Technical Training for Delinquent Youth in Placement and on Aftercare." Presentation at Center for Juvenile Justice Reform conference, Georgetown University, Washington D.C.

Breedlove, Tom. "A Closer View of the Missouri Division of Youth Services and Juvenile Justice Systems." Presented October 29, 2007. www.dss.mo.gov/dys.

Child Lures Prevention. "Team of Sisters to Lead Award-Winning Child Personal Safety Program: Child Lures Prevention/Teen Lures Prevention." Press release, March 17, 2009, www.childlures prevention.com.

JWB Children's Services Council of Pinellas County Planning Department. "Juvenile Delinquency: The Need for Small Residential Care as an Alternative to Larger Institutions." Fact sheet issued 2008.

New York Times. "Delinquency and Prevention." April 10, 2009.

New York Times. "The Right Model for Juvenile Justice." October 28, 2007.

St. Petersburg Times. "State seals fate of San Antonio Boys Village." September 12, 2009.

White, Bobby. "Youth Prison Model Sets High Bar." Wall Street Journal, October 12, 2009.

CHAPTER 28
Solving the DMC Problem: A Case Study in Florida

[1]Jefferson, Rhyna and Randy Nelson. "Disproportionate Minority Contact (DMC): Exploring Minority Overrepresentation in the System." Presentation to "Examining Zero Tolerance: A Summit on Florida's Students" conference, Kissimmee, FL, August 11, 2008.

[2]Lindsey, Michael L. "DMC Best Practices and Principles." www.nestorconsultants.com.

[3]Cheives, Barbara. Email correspondence to author author, January 5, 2010.

[4]Forman, James et al. Presentations to "Passages, Prevention, and Intervention" conference, University of Florida College of Law, February 19–20, 2010.

[5]Canada, Geoffrey. Reaching Up for Manhood. Boston: Beacon Press, 1988.

Lindsey, Michael L. "The Impact of Waivers to Adult Court, Alternative Sentencing, and Alternatives to Incarceration on Young Men of Color." Report issued by the Joint Center for Political and Economic Studies Health Policy Institute, Washington, D.C., 2006.

Marsh, Shawn C. "The Lens of Implicit Bias." Juvenile and Family Justice Today (Summer 2009).

CLOSING ARGUMENT
Members of the Jury

[1]Wikipedia. "Declaration of the Rights of the Child." http://en.wikipedia.org/wiki/Declaration_ of_the_Rights_of_the_Child.

[2]Sullivan, Irene. Transcript of Stetson University College of Law phone conference held by author.

[3]Kaye, Judith S. "Hats Off to Claire Flom and Her Special Vision: Education and the Importance of Being Involved." Lecture sponsored by the Feerick Center for Social Justice at Fordham Law School, New York, NY, March 25, 2010.

[4]Sondheim, Stephen. "Gee, Officer Krupke" (lyrics). www.westsidestory.com.

Bilchik, Shay. "The Ebb and Flow of Juvenile Justice in America." Keynote speech to "Passages and Prevention" conference, Gainesville, FL, February 2010.

Butts, Jeffrey A. "Whose Problem? A View from the United States." Debating Youth Justice: From Punishment to Problem Solving? www.kcl.ac.uk/ccjss.

Collins Center for Public Policy. "Smart Justice." February 2010.

Harlem Children's Zone. Development office handouts, downloaded from www.hcz.org.

Harlem Children's Zone. "Harlem Children's Zone Evaluation Highlights from July '08–June '09." Newsletter, October 2009.

Justice Policy Institute. "The Costs of Confinement: Why Good Juvenile Justice Policies Make Good Fiscal Sense." *Justice Policy Institute Newsletter,* May 2009.

St. Petersburg Times. "Should Dozier Be Shut Down?" March 9, 2010.

INDEX

ABOUT THE AUTHOR

A NATIONALLY RECOGNIZED speaker on juvenile justice and truancy matters, Irene Sullivan is an award-winning Circuit Court Judge in Florida's Unified Family Court, handling juvenile delinquency, dependency, and domestic violence cases. She is also a vice president of the National Truancy Prevention Association, a member of the Blueprint Commission to reform juvenile justice in Florida, and a member of a statewide taskforce on Disproportionate Minority Contact. In addition, she serves on advisory boards of Stetson University College of Law, the Juvenile Welfare Board, the Ounce of Prevention of Florida, Inc., and PACE Center for Girls. Judge Sullivan is the mother of three adult children and grandmother to five truly "grand" kids.